Praise for *No Bullshit Social Media*

"A book like this deserves a no bullshit testimonial: The social media world is so full of it, I really didn't think anybody had the guts to put out a book like this on it. If someone tells you social media is crap, throw this book at them and demand they read it."

—**Scott Stratten**, international bestselling author of *UnMarketing: Stop Marketing. Start Engaging*

"Jason and Erik don't screw around with wishy-washy theories or starry-eyed notions. If you're looking for sound advice on how to use social media to grow your business (and who isn't?), this book is your guide."

—**David Meerman Scott**, bestselling author of *Real-Time Marketing and PR: How to Instantly Engage Your Market, Connect with Customers, and Create Products that Grow Your Business Now*

"I've been famously quoted as saying, '99.5% of social media experts are clowns,' but watching Jason over the course of the last five years makes me feel pretty confident that he's in the other .5%."

—**Gary Vaynerchuk**, cofounder, VaynerMedia; author of *The Thank You Economy*

"Jason and Erik are the real deal. They blend heartfelt sincerity with technical know-how and experience. This book gives you a lot to chew on, and if you let it, gives you a serious step up on your competition."

—**Chris Brogan**, coauthor of *Trust Agents: Using the Web to Build Influence, Improve Reputation, and Earn Trust*

"Finally, a book that hits the topic of social media in a way that makes it real, practical, and important."

—**John Jantsch**, author of *Duct Tape Marketing and the Referral Engine*

"Social media marketing can drive real business results and *No Bullshit Social Media* delivers straight-talking guidance to help brands succeed."

—**Peter Kim**, chief strategy officer, Dachis Group

"Forget everything you thought you already knew about social media marketing. Chuck it. Start over. Then, turn to page 1 of Falls and Deckers's *No Bullshit Social Media* guide and learn from the masters."

—**Todd Defren**, principal, SHIFT Communications; blogger, PR-Squared

"Deckers and Falls crystallize the relevant aspects of social media marketing in an exciting and informal way. Not just for marketing types, *No Bullshit Social Media* is a must-read for anyone who has a passion to grow their business by learning how to listen and dialog with their customers."

—**Scott Applebee**, vice president marketing, Travelpro International, Inc.

"Finally! A no-nonsense marketing book from guys deep within the social media trenches. This book is a must-read for any business that's struggling with social media marketing."

—**Michael A. Stelzner**, CEO, SocialMediaExaminer.com; author of *Launch: How to Quickly Propel Your Business Beyond the Competition*

"I punched the wall with enthusiasm after reading this book! No joke. This is the best bare-knuckled approach to social media marketing I have ever read. Erik and Jason tell it to you straight. Every CEO, entrepreneur, and business professional should read this book and spit out the BS!"

—**Kyle Lacy**, author of *Branding Yourself* and *Twitter Marketing for Dummies*

"Pop! Finally a book that bursts the hype balloon around social media and delivers a real recipe for how to use it to actually build your business. Falls and Deckers call out the fools and phonies and pull no punches while doing so. This book delivers clear-headed, no-nonsense, proven advice that you'll gobble up like candy—especially if you're a doubter about the whole social media craze."

—**Jay Baer**, coauthor of *The Now Revolution: 7 Shifts to Make Your Business Faster, Smarter, and More Social*

"Jason Falls and Erik Deckers waste no words getting right to what works and what doesn't. You couldn't find two more qualified people to deliver the clear story on how social media can grow your business—using the speed and reach of the Internet to make real relationships. Buy this book now!"

—**Liz Strauss**, brand strategist, community builder, founder of SOBCon

"Ripping off a Band-Aid never feels good, but that is exactly what Falls and Deckers do as they cut right to the point and tell you exactly how your company needs to approach social media if it wants to be successful. No kissing your boo-boo in this book!"

—**C.C. Chapman**, coauthor of *Content Rules: How to Create Killer Blogs, Podcasts, Videos, Ebooks, Webinars (and More) That Engage Customers and Ignite Your Business*

"Stop. Put this book down! Step away from the book. Honestly, we'd prefer that you not read this book. We're quite happy to continue to run laps around your business, and the last thing we need is for you to start trying to satisfy your customers by applying what you'll learn here."

—**Joe Sorge**, entrepreneur, small business owner, burgerwhisperer, coauthor of *#TwitterWorks: Restaurant 2.0 Edition: How social media built a restaurant, a pizza truck and thousands of relationships*

"*No Bullshit Social Media* advances and distills Jason and Erik's unique and thought-provoking insights about why, and how, we should use what they so simply demonstrate is the most powerful marketing tool available to businesses today—social media."

—**Kevin Taylor**, aka @telecomtails; former president, Chartered Institute of Public Relations; founder, Robertson Taylor PR; European lead for Global Results Communications

"Many business leaders are still trying to understand the value of social media communication. Falls and Deckers take the key questions and challenges head on, back them up with examples, and spare you the frustrating jargon and hyperbole. If you're an executive trying to get your arms around social or need your boss to better understand, this book is the place to start."

—**Amber Naslund**, VP Social Strategy, Radian6; coauthor of *The Now Revolution: 7 Shifts to Make Your Business Faster, Smarter, and More Social*

"Kick-ass straight-talk about how social media has emerged core to businesses' bottom line success. A must-read, with no holds barred."

—**Stacy DeBroff**, CEO and founder, Mom Central Consulting

"This is a book I'm excited about. Not just because it sounds straightforward (that 'No Bullshit' thing!), but because it is. Social media isn't all Rainbow Brite, snuggly puppies, and big group hugs. It's real. It's actionable. It works. So what are you waiting for?"

—**Ann Handley**, chief content officer, MarketingProfs; coauthor of *Content Rules: How to Create Killer Blogs, Podcasts, Videos, Ebooks, Webinars (and More) That Engage Customers and Ignite Your Business*

"Jason and Erik offer something often in painfully short supply in the social media world: business sense. No kumbaya, no fluffy talk about engagement or conversation, just real advice crafted with business needs and a bottom line in mind."

—**Christopher Barger**, senior vice president of global programs, Voce Connect

"'Yes you can!,' President Obama's slogan from his first presidential election campaign, is an apt label to apply to Jason Falls and Erik Deckers's treatment of social media and its dynamic place in business and marketing. Falls and Deckers pepper their book with credible case studies to illustrate the compelling differences social media marketing can make to any business, large or small. *No Bullshit Social Media* offers you actionable insights that will help you believe that you, too, can realize benefits that social media marketing can bring to your business."

—**Neville Hobson**, ABC (Accredited Business Communicator), communication consultant, digital media entrepreneur, blogger, copresenter of the *For Immediate Release* podcast series, founding senior research fellow and advisory board member of the Society for New Communications Research, volunteerism leader with the International Association of Business Communicators (IABC)

"Jason Falls and Erik Deckers continue to deliver 'Pristine and Straight Arrow Insights' into social media marketing. Their book *No Bullshit Social Media* is just that: no B.S. This book is common sense from cover to cover!"

—**Ramon De Leon**, social media visionary and international speaker, Domino's Pizza Chicago

"In an era when everyone from kids to grandparents has mastered social media, too many business people are still asking, 'Do I dare?' This no-B.S. read says loudly and clearly, 'Hell, yes!' It's a smart, succinct combo of why to and how that persuasively pounds home its social-media premise: 'You better play, or you're gonna pay.'"

—**Bruce Hetrick**, president and CEO, Hetrick Communications

"Enough of the excuses! No more saying that you don't 'get' social media or that you're too old/out of date/not geeky enough to use today's tools to market your business. Get off your butt, buy this book, and start growing! 'Nuff said."

—**Sarah "Intellagirl" Smith-Robbins**, PhD, Director of Emerging Technologies, Kelley Executive Partners at Indiana University; Marketing faculty, Kelley School of Business, Indiana University

NO BULLSHIT SOCIAL MEDIA

The All-Business, No-Hype Guide to Social Media Marketing

JASON FALLS

ERIK DECKERS

800 East 96th Street,
Indianapolis, Indiana 46240 USA

No Bullshit Social Media

Copyright © 2012 by Pearson Education, Inc.

ISBN-13: 978-0-7897-4801-0
ISBN-10: 0-7897-4801-0

Library of Congress Cataloging-in-Publication Data

Falls, Jason.
  No bullshit social media : the all-business, no-hype guide to social media marketing / Jason Falls, Erik Deckers.
    p. cm.
  ISBN-13: 978-0-7897-4801-0
  ISBN-10: 0-7897-4801-0
1. Internet marketing. 2. Social media—Economic aspects. 3. Online social networks—Economic aspects. I. Deckers, Erik. II. Title.
  HF5415.1265.F35 2012
  658.8'72—dc23

                    2011027856

Printed in the United States of America

First Printing: September 2011

Trademarks

Warning and Disclaimer

Bulk Sales

Que Publishing offers excellent discounts on this book when ordered in quantity for bulk purchases or special sales. For more information, please contact

> U.S. Corporate and Government Sales
> 1-800-382-3419
> corpsales@pearsontechgroup.com

For sales outside of the U.S., please contact

> International Sales
> international@pearson.com

CONTENTS AT A GLANCE

TABLE OF CONTENTS

About the Authors

Jason Falls is a consultant, speaker, strategist, and thinker in the world of digital marketing and social media. He is the owner of Social Media Explorer, a social media consulting service, as well as Exploring Social Media, a learning community. He works with corporate clients, developing and managing their social media and PR strategies. He is a highly sought-after speaker, traveling around the country to speak to various trade associations, conferences, and corporate groups.

Erik Deckers is the co-owner and vice president of creative services of Professional Blog Service, a ghost blogging and social media agency. His company works with both small businesses and large corporations. Erik has been blogging since 1997, and he speaks widely on social media topics for personal branding, business, crisis communication, and citizen journalism. He is also a newspaper columnist and award-winning playwright.

Dedication

To Nancy, Grant, and Katie. Thanks for sharing, so that I can.
Jason

To Toni, Madison, Emmalie, and Benjamin. You're why I do anything.
Erik

Acknowledgments

Social media is a community first. One of the cool things about this community is that we help each other, even our competitors. So we want to thank some very special people who made this book possible.

First, thank you to Katherine Bull, our editor at Pearson, for making sure we could do our work and that we got our work done. Special thanks to Brandon Prebynski and Leslie O'Neill for the editing work that made the book so much better than it would have been. (We especially want to thank Leslie for being the willow in the windstorm of putting up with our grumblings.)

Thanks to Karen Annett for copy editing and making this book look so damn good, and to Betsy Harris for keeping us on task and making sure everything is done properly! Thanks to the rest of the support team at Pearson for believing in our off-beat approach.

We also want to thank people in our community. Without working with you, learning from you, and sharing ideas with you, we wouldn't be able to write a book like this. Your generosity of time, knowledge, and ideas made this book possible. So thank you, in no particular order, to Paul Lorinczi, Kyle Lacy, Lorraine Ball, Doug

Karr, Jay Baer, Darrin Gray, Sarah Robbins, Scott Stratten, Amber Naslund, Scott Monty, Chris Brogan, Nick Huhn, Tamar Weinberg, DJ Waldow, Aaron Marshall, and Dean Holmes. Also, thanks to Gary Vaynerchuk, whose line, "If you're not using Twitter because you're in the camp that thinks it's stupid, you're going to lose," became the seed of an idea that resulted in this book.

We would be remiss if we didn't thank our teachers over the years. You don't become a writer or professional without help. Jason would like to recognize Jeanne Williamson Clark for teaching him how to write and Modena Sallee for making him want to. Jason also tips a cap to Dan Burgess, Todd Spencer, and Dave Wilkins of Doe-Anderson for giving him the confidence and freedom to work with clients when few knew what social media was. Erik wants to recognize his friend Joel Hedge for giving him his first writing break, Carmon and Jan Wenger of WE International for teaching him enough about business and marketing to become the kind of professional to write a book like this, and his mom and dad for instilling a love of the written word in him.

(Erik would also like to thank Jason for saying yes to a late-night text, asking him if he would like to write a book, after spending the previous two years swearing he never would. Jason would like to thank Erik for talking him out of being such a curmudgeon and putting his ideas down on paper.)

Finally, Erik would like to especially thank his wife, Toni, and his children, Maddie, Emma, and Ben, for their unwavering support, love, and hugs. Jason would like to thank his wife, Nancy, and his children, Grant and Katie, for giving him the freedom, the support, and the reason to do what he does. And finally, his mother, Sara George, for getting him to the point he could.

We Want to Hear from You!

As the reader of this book, *you* are our most important critic and commentator. We value your opinion and want to know what we're doing right, what we could do better, what areas you'd like to see us publish in, and any other words of wisdom you're willing to pass our way.

As an editor-in-chief for Que Publishing, I welcome your comments. You can email or write me directly to let me know what you did or didn't like about this book—as well as what we can do to make our books better.

Please note that I cannot help you with technical problems related to the topic of this book. We do have a User Services group, however, where I will forward specific technical questions related to the book.

When you write, please be sure to include this book's title and author as well as your name, email address, and phone number. I will carefully review your comments and share them with the author and editors who worked on the book.

Email: feedback@quepublishing.com

Mail: Greg Wiegand
           Editor-in-Chief
           Que Publishing
           800 East 96th Street
           Indianapolis, IN 46240 USA

Reader Services

Visit our website and register this book at quepublishing.com/register for convenient access to any updates, downloads, or errata that might be available for this book.

Introduction

Change or Die?

"Daddy, where did you hear about Osama bin Laden's death?"

"On Twitter, buddy. On Twitter."

It's three days after Osama bin Laden was killed by U.S. forces, and the Internet world has been abuzz with how we heard the news several minutes before the mainstream media made the announcements.

Welcome to the world of social media, where people are not just talking about the news, they're breaking it.

What do social media and the news have to do with social media and the business world? Everything. In both cases, social media is changing the way people communicate and gather information. It's changing how people share news, share opinions, and share personal events. Social media has made word-of-mouth marketing one of the most powerful marketing tools available.

At least it is for those companies taking advantage of it. The companies that aren't using social media marketing may get stung, or even hammered, by its users, and never even realize it.

Can you imagine getting a phone call from a reporter from the *Daily Mail* in London asking you for your reaction to the tens of thousands of angry blog posts, Twitter messages, and Facebook updates about a seemingly innocuous comment your CEO made at a small conference two days ago?

Your first thought is "What's Twitter?" Your second is, "Why is this reporter calling us? How did they even hear about us?" Your third is "Wait, did she say she was from the **London** *Daily Mail*? As in England?!" That's when you realize this social media thing has a worldwide reach.

What you didn't realize—until now—is that most of those people were blogging, posting Twitter messages, and updating their Facebook statuses about the thing your CEO said, right as he said it. Those messages reached hundreds of thousands, if not millions, of people, in a matter of a few hours.

Don't think it can happen? We wouldn't have written this book if it didn't. A lot. To big companies. The news about Osama bin Laden scooped CNN by several minutes, and Twitter messages were being sent at a rate of 4,000 per minute while President Barack Obama was announcing the news to the world. The only other time Twitter reached that rate was during Super Bowl XLIV this past February. The immediacy of social media channels isn't just kicking traditional media's butt in first-to-market for news. Journalist Sarah Lacy was raked over the coals on Twitter by audience members watching her 2008 South By Southwest Interview with Facebook CEO Mark Zuckerberg. Her reputation as a journalist was publicly questioned and potentially damaged before she even got off stage. One audience member even approached the question-answer microphone during the session and asked, "Has this been a rough interview for you?" directing the question not at Zuckerberg, but Lacy, who was clueless as to the public reaction.

We're going to say it several times in these pages. Social media is not going away. It's only going to get bigger as more people use it and learn to share with each other. More people are going to share news, information, and personal events, and it's going to eclipse traditional marketing and advertising channels. And your company is going to be right in the middle of it as you deal with customers, announce company news, experience down-turns or crises. Tuning out social media for a few minutes as Sarah Lacy is one thing. While Lacy recovered (somewhat) and is still a successful journalist, if you tune out your audiences and their voices on social channels, it could be the difference between a successful business and an unsuccessful one.

Social media is going to become like the ocean: You never want to turn your back on it.

What Is Social Media Marketing?

Social media marketing has had more effect on the communication world than any technology since television. Even such a dramatic change to the television land-scape like cable was nothing more than segmented television. You still sent market-ing messages the same way: through 30- or 60-second advertisements that interrupted the programming people tuned in to see.

Wireless communications simply added short text messages to telephone technol-ogy. Advertisers still delivered a message to a phone that you hoped the receiver paid attention to. They could respond, but seldom did.

The Internet presented a vast new universe for companies to explore and build out-posts for customers to find and perhaps even browse around. But most websites for company communications were simply versions of printed brochures viewed through a web browser well until the mid-2000s. Even today, some corporate web-sites still suffer from online brochure syndrome. But with the advent of social net-working platforms and blogs—which captured Internet users' imaginations throughout the 2000s as their online experience became less about receiving and also about sending messages, or even having conversations—corporate websites began to evolve, too. The Web was no longer static. It was dynamic. The near- to real-time nature of today's communications platforms make it possible for the Internet to be a living, breathing thing, kept alive by its own users who contribute, write, ask, respond, and interact. The two-way nature of conversations in social media channels presents a fundamental shift in how companies communicate with their customers. *Now they can talk back to you.*

Nothing in the history of marketing has let us consumers communicate with our favorite brands in so public a manner. Sure, we could make a phone call, send a let-ter, and tell a few friends about our good and bad experiences, but the phone call could be ignored, the letter could be thrown away, and we would lose energy after we told four or five friends. Now, we can tell our favorite companies how we feel about their brands and let thousands of our friends know about it at the same time.

Social media sites—blogs, social networks, community-manicured news sites, and photo- and video-sharing platforms—add an element few marketers and business owners expected: conversation. Sure, many companies had on- or offline customer service functions before social media existed. And yes, those channels provided cus-tomers the opportunity to respond and even have a back-and-forth exchange with the company. But these conversations were primitive at best when compared with what social media sites are doing today.

No longer are marketing communications about the company spraying sales talking points out to as many people as it could, hoping a few of them would hear or read those points before making a purchase. Fundamentally, social channels are different because companies can send messages to their audiences and the audiences can send messages back ... and even send messages to other customers without the company's blessing or even knowledge.

(Cue the thunderclap and sinister music.)

This is the part that freaks out a lot of businesspeople: the idea that their customers can and already are talking about them. They can't quite get comfortable with that idea, and will hide from, squash, ignore, abuse, or even sue the people who do it, because they're so afraid of the power their customers have.

Social media didn't change marketing from a monologue to a dialogue—it changed it to a *multilogue*. Now, companies can talk to customers and customers to companies, but customers can also talk to other customers, prospects, and the public in general. While initially shocking to the systems of the corporate world, which is used to controlling the marketing message, smart companies see this new world as an opportunity. For the first time, they can watch people talk about them, often in real time, and use that listening to gain insights about what their customers want and even to intervene when customers seek advice and support.

Still, many companies—especially small businesses or those in regulated and conservative industries—shy away from the multilogue, often needlessly. Whether the new dynamic of uncontrolled conversations worries them or the uncertainty of regulatory or legal interpretations of even basic definitions of *marketing* and *advertising* are holding them back, those companies understandably play it safe. Many of you reading this book are part of that group. Don't worry: You're not alone. (And you're reading this book, so you'll soon separate yourself from the safety of what you know to participating safely in the new world of social media marketing, much to your competition's chagrin.)

But by standing on the sidelines and riding the bench, some of these companies are seeing now they've perhaps fallen behind. Some may even feel as if they've missed the boat: that marketing communications has changed course, set sail, and left them behind. If you feel you've missed the boat, you haven't.

In fact, social media and online marketing continues to mature. Although there are still no real rules of social media marketing, enough companies have blazed trails, built case studies, and even monitored consumer behavior in relation to corporate behavior on social media sites to create an accepted standard for "good behavior." There's more proof in the social media pudding today than there was even a year ago. There are best practices to follow, some do's and don'ts to be aware of and, in some cases, even some rules, regulations, and interpretations to help guide companies and their efforts in the social media space.

Social media marketing is no longer in its infancy. It would be premature to call it fully matured—social media, like all other marketing channels, is still evolving and will continue to do so for years to come. But the social media marketing world now knows that companies need business outcomes from their social media efforts, namely increased sales, profits, and market share.

When the early social media evangelists pushed companies to "join the conversation" and "engage with their customers," they rarely mentioned driving business or measuring success. The single-most talked about subject in the social media marketing world in the past two years has been measuring its return on investment, or ROI. As an industry, we're defining the answers to that, and other questions. We're becoming more adept at not just doing social media tasks or implementing social media marketing strategies and programs, but also at accounting for the business side of the equation. Social media marketing is no longer an unclear world. While it's not yet in crystal focus, we've reached a point where most businesses need to take it seriously and the requisite business conversations that help us quantify and understand success and failure there are happening.

The social media marketing world is growing up. And it's ready for you to ask it out on a date.

This book will help you not only understand the culture-shifting philosophies that make up marketing in the social media world, but also the strategic reasons social media marketing is used for business. It will

- Help you understand what social media can do for your business

- Help you decide what you want it to do for your business

- Show you how to measure what it can do for your business

It is not an introduction to social media, but to social media marketing strategy. It peels away the touchy-feely advocacy of early evangelists and gets down to business, because you are a businessperson. You don't have time for frivolity, games, and all that bullshit. You need to know the time and money you spend on social media is accomplishing something for you. You need the *No Bullshit* take on social media marketing.

Part I: "Social Media Is for Hippies. Social Media Marketing Is for Business."

The social media purists laid a healthy foundation for us all. Joining the conversations and engaging with your customers, providing value to earn trust and influence, and other gospels they preach are critical to companies understanding the ethos of social media. But the purists only take us halfway there. A company requires a back end to the ethos that has something to do with driving business. Part I will give you a gut check to make sure you're focused on social media marketing and in using it to move the needle on strategic business drivers. It will help you understand the difference between social media and social media marketing and level with you about what social media marketing can do. Those insights will come from these chapters:

- **Chapter 1, "Ignore the Hype. Believe the Facts."**—Learn what social media marketing can do for your business so you can understand better what you get in return.

- **Chapter 2, "It's Not Them; It's You!"**—Understand that your hesitation with social media has less to do with the fact your audience has changed and more to do with the fact you haven't.

- **Chapter 3, "Your Competition May Have Already Kicked Your Ass"**—We'll zero in on audience drivers that show social media marketing is almost required, address concerns from the business-to-business crowd, and review examples of successful social companies we hope aren't your competitors.

- **Chapter 4, "Here's the Secret: There Is No Damn Secret!"**—Check off five mind-set shifts that can make you a successful social media marketer.

Part II: "How Social Media Marketing Really Works"

Now that we've seen what social media marketing can do and prepared our mind-sets to ensure we can successfully manage social media for our businesses, we'll take a deeper look at each business benefit. The chapters in Part II will not only dissect how to plan for and measure each business driver, but will also present case studies and interviews we've conducted with business owners and marketing managers out there getting social media done. The chapters in this part include the following:

- **Chapter 5, "Make Some Noise: Social Media Marketing Aids in Branding and Awareness"**—Traditional marketing methods and their metrics have lied to you for years. Learn how these new mediums help you reach customers and build awareness and a case for your brand.

- **Chapter 6, "It's Your House: Social Media Marketing Protects Your Reputation"**—Whether through responding to online conversations about you or using social media content to protect your standing in search engines, protecting your reputation is a critical business focus social media marketing can anchor.

- **Chapter 7, "Relating to Your Public: Social Media Marketing and Public Relations"**—Public relations used to be as much about the media as the public. Now the public is the media and public relations has changed.

- **Chapter 8, "The Kumbaya Effect: Social Media Marketing Builds Community"**—It's one thing to preach about the holy grail of social media (building a community of brand loyalists to market your product for you); it's an entirely different one to show how to build one you can measure and drive business with.

- **Chapter 9, "It's About Them: Social Media Marketing Drives Customer Service"**—Whether it's building greater customer satisfaction or cutting costs, using social media marketing for customer service can change both perceptions and company cultures.

- **Chapter 10, "Get Smarter: Social Media Marketing Drives Research and Development"**—We'll look at collaborating with customers and show how companies can use social media marketing to, in some instances, replace research and development efforts with online social efforts.

- **Chapter 11, "It's All About the Benjamins: Social Media Marketing Drives Sales"**—How many social media evangelists have told you that you can't sell through social media? We'll show you how they're wrong and you can.

Part III: "Get Off Your Ass, Would Ya!"

Now you've got the keys to the car and a map to point you toward your destination. But there are some practical tips to the route you'll need some help with. This section will solidify your confidence and help overcome those lingering hesitations you may have by giving you practical pointers to putting your social media plans into action.

What you're trying to run is a business, not a hobby. As a result, you'll need to address company policies, business goals, and accountability for both internal and external activities. But we'll also leave you with some parting thoughts to make the business drivers you learned about in Part II more practical to apply to your business. In this section, these chapters will help you:

- **Chapter 12, "Remedy Your Fears with Sound Policy"**—Whether your company is already highly social or heavily regulated, strong social media policies are imperative for your success. We'll walk you through how to create social media policies for your employees and your audiences.

- **Chapter 13, "Assign Responsibility and Be Accountable"**—The larger the organization, the more unclear the answer to who owns responsibility for social media. This chapter will help you decide who should own responsibility for social media marketing in your business.

- **Chapter 14, "This Is NOT a Sandbox. It's a Business."**—Although experimentation in new mediums is almost necessary for you to learn how to use these channels appropriately, you have to remember that you're not playing a game here. Social media marketing is about business.

- **Chapter 15, "Being Social"**—This is our parting shot to help you marry the philosophies of the social media purists and the No Bullshit approach to social media marketing presented in the previous chapters.

And that's No Bullshit Social Media. Although we make no claims to know and understand your specific business, we will present ideas, arguments, and case studies here to help you apply these ideas and the no-nonsense approach to your organization or business efforts. Everyone's experience will vary, but at the end of this book, you will have both the knowledge and confidence needed to approach social media as a business...for marketing...and not just as someone wondering if the chatter can do something for your business.

Enjoy!

1

Ignore the Hype.
Believe the Facts.

You're afraid of social media, aren't you? It's okay to admit it. It's a little terrifying to us, and we do this for a living.

A lot of businesspeople, especially C-level executives, VPs, and directors, are afraid of it because they've never used it. That lack of understanding breeds more contempt than familiarity because they don't understand that it can be used for business and certainly not how it can be used for business. And then there are the common fears that creep in. "People might say something bad about my company" is a popular one. (Hint: It's not that they might. If your product or service is such that people might say something bad about it, they already are. But by not participating in social media, you're not aware of it.)

But social media is not-so-slowly creeping into the business world. Despite some business leaders' attempts to hide from it, and lots of business owners and managers shying away from it, social media has arrived. Forward-thinking companies are not only starting to use Twitter, Facebook, LinkedIn, and blogging as a way to reach customers, those companies are surging past the competition to do so.

The ones who aren't using social media? They're choosing from myriad reasons why they're afraid of it.

Australian social media professional Jeff Bullas identified 28 of those reasons, and wrote about them on his blog:[1]

1. It is detrimental to employee productivity.

2. It could damage the company's reputation.

3. Security risk.

4. Fear of the unknown.

5. We already have information overload.

6. Don't know enough about it.

7. So much of what's discussed online is shallow and we have real work to do.

8. We don't have the time or resources to contribute and moderate.

9. Our customers don't use it.

10. Traditional media is still bigger, we will use Social Media when it is more mainstream.

11. It doesn't fit into current structures.

12. No guaranteed results.

13. The tools to measure and analyze Social Media aren't mature enough yet.

14. We are in B2B and who wants to hear about our boring product on a blog or Twitter.

15. We will lose control of our brand and image.

16. Upper management won't provide support.

17. Waiting on ROI (return on investment) with facts and figures.

18. We are afraid of making a mistake.

19. Lack of experience.

20. Ignorance.

21. Unwilling to be transparent.

22. Confusion.

23. No money.

24. No expertise.

25. Lack of leadership.

26. Terrified of feedback and truth.

27. The "newness" of it, going to wait.

28. High degree of skepticism.

If you're not using social media, how many of those reasons did you find yourself nodding at? If your company is using it, how many of these objections did you have to overcome to convince your boss to let you use it?

This book is called *No Bullshit Social Media* for a reason. We're not screwing around, feeding you a line, or trying to teach you how to use something you're not yet convinced will entirely work.

We're going to give you information about why social media marketing is important to your business. We're not going to couch this book in marketing speak or use business school jargon. This is the no bullshit book.

We want you to understand four things:

1. Social media is the wave of the future. It's not going away.

2. The companies that will succeed over the next 10 years are the ones that embrace social media marketing.

3. The companies that will fail over the next 10 years probably won't embrace social media marketing—most likely because of the fear we hope to eliminate.

4. Social media marketing can be real. It can be actionable. And it can be measured.

Social Media and the Hype Cycle

No single subject has exploded into society and the business world the way social media marketing has.

In 2004, there were no books in your favorite bookstore that even used the term *social media*. Only James Surowiecki's *The Wisdom of Crowds* even considered this soon-to-be-emerging niche of marketing.

Fast forward to 2008: You couldn't swing a dead laptop without hitting a handful of "social media consultants." Few people in the mid- to late-2000s could accurately describe social media properly, much less prescribe marketing strategies and tactics for it. It was a newborn environment, full of experimentation and exploration. There were no rules or best practices. Businesses were curious, but only a little bit. Small businesses were willing to try it because they needed any advantage they could get. But the larger businesses were unwilling to try it, usually for one of the previous 28 reasons.

With information explosions comes the inevitable hype cycle, first described by Jackie Fenn of Gartner Research in January of 1995. After the market is set on fire, with talk about this hot new thing, the "trough of disillusionment" hits: People remember the "dot-bomb" era, and wonder if the "next big thing" is just a fad. (*Hint*: Facebook, the world's biggest social network, is valued at over $50 billion; it's not going away anytime soon.)

But the companies that embraced it in the 2007–2009 time frame learned how to use the tools, and reached a plateau of productivity. These companies learned how to actually process the information (or product, style, methodology, etc.) and use it in a practical, sensible manner. These companies discovered it was real, actionable, and measurable.

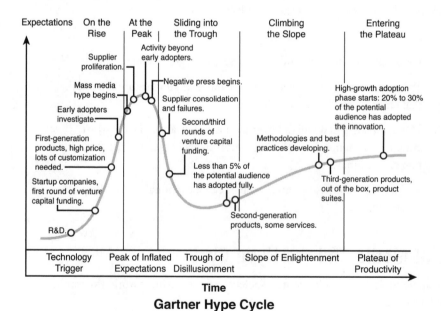

Gartner Hype Cycle

Figure 1.1   Gartner's Hype Cycle demonstrates the cycle of peak interest, followed by a dip in interest—the trough of disillusionment—followed next by the plateau of productivity. Source: Gartner's Hype Cycle Special Report for 2010, August 2010.

We think the first domino in the chain of events that brought social media into being as a communications channel, not just underground forums on nerd websites, was the publishing of *The Cluetrain Manifesto*,[2] the twenty-first century's 95 Theses nailed to Corporate America's door, declaring, "Markets are conversations." The proclamation in the 1999 work by Rick Levine, Christopher Locke, Doc Searls, and David Weinberger insisted that companies must join the customers in these conversations in order to survive. Consumers were sick and tired of being talked at. They wanted to be talked with.

Social media reached its peak of expectations in 2009 and early 2010. Facebook exploded into the hundreds of millions of members and early corporate social media adopters such as Dell began sharing sales data from social programs. Companies and their marketing managers worked themselves into a frenzy, trying to grab social media's reins and hang on for the ride.

Many of those marketers who were frothing at the bit dove into Facebook to sell their wares, blasted links to their websites on Twitter many times a day, and set their unwitting PR teams on blog comments to promote, promote, promote. They did it old school, with old school results: They got spanked.

Their return on investment was either nothing—or a public relations nightmare when bloggers called them out for spamming their comments with one-way, blast marketing messages.

Unfortunately, reality and the trough of disillusionment hit those marketers hard.

Turns out, *Cluetrain* was right. The marketplace has changed. Customers are in control, not the marketers.

You can't treat social media like TV, newspapers, or billboards. More is not better.

Maybe you see the trough of disillusionment not as the next step in the hype cycle of social media, but rather as the first indication that the fad is over.

You would be wrong.

Businesses that will succeed in their marketing efforts in the coming years have turned the corner—not their heads—toward the slope of enlightenment and are moving toward the plateau of productivity. While the "hype" is quieting, it is not because social media is a fad that is going away. It is because people using it are starting to see it for what it really is and can do and are using it that way. People who ignore social media because they think the fad is over are just treading water while their competition swims by them.

The businesses that will succeed are no longer saying, "I want a blog!" or "We need a Facebook page!" Instead, they're saying, "I want to engage my customers using social media strategically."

Just by purchasing this book, you've identified yourself as someone who is ready to look at social media as a real marketing tool with real potential to improve sales and profits.

Would it surprise you to learn that social media marketing, as we know it today, isn't just some surprising development spawned by tech startups and Gen Yers reeling after the dot-com bust of 2000? Would it shock you to know that the era of consumer-centric marketing began in the minds of traditional marketers in parallel with the information and technology explosion of the last decade?

Philip Kotler, author of more than a dozen books on marketing, discussed several interesting precursors to social media marketing in his 1999 book, *Kotler on Marketing: How to Create, Win, and Dominate Markets.*[3]

In a decade-old comparison of successful business practices, he shows a clear transition from "be product centered" to "be market and customer centered." He says:

> "Old marketing thinking is, fortunately, now giving way to newer ways of thinking. Smart marketing companies are improving their customer knowledge, customer connection technologies, and understanding of customer economics. They are inviting customers to co-design the product. They are ready to make flexible marketing offerings. They are using more targeted media and integrating their marketing communications to deliver a consistent message through every customer contact. They are utilizing more technologies such as video-conferencing, sales automation, software, Internet web pages, and Intranets and Extranets. They are reachable seven days a week, twenty-four hours a day at their 1-800 customer telephone number or by e-mail. They are better able to identify the more profitable customers and to set up different levels of service. They see their distribution channels as being partners, not adversaries. In sum, they have found ways to deliver superior value to their customers."

In 1999, Kotler also predicted that by 2005, every product, even business-to-business offerings, would be available over the Internet and that retailers would have to find, "imaginative ways to exceed customer expectations."

This is what social media marketing is: Exceeding customer expectations, often but not always, in the online world, through human connection and relationship building.

Social media, then, is simply defined by the channels we use to achieve that. Blogs, social networks, podcasts, question-and-answer forums, email, and more are simply the strings between the tin cans that we use to communicate with our customers. The channel is social because the technology makes it easier.

Certainly, much of our focus is on the Internet and online tools to achieve this communication. But a bulletin board (the corkboard type with thumbtacks, not the online forum type) is also a social medium if your intent is to use it as such. Just post a question on the bulletin board for those passing by; provide a pen, note cards, and an envelope for folks to respond; then post those responses with your comments next to the question sheet tomorrow and you have social media.

Even a conversation with a group of people over lunch is a social medium. The key is understanding how to use a medium that is primarily social for marketing purposes.

The Problem with What Social Media Purists Preach

It's really kind of sad that social media marketing advice evolved the way it did. Social media enthusiasts in the mid-2000s interpreted and preached the principles of the *Cluetrain* with a vengeance.

Their themes included "talk with your customers, not at them," "engage your audience," and the ever-popular (and really annoying) "join the conversation!"

This last talking point even became the title of social media pioneer and agency entrepreneur Joseph Jaffe's book.

Join the Conversation[4] did an excellent job of pounding the purist drum and pointing businesses down the road of changing their traditional ways to connect or reconnect with a dissatisfied consumer. But for all the talk of collaboration and community, the book only offered real-world case studies of companies that made marketing missteps, but never really talked about whether or not "conversational marketing" actually works.

Unfortunately, Jaffe's gaffe was the loudest song being sung by social media evangelists in the late 2000s. They would talk about the touchy-feely part—we call it the Kumbaya Effect—but they conveniently overlooked the other half of the equation: the bottom line.

To be fair, this was when social media marketing was just getting started, and the evangelist needed to spend a lot of time teaching businesspeople how to just listen to the new, connected customer. He or she didn't have time to focus on harder topics such as how to measure conversations or the ROI of social media.

The social media purists even had us convinced. In October 2008, Jason wrote a blog post on SocialMediaExplorer.com called "*What Is the ROI for Social Media?*" that still garners a fair amount of traffic and discussion. He wrote:

"The problem with trying to determine ROI for social media is you are trying to put numeric quantities around human interactions and conversations, which are not quantifiable."

(This is the business equivalent of your kids finding photos of you wearing your favorite clothes 20 years ago.)

Thankfully, Jason's opinions have evolved in the years since. His focus is now on social media measurement and monitoring for his clients, cutting out the purist's bullshit and getting down to the business at hand.

Social business and technology analyst Jeremiah Owyang of The Altimeter Group confirmed that you can, in fact, measure social media and its return on investment:

"Human interactions can certainly be measured. You can measure time spent together, eye contact, words exchanged, sentiment, tone and body language. Now with the digital mediums like social, you can find attributes that also relate to those: time on site, words exchanged, sentiment and tone... but not body language.

"To truly measure ROI, the interactions and engagements in the social space have to be measured in one of the two following ways: 1) Specific actions have direct trackable activities that lead to generating a lead or transaction. This could be a unique URL, cookie or even registration code. Or 2) Track it post-purchase by asking questions right after or running a survey to all customers later."

Owyang often cites his boss, Charlene Li, and her case study of defining the ROI of corporate blogging for General Motors and the GM Fastlane Blog.[5] When Li was with Forrester Research, she helped devise a measurement system that included translating the number of unique blog readers to the cost of reaching the same number of people via a regular advertising channel. She then determined the time and financial costs of blogging to produce an "ROI of Blogging."

But Asking About ROI Is Asking the Wrong Question

So measuring social media and its value to a business has been—and is being—done. But this notion of a return on investment (ROI) is bothersome. We don't want you to think of social media marketing in terms of ROI. And no, we're not contradicting ourselves. We want you to think in terms of what social media marketing *can do for your business*. Those are two distinct ideas.

Asking "what's the ROI of social media" is pretty foolish. You should actually ignore the question...at first.

"What's the ROI?" is a cop-out question asked by people who don't understand all of what social media marketing can do for their business. It is also a financial metric, so asking that question implies that all you can get out of social media is money.

Social media consultant and author Scott Stratten once said during a speech, "The next time someone asks you about the ROI of Twitter, substitute Twitter with the word 'talking.'"

"What's the ROI of 'talking?'" he asked. "How much money do you make with this new 'talking' business? I don't understand why you're 'talking' to customers all the time."

Another social media author and public relations expert, David Meerman Scott, once shouted during a podcast interview, "What's the ROI of your secretary?!" His point was that you don't measure the ROI of the person who answers the phones at the front desk.

Although the three true business metrics—revenue, cost savings, and customer satisfaction—can certainly be affected by strong social media marketing, so can other areas of your business and marketing efforts. What if you want to enhance the awareness of your product? Do you measure that in dollars? No. Thus, ROI is often the wrong measure to apply.

Even if you are going to use social media marketing for a money-driven purpose, asking the ROI question first is out of order. You're asking what the ROI of your social media marketing efforts is *before you ever get started.*

The smart approach to gauging your potential success in social media is first knowing what social media can do for your business. You then set goals within those expectations for your efforts. You can gauge an ROI, but only if your goal is financial success and you've implemented some activity toward those goals.

Now, this is not to say that social media should not be measured. It absolutely should. That's how you'll know it's working. You should be measuring all of your marketing efforts, whether it's a print ad, a TV commercial, a trade show, or a direct mail piece. But we're willing to bet no one asked about the ROI of those things before you bought them. (We're also willing to bet that a lot of people aren't measuring them afterward either.)

If you ask the ROI of social media question before you ever get started, you're setting yourself up for failure because you don't know what you're trying to measure.

The honest answer to the ROI question for your business before you start a social media marketing effort is, "I'm not sure. I can't make any predictions or promises. I know what I've done for other companies, but every situation is different, and we won't know how you'll do until we try it."

This brings us back to why you might ask the ROI question in the first place. People who do ask typically ask out of fear. If they can be assured that they'll succeed, they'll try it. Otherwise, it's "What's the ROI? How much money will we make? Can you guarantee our success?"

Those who ask these questions don't understand social media marketing isn't just about sales; it can also be about customer service and satisfaction, reputation protection, loyalty and advocacy building, research and development, and more.

And we're not going to play along with the social media hippies and tree huggers and say ROI should stand for something warm and fuzzy, like "return on interaction" or "return on innovation" or "return on conversation because we're really bad with acronyms." ROI is ROI and always will be.

What you might get out of social media marketing is specific results. Just like other areas of marketing and communications, they might be good...or they might be bad. But asking what they're going to be at the beginning of your journey is like asking the final score before the game starts.

Knowing what you can get out of social media marketing makes it much easier to determine your goals, set expected levels of accomplishment, and ultimately measure what you're getting out of it all. Again, we're *not* talking exclusively about measuring your return on investment (ROI). Yes, you will invest money in your social media marketing efforts, just like you would public relations, letterhead, or even the graphic design of your company brochures. Yes, you should expect to see a return on the money you spend, but you should focus the ROI metric on your whole marketing efforts. Trying to drill down an ROI on one piece is, as we've illustrated, sometimes illogical. (That letterhead ROI is tricky, isn't it?)

But, to paraphrase a common theme from social media measurement expert Katie Paine, "You're not always investing in a financial transaction, so you're not always going to get a financial result." There are times when your results will be intangible but still important and useful.

For example, if you're facing some negative news about a product recall, your goal should be to protect your brand's reputation. Your measure of success won't be an increase in sales or profits, but rather an increase in positive reputation indicators, a reduction of negative search results on Google, an improvement in positive search results, or a reduction of angry phone calls to customer service. Still, if you're using social media to drive sales, facilitate research and development, or even enhance customer service, you *can* track financial results that come from audience members you've cultivated through social activities, or even retention rates among the same crowd. These measures can certainly produce dollar figures on a spreadsheet that will make the "dollars-first" executives take note.

Seven Things Social Media Marketing Can Do for Your Business

It's vacation time. You load your family in the minivan, pull out of the driveway, and say, "Okay! Where are we going on vacation?" As you pull away from the house, you realize you didn't buy gas, book plane tickets, pack, study the map to know your route, make reservations at a hotel, or arrange for someone to feed the dog. Worst of all, you left without even knowing what your destination was.

That's what happens when you don't create goals for a business venture. Even something as simple as signing up for a single social network to do a few tests shouldn't be left to chance.

To understand what you're going to get out of anything, you first have to have goals just to measure whether your efforts are successful. If you don't, you're racing down the highway toward your unknown destination: You're lost, but you're making great time.

Starting with Chapter 5, "Make Some Noise: Social Media Marketing Aids in Branding and Awareness," we're going to dive deeply into the seven things social media marketing does for your business:

- Enhance branding and awareness
- Protect brand reputation
- Enhance public relations
- Build community
- Enhance customer service
- Facilitate research and development
- Drive leads and sales

In our experience, these seven areas cover just about everything you can expect your business to accomplish using social media marketing. And the three core business metrics—increasing sales, decreasing costs, and improving customer satisfaction—are built in to many of them, implicitly and sometimes explicitly.

The strategic approach to social media marketing is to review these seven areas, identify which are a good fit for your organizational goals, then map your goals, objectives, and, eventually, measures of success from there.

1. Enhance Branding and Awareness

The image of your product in the market. Its perception to others (and not you).

It is important to look at your brand from the eyes of your customers, partners, and vendors (your stakeholders), not your own. Because you eat, sleep, and breathe your brand, you're going to have an extreme, one-sided perception of it. Negatives will be excused away; positives may be lauded louder than they should.

The marketplace's perception of your brand is far more accurate and indicative of your company's value. Social media marketing can build a more positive brand and increase the public's awareness of you.

Social media marketing can:

- Increase awareness of your brand.

- Increase the reach of your brand messaging.

- Increase online conversations about your brand.

- Increase consumer preference for your brand over competitors.

- Increase your brand's Q-Score, or online appeal and familiarity.

- Increase your brand's online conversational market share—the percentage of industry conversations mentioning you versus your competitors.

2. Protect Brand Reputation

Upholding a positive perception of the brand.

Though considered a subset of branding and awareness, protecting brand reputation is important enough to set aside as its own topic. Sometimes, you need to respond to a crisis, and no amount of marketing speak is going to save you. It is important for a company to listen to online conversations to mitigate any negative (and amplify any positive) claims or conversations. But doing so also protects the reputation of the brand in the eyes of the search engines.

Google doesn't rank your company first in keyword searches because you deserve it—or because you do good and wonderful things. It prioritizes search results it considers the most relevant based on the keywords entered in the search box and what kind of information is being discussed lately. That means, if a lot of people are angry about your company, their complaints are what will be found on Google.

If you want to be the top result for certain keywords, you have to earn it by optimizing your site and its content for search. Social media marketing can

- Increase positive online mentions and sentiment of the brand

- Decrease negative online mentions and sentiment of the brand

- Mitigate all negative online mentions of the brand

- Rank in the top-five search results on Google, Yahoo!, and Bing for targeted keywords

3. Enhance Public Relations

Building and maintaining relationships with various audiences, or publics, which reflect positively upon the company, organization, or person.

Social media is closely aligned with public relations because the platforms that make up its world are populated by the public. As companies develop strategies and tactics to communicate with their audiences, they look for mediums the audiences watch, read, or listen to. Social media platforms have become one of those mediums.

As a result, social media marketing has evolved as a convenient extension of public relations, incorporating elements of media relations, crisis communications, event planning, community relations, internal communications, and more. In fact, almost every facet of a traditional public relations program has some sort of translation into the online and social media world.

Social media marketing can

- Build and maintain relationships directly with customers and stakeholder groups

- Publicize organization initiatives through blogger and influencer outreach

- Improve the communications success of community or internal initiatives

- Facilitate critical crisis communications in often a more expedient fashion than traditional media

- Empower greater public participation than traditional approaches by removing a media filter between a company and its public

4. Build Community

Growing an audience of consumers (of product or content) to serve as an advocacy or word-of-mouth marketing channel.

This is sometimes considered the golden cow of the social media world. Building community ultimately makes a social media marketer's job easy. Community means loyal customers, raving fans, and product evangelists.

With loyal fans and advocates rushing to defend your company when it is criticized, or amplifying your new ideas and messages to the market, strong brand communities and their advocates move a brand into gold-standard territory. Think of Apple iPhone users, Moleskine notebook fans, or the Maker's Mark Ambassadors Club.

Whether cultivating that community through a robust, branded social network or just informally connecting enthusiasts with your company in loosely tied conversations, brands are doing it.

Social media marketing can

- Increase your number of fans, followers, friends, or readers
- Grow your opt-in email marketing list
- Increase the number of your affinity or loyalty club members
- Increase fan-generated advocacy and promotion of your brand initiatives
- Increase fan-generated defense of your brand in negative conversations

5. Enhance Customer Service

Facilitating customer needs through proactive and reactive communications (on- and offline).

Enhancing customer service is the most popular way of using social media marketing, perhaps because it is the easiest of the seven functions to fulfill. When all you have to do is ask "how can I help" to someone complaining on Twitter, customer service through social media can not only reduce the call center costs, but can also even boost word-of-mouth marketing.

Social media marketing can drive customer service in a few ways. Note the overlap with reputation protection. This is important because a lot of customer complaints can produce similar reputation results as a product crisis.

Social media marketing can

- Increase your customers' satisfaction levels
- Reduce your call center costs
- Increase positive online mentions and sentiment of your brand
- Decrease negative mentions and sentiment of your brand

6. Facilitate Research and Development

Idea generation, improvement creation, and market research.

Some companies have benefited greatly by getting ideas, complaints, and suggestions from their customers. This collaboration, sometimes called "open source" collaboration, enables the product development department to get new ideas and the marketing department to see what their customers need. Dell's IdeaStorm, a product and feature suggestion and voting site, is the most popular example of social media marketing as research and development (R&D).

If building community is the golden cow of social media marketing, facilitating research and development within that community is nirvana. By tapping into the vested interest and intelligence of your customers, fans, and even detractors, you can harvest ideas that lead to new products, product features, and even profits.

Social media marketing can

- Generate new product ideas for your company

- Improve your product features

- Improve your service lines

- Generate market research for your company

- Generate sales for your company from R&D activities

7. Drive Leads and Sales

Sales of products or services or leads which produce them.

Yes, social media marketing can drive leads and even sales. And no, it's not just some mystical, magical by-product of "joining the conversation." You can prescribe goals and objectives around sales using social media. And you can measure them accordingly.

Social media marketing can

- Generate leads and sales from blog visitors

- Generate leads and sales from social channel interactions (Facebook, Twitter, etc.)

- Increase conversion rates

- Increase repeat and referral business

When You Add "Marketing," It's About Business

The formative years of social media marketing are behind us. This is not an exploratory time anymore. Social media professionals are helping businesses grow through emerging technologies. When you add the word *marketing* to *social media*, it's about business. Draw that line to the bottom line, or go home.

A few years ago, the social media purists got the marketplace all hyped up about just that: hype. Let's gather in a circle and sing, "Kumbaya," with our beloved customers. Let's "join the conversation" and "talk with, not at" them. Let's "engage" and become a "social business."

It sounds nice, in a very holding-hands-in-a-circle kind of way, but that can't be all we do. We have to make money, or else we cease to have a profitable business.

Still, the tree huggers and hippies of the online world got half of the equation right. We do have to join the conversation. The new consumer requires us to engage and talk with, not at them. We can probably forego the "Kumbaya" circle, but turning traditional marketing around to focus on the consumer and not the brand is imperative for successful online marketing today.

So let us take that direction and do what we do best: Make social media about business.

Social media marketing becomes realistic, actionable, and measurable when you approach it strategically. That is, implement one or more of the seven things social media marketing can do for your business and do the following:

- Set goals your company wants to focus on
- Create measurable objectives within each that accomplish your goals
- Produce strategies or concepts to execute that accomplish your objectives
- Create tactics or tasks that accomplish your strategies or concepts
- Build measurement systems to evaluate the implementation of your plan

None of these five items are new to anyone who has taken a business or marketing course where strategic communication planning was covered. As Jason often says, "This ain't rocket surgery."

What seems to be difficult for most businesses is not thinking strategically, but rather remembering to do so. Today's pace of business is frenetic at best. We've forgotten to focus, to ignore the shiny, new object and get stuff done. With the ever-changing world of technology and social media tools, it's easy to—LOOK! A SQUIRREL!—be distracted by the new tool or strategy.

It's hard to plan, launch a course of action, and stay the course while integrating market changes as they arise.

By grounding your social media marketing in a strategic approach—setting goals, measurable objectives, producing strategies, creating tactics or tasks, and measuring it all—you have a plan. Installing a measurement system for control and evaluation helps you execute the plan. And executing the plan is as easy as working backward: Accomplish the tasks or tactics that execute the strategies or concepts. Those meet the objectives, which then accomplish the goals.

What happens when you approach social media marketing strategically? You see past the hype and understand that social media marketing can be real. It can be actionable. It can be measured. You acknowledge and even embrace the Kumbaya philosophies of joining the conversation, building relationships, and talking with, not at, customers.

But you don't stop there.

You view social media marketing through the eyes of your business and your customers. You see where you can provide value and where value can then return to your business.

And when all that happens, you lose your fear.

Again, it's not hard to plan. It's hard to remember, or make time, to plan. And execution is sometimes challenging, but it shouldn't be hard.

This is, after all, just communicating.

Endnotes

1. Reprinted with permission. http://www.jeffbullas.com/2009/08/08/28-reasons-why-the-ceo-is-afraid-of-social-media/.

2. Levine, Locke, Searls & Weinberger, The Cluetrain Manifesto. Basic Books, 2000.

3. Philip Kotler, *Kotler on Marketing: How to Create, Win, and Dominate Markets.* Simon & Schuster, 1999.

4. Joseph Jaffe, *Join the Conversation.* Wiley, 2007.

5. General Motors Fastlane Blog, http://fastlane.gmblogs.com.

It's Not Them; It's You!

We hear all kinds of reasons from executives and business owners who don't think they should use social media marketing. It's a fad; it will give our customers a chance to complain about us; or our personal favorite, our customers aren't using social media.

Gary Vaynerchuk said in his best-selling book, Crush It, "If you're not using Twitter because you're in the camp that thinks it's stupid, you're going to lose. It's as simple as that. It doesn't matter if you think it's stupid. It's free communication, and there's a crapload of users."

The very real fact is that your customers are using social media platforms already. They are using them in staggering numbers. If your company is not using social media for marketing, to listen to your customers, and to aggregate valuable data, you're missing out on the biggest, most popular channel of communication there is.

In the spring of 2011, roughly 310 million people lived in the United States. Almost twice that many people had Facebook accounts.[1] And, according to Facebook, roughly 30% of its users are from the United States. That's 150 million U.S. Facebook users, which means nearly one in every two people you talk to today will likely have a Facebook account. An iStrategyLabs analysis of Facebook users in late 2010 showed 71% of U.S. web users are on Facebook.[2]

Are you ready to turn your back on half your audience?

"But our target audience just doesn't use Facebook," you say. Really?

No age group has less than 22.8% growth on Facebook over the last year. The fastest growing? 18- to 24-year-olds. The second-fastest? 55-plus.

But that's just one platform. The world of social media is far more vast:

- There are 200 million accounts on Twitter.

- There are more than 100 million users on LinkedIn.

- The average time spent on Twitter is 2 hours, 12 minutes per month.[3]

- The average age of Twitter users is 39.

- The average age of LinkedIn users is 44.[4]

According to the Pew Internet & American Life Project's fall 2010 tracking survey, 95% of all U.S. adults with a household income of $75,000 or more use the Internet and own a cell phone. For those with an income of less than $30,000, 57% use the Web while 75% have cell phones.

Comscore tells us four out of five web users visit a social networking site on at least a monthly basis.[5] TNS Global Research's Digital Life survey shows 46% of global users visit a social networking site every day.[6] Their findings go on to say that 29% of global users actively look for brands to interact with online. There are nearly 6.9 billion people in the world, so that's 2.41 billion people looking for brands like yours.

So, 29% of the global web population is actively looking to interact with brands through social networks and you're satisfied with your 0.2 to 0.3 average click-thru rate on a banner ad?[7]

And while we're at it, how about mobile marketing? The cell phone and smartphone devices account for five billion people worldwide.[8] The International Telecommunications Union expects mobile devices accessing the web to surpass the access from desktop computers within five years. Why? So people can stay hyperconnected to their friends and family through social networks they access through mobile devices.

We could keep hurling statistics at you like a hyperactive 10-year-old in a snowball fight, but we won't. Suffice it to say, your customers are plugged in, turned on, and social media users. So why aren't you? Or what are you going to do now to capture their attention when it has shifted to more interactive and dynamic conversation-based websites?

Today's Consumer Is Different. You're Still the Same Old Dinosaur.

A lot of businesses we talk to are still relying on traditional marketing methods, focusing on TV and radio commercials, print ads, billboards, and trade shows. Thinking of social media as a marketing channel is laughable to them. As a result, they "get some social media," perhaps by starting a Facebook page or Twitter account where they just automate blog post promotions but then relegate it to such low priority that an intern is in charge of it. While the business owners are satisfied they "got some social media," the employee put *in charge of the marketing of the company* through this emerging channel is not a full-time employee nor well versed in communicating on behalf of the company. If the intern is lucky, he or she doesn't have to fight with IT or the compliance department to have access to social media sites from a work computer.

"Our customers aren't using social media," seems to be the common response from the executives of these companies.

"How do you know?" we ask.

"Well, because I don't use it."

Well, your customers are, and if companies waited until the CEO adopted technology before implementing its use, our best digital device would be the abacus. It's also unlikely your customers will tell you they want you to use social media to communicate with them. They'll just migrate to the competitors that are and you'll be left with your "I don't use it" CEO who is selling products to "I'm no longer using you" customers.

If a company is not using social media platforms, it has no way of knowing whether its customers are using it. Do you really believe your customers aren't? Go to Gist.com and upload your customer email list. That service will show you how many of those email addresses are connected to accounts on Twitter, Facebook, LinkedIn, and more. Trust us...more of your customers are using social media than you think.

Or you could just look at the broad use numbers:

- 77.3% of the people in the United States are on the Internet.[9]

- 65.8% of U.S. adults with an Internet connection use social media in some form or function.[10]

- 77.4% of all North Americans are online.[11]

- 1.9 billion people are online worldwide.[12]

Think of the numbers for a minute: 77% of U.S. homes have Internet access and 65% of them are on a social network. That means 50.8% of the people in the United States are using social media.

That's half of your customer base, half of your vendors, and half of your competitors. And if social media use is that widespread, and even half of your competitors are already using it, that means they're reaching half of your customers on a channel you haven't even considered using.

Despite these numbers, a lot of executives and business owners still dismiss social media out of hand. They think it's a fad, that it's not important, or that it consists of websites full of only angry people who live in their parents' basements.

Target made this blunder by underestimating the blogosphere when it told a blogger it doesn't "participate in nontraditional media." The company realized the error when that same nontraditional media reared its ugly head and dropped a PR hammer on them.

In 2008, Amy Jussel, the founder of ShapingYouth.org, complained on her blog about a new ad campaign the retail giant had created, including a woman laying on a large Target emblem, arms and legs spread like she's making a snow angel. She believed "targeting crotches with a bull's-eye is not the message we should be putting out there." Jussel called Target's public relations team, asking for a comment or response to her questioning of the ad. A PR spokesperson wrote to Jussel and said, "Unfortunately we are unable to respond to your inquiry because Target does not participate with nontraditional media outlets. This practice is in place to allow us to focus on publications that reach our core guest."

What Target failed to realize is that their core guests—*people*—write blogs and read blogs.

Their "core guests" turned the discussion from whether the ad was sexually suggestive to whether Target hates social media practitioners. Many bloggers, even those with thousands of readers, began pounding Target with not-so-nice things written about them.

Target's readers were more than a little irritated with the retail giant, many of them promising never to shop there again. The public outcry was enough that a spokesperson said they would review the policy and consider adjusting it. Not only did they, but Target now even responds to public questions asked of the company on Twitter. Although it did not begin as a major shift in thinking, Target at least realized that blogging was fast shedding its "nontraditional media" skin and becoming a real source of news and opinion.

Your customers are using social media platforms, they're comparing notes about the products and services they buy, and they're discussing which ones they like the best. They're even talking about you. But the Internet is not a dictatorship and you aren't in control. This is why you hear the call to "participate in the conversation." You won't control it. But by participating, you can at least respond, be accountable, and hold others as such. Still, you need to understand a thing or two about control.

You Never Controlled Your Message

Another worry for a lot of executives, business owners, and the lawyers (especially the lawyers) is that if a company has a blog, Facebook page, or Twitter account, these platforms offer people the opportunity to say bad things about the company. Why open that door?

The door has been open for years. You just haven't been able to see what's on the other side. Twenty years ago, there were several million water coolers around the world. People were talking about you around a few of them. The difference today is that there's one, big water cooler with several million people around it...and you can hear what most of them are saying.

If you have a bad product, poor customer service, or lousy policies, customers are already saying bad things about you. They're complaining, telling their friends, or writing angry letters and have been for years. Thanks to technology, they can now complain on Facebook to several hundred friends, or write a blog post that's read by thousands.

It happened to Dell back in 2005, when journalist Jeff Jarvis wrote a blog post called "Dell lies. Dell sucks" on his BuzzMachine.com blog. Jarvis, the founder and creator of *Entertainment Weekly* and former TV critic for *TV Guide* and *People*, said later in an interview, "I learned some time ago that you can search Google for any brand, followed by the word 'sucks,' to find out how much ill will is attached."

Jarvis's post exploded. Dell was embarrassed. And when the company finally took note and offered to replace Jarvis's computer, the damage was done. He refused and purchased a Macintosh Powerbook.

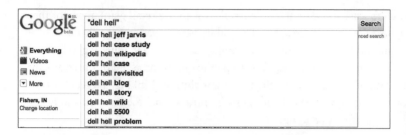

Figure 2.1   Dell had some serious reputation problems when the phrase "Dell hell" started gaining its own prominence in Google searches.

Clearly, it did not matter whether Dell had a social media presence or not; people were already saying bad things about the company. At first unaware of Jarvis's post, Dell suffered badly. To its credit, Dell learned from the incident and now has one of the more robust, engaged, and successful social media presences of any company.

So people are going to complain, especially if you give them reason. Would it surprise you that we think the best place for them to do it is actually on your website or your company's social media outposts? We're not nuts. Here's why.

If you can easily find the complaints on your site, you can respond to the complaint and fix the problem faster, respond to the customer, and share your response with other site visitors. This way, when someone else comes to the site and sees the complaint, they'll also see that you fixed it as well. They'll be more impressed that (1) you're willing to admit a mistake, (2) you fixed it, and (3) you didn't mind doing it out in the open.

People only have so much time and energy to complain. If they complain about you on your site—where you can easily see it—then they're less likely to take the extra time to complain about you on another site you never even knew about. This way, you're allowing people a chance to vent and complain, feel like they've been heard, and then go about their day.

Keep in mind this assumes you will actually respond to the person's complaint and fix the problem. Don't just put up a blog or place for people to complain if you don't plan on doing anything about it. Companies that pretend to listen but don't actually do anything about it will get a double whammy: people complaining about the company's actions and then complaining about their inaction. Only now they're likely to make it much more public.

If Social Media Can Help Overthrow a Government, What Will It Do to a Company?

In February 2011, the world got to see the power of social media when wielded by an unhappy public. The people of Egypt, fueled by messages posted on social networks, protested the actions of President Hosni Mubarak, high unemployment, and rising prices. Protesters were sharing information via Facebook, Twitter, and YouTube, telling the world what was happening in their country.

As the protests grew, the government caught on and blacked out the Internet. The subsequent outrage made matters worse and Mubarak was forced out of power. Although protests have existed for centuries before social media, this time the social connectivity of the Internet played a significant role in helping topple an oppressive regime.

And although other governments who have dealt with protesters tried different techniques, like shutting off cell towers and community Wi-Fi networks, they have all tried shutting off two of the biggest communication networks in the world, all with similar degrees of success: none at all. Even when Egypt shut off the wireless Internet and cell networks throughout the country, activists fired up old dial-up modems to communicate with each other, as well as the outside world.

But there are lessons that business leaders can learn from these protests as they relate to social media and your customers.

- People are talking about your organization, whether you know it or not. In the protests, the governments were caught off guard because they didn't know people were upset or trying to organize. They didn't know what was happening until they looked out their windows and saw an angry crowd of people.

  If customers are not happy, they're not going to call your customer service department, send an angry fax, or write a postal letter. Some might, but still more of them will tell their friends on the biggest, most widely read channels of communication in the world.

- People will find a way to talk about you. Even though these different governments tried to shut off the Internet to quell the protests, people found a way around it. When they couldn't access it through their Wi-Fi networks or mobile phones, they found other, sometimes older, ways to communicate.

  It doesn't matter whether you refuse to put up your own blog with a comments section, block those comments, get your legal department to write a nasty letter to some of the worst offenders, or ignore social media altogether. People will still find a way to talk about you. They may need to go outside the regular arena to do it, but they'll find a way to air their grievances and make sure other people know about it.

- If you make enough people angry, you'll be replaced.

When you don't address customers' needs or answer their questions—or if you don't give them a place to feel like they've been heard—they will oust you from their own buying habits. And in today's share-first environment online, they'll tell everyone they know, too.

It's Not About Being on Social; It's About Being Social

Using social media for business isn't just a matter of signing up for a couple of social media accounts, turning them over to your intern, and waiting for the electronic world to beat a path to your door. It didn't happen with your first fax machine, email system, or website, so it's not going to happen with your social media presence either.

If you build it, they will not come. You have to build it, tell everyone it's there, and then be there when they show up.

Using social media for business means actually using it. This is a communication device, which means people are expecting you to be there, to talk with them, to listen to them. They expect you to have conversations with them.

Remember, we told you that the hippies and tree huggers had half the equation right. Social media is about having conversations and engaging with your customers. But when you add the word *marketing* to *social media*, it becomes about business.

The world of social media is another marketing and communication channel, just like all the other channels you already use. The only difference is that this is a channel where the people aren't looking to be pitched, sold, or persuaded. In fact, many of them are purposefully avoiding a sales job. They want you to talk with them, to have relationships with them, and to listen to them.

Usually when an angry customer says she's telling all her friends never to patronize a company again, she'll tell a few people, and that will be the end of it. When Heather Armstrong does it, she tells a million people all at once.

Armstrong was famously fired in the mid-2000s for blogging. Her subsequent Internet fame led to an incredibly well-trafficked blog (Dooce.com). In 2009, Armstrong purchased a $1,300 washing machine, which stopped working properly. After a repairman made several visits, none of which actually repaired the machine, she called a help line to no avail. While waiting on hold for the customer service rep's supervisor, she sent a tweet (a Twitter message) to more than one million followers: "So that you may not have to suffer like we have: DO NOT EVER BUY A MAYTAG. I repeat: OUR MAYTAG EXPERIENCE HAS BEEN A NIGHTMARE."

Three minutes later, she wrote, "Have I mentioned what a nightmare our experience was with Maytag?" She followed that with three more tweets that mentioned her displeasure with Maytag, calling them out by name.

She was contacted by a number of appliance stores, and then received a tweet from @WhirlpoolCorp, the Twitter account of Maytag parent company Whirlpool, asking for her phone number. The next day, she received a call from Whirlpool's headquarters, who sent out a new repairman, overnighted some parts, and the day after, she had a working washing machine.

Although some organizations would have ignored the Dooce Twitter account because she was a nontraditional media outlet, the fact is, she is able to reach 1.5 million people via Twitter and 300,000 people per day with her blog. There are TV shows that don't reach a few hundred thousand people at all. (CNBC barely gets 200,000 viewers in a single day.) Numbers like these are big enough that, in 2009, Forbes named her one of "The Most Influential Women in Media."

Maytag/Whirlpool was lucky because they monitored social media and knew there was a problem as soon as Armstrong tweeted it. But the damage she could have done to their reputation could have meant a significant loss in sales, and they never would have known why it happened. But the fact that they were present, using it, and listening to their customers saved them from serious reputation damage.

The lesson learned is that just having an account isn't good enough. It is only the first step. The follow-through is actively monitoring, participating in conversations, and making sure social media doesn't "Dooce" you.

From washing machines to television programming, participating in the conversation is proving fruitful for companies. Charles Miller and his team of e-communications responders at DirecTV seek out customer's concerns by monitoring a variety of social media sites. DirecTV is a huge company that serves millions of customers around the world. Their U.S. operation serves several million customers alone.

When an avid sports fan tweets a complaint that the big game isn't on a certain channel as advertised, Miller and crew spring into action, routing the issue to the broadcast department to see if there's an issue. This happened in September of 2009 when a user complained about the ESPN reception for a Georgia Tech versus Clemson football game. Within a few minutes, the official DirecTV Twitter account responded with assurance they were working on the issue and instructions to watch the regular resolution on a different channel.

An hour later, the official account told fans the high-definition channel was restored and they could switch back. The resulting tweets showed appreciation and cheers for DirecTV, not dissatisfaction that there was an issue in the first place.

What DirecTV did is not just sign up for an account, but monitor it, use it to participate in conversations with customers, and, ultimately, be social.

Baltimore's 1st Mariner Bank is another example of a brand being social, not just using social media. Whether you look at its Twitter account (@1stMarinerBank) or Facebook page (www.facebook.com/1stMarinerBank), you see helpful posts about managing your finances, links to interesting articles and events that affect the Baltimore area, and back-and-forth conversations with followers and fans. If customer service issues arise, they're quickly routed to private channels (financial industry regulations and privacy concerns keep users as well as the bank from discussing much publicly), but the institution uses its accounts to primarily be social.

They share good content and engage in conversations.

Social media marketing is about being social with a purpose. It means listening to what your customers are saying. Listening to what they're complaining about, and then fixing it; listening to what they're asking, and then answering it; listening to what they're happy about, and then thanking them; and listening to what they're telling their friends about, and then rewarding them when appropriate.

Of course, that does mean letting go and letting your employees talk to your customers—even if it's just a few members of your marketing or PR team. By now you know your customers can and will talk about you. So, you need to let your employees talk with those customers to keep them happy.

If You Don't Trust Your Employees, You Hired the Wrong People

A lot of companies don't feel they can trust employees to use social media tools and communicate with customers. The excuse we often hear from executives is, "We need to ensure we stay on message." The real reason, however, is that these companies just don't trust their employees. (Some companies actually say this outright.)

If your employees can't be trusted to pick up the phone and talk to customers, if they can't field a question from a customer who walks into your store, if they will likely sneak and play Angry Birds or send personal messages to family and friends if given access to Facebook at the office, then you're right. You can't trust them to talk to customers online.

But if those scenarios are true, you've hired bad employees.

By saying you don't trust your employees to communicate with your public, you're essentially saying you hired people who will put out bad or incorrect information, or won't communicate to your customers properly. If, however, if you trust employees to answer customer service calls and give them the ability to accept returns, give credits, and speak on the company's behalf, then you can trust them to talk to customers online. These employees make decisions that can affect the company's bottom line every day. You're trusting them to provide good customer service to create repeat customers.

You trust your salespeople to speak to your customers without you. You trust them to go to meetings and represent your company in the best possible light, and to do everything they can to get the sale without giving away profit margin. You don't go on all the sales calls with them, watching over their shoulders as they give their presentations, negotiate the best possible terms, and approve every detail and decimal. Your salespeople are directly responsible for your bottom line. Their successes and failures mean you either have a great year or a bad year. The better they do, the better the company does. So you provide them with the tools to get the job done and to be as successful as they can be.

You trust the people you hired to count and spend your money. You trust the people you hired to write sales brochures and organize trade shows. You even trust the people you hired to produce your product, put it in a box, and stick it on a truck.

But while most companies trust these employees, they don't trust those same employees to write 350 words three times a week on a platform where errors are easily fixed. They don't trust people to send Twitter messages that are 140 characters long. They don't trust people to keep an eye out for Facebook messages about your company.

They're thinking about it the wrong way.

Tony Hsieh is the CEO of shoe and apparel company Zappos. His company has sold shoes online since 2000. It's not a big deal because a lot of people sell shoes online and in stores. But as the technology became available, Hsieh trusted his employees to write blog posts and to tweet about life at Zappos.

They didn't have to run anything through legal; they didn't have to have anyone check everything over first. They just did it. They tweeted and blogged about everything in the company—co-workers, projects, customers, big deals, bad days—and provided some excellent customer service to boot. They used customer service phone calls, blogging, and Twitter to build deeper emotional connections with their customers. They communicated with their customers, rather than hammering them with a steady barrage of commercial messages.

Within eight years of launching the company, they were selling $1 billion worth of shoes and apparel online, two years before their initial projections. The following November, Hsieh sold Zappos to Amazon for $928 million in a stock exchange.

Maybe it's just a coincidence, but a company that trusted its employees to communicate with its customers over the phone and through social media was selling

$1 billion worth of shoes eight years after they started and sold for 93% of that total the year after.

Letting employees communicate freely goes against the grain of a lot of corporate types because they're used to controlling every message, but we've already established you're not controlling customer service reps' responses or salespeople or company presentations. (You're certainly not controlling whether your customers are talking about you.) You need to give your staff the same amount of trust to communicate online.

We're not saying you need to allow all of your employees the chance to be official or unofficial company representatives on social media sites. We know there are some employees who, when they miss a day of work, things go more smoothly. However, you also have those employees who are outstanding, trustworthy, and true ambassadors for your organization.

These employees are your social media opportunity waiting to happen. You can create guidelines and policies to give them parameters for online communications, but don't be afraid of your own best evangelists. Plug them in and turn them on.

But don't let other departments stand in their way.

Don't Blame It on IT, Compliance, or Legal

Surprisingly enough, when a company does say they'd rather not dive into social media marketing, the decision is inevitably made by a department other than marketing. In our experience, it's usually the people from the legal department, compliance, or IT.

This isn't a rant about tattletales and sticklers. We respect and embrace the role of each of these business units. Typically, when they raise objections about social media marketing or your company's Internet plans, they're only looking out for the best interests of the organization. Lawyers are supposed to minimize risk. Compliance is supposed to ensure regulations and rules are followed to keep the company out of trouble. IT is often on the lookout for security and technical breaches that can adversely affect how the company's infrastructure works.

But there are times when the overprotective parent says "no" because that's an easier answer than "yes." Saying "yes" means having to account for new policies, new procedures, and new checks and balances. It brings about change, which many people are resistant to.

The "no" is often followed by justifications like network security, governmental regulations about privacy, privileged information, trade secrets, financial regulations, or anything else they're paid to worry about.

There's a very easy way your company can avoid violating privileged information/secrets/regulations through social media:

Don't violate privileged information/secrets/regulations through social media!

As flippant as that sounds, it is that easy. Think of all the ways we can't violate secrets and privilege now. We can't share private information on the phone with a friend, email it to our spouse, or fax it to a former co-worker. And we can't tell anyone in person.

The same rules and laws still apply to the Internet and social media because it's just one more communication tool. You talk to people, they talk back. You share information, they receive it. Regardless of the communication channel, you know not to violate that secret information. Social media activity does not suddenly render people stupid or oblivious. Social media doesn't trick people; it doesn't lull us into a false sense of security. We don't violate privilege or trade secrets just because we have a new way to talk to people.

The best social media policy writing is typically done by adding the words "online and offline" to strategic places in the company code of conduct or ethics. You have these privacy and proprietary information clauses incorporated into employee communications...or you should. Simply clarify that the policy also applies online.

Social Media Doesn't Violate Company Policy. People Violate Company Policy.

If you trust your employees not to violate privileged information/secrets/regulations with the other forms of communication already in your office, then you should trust them not to violate these same rules on social networking. Let them exercise the same judgment you hired them for, rather than hindering them by letting someone who doesn't understand marketing—legal, compliance, and IT—tell them what they can and can't do. After all, marketing doesn't ask to edit legal briefs or maintain software and network updates.

Please know that we're not just trying to sell you a bill of goods. There are times when employees mess up, say the wrong thing on Twitter, share information they shouldn't have in the comments of a blog post, and more. But Twitter, blogging, and social media aren't the cause. They're the channel. The employee violated the policy. And he or she didn't need the Internet to do so.

When an employee of New Media Strategies, then social media agency of record for Chrysler, popped off on Twitter about the bad drivers in Detroit in the spring of 2011, he or she did so using an expletive and accidentally posted the tweet on Chrysler's account, not his or her own. According to media reports, New Media Strategies fired the employee, and Chrysler fired the social media agency.

But the incident was an isolated incident. Chalk it up to human error, but know that human error will happen. The last time an employee of your company shared private information with an inappropriate party or mouthed off about his or her supervisor within earshot of someone else in the office, it wasn't because of his or her cell phone. And if it ever happens online, it will not be Twitter's fault, or Facebook's, or your blog's. It will be human error, which you account for with strong company policies and education (see Chapter 12, "Remedy Your Fears with Sound Policy").

So What Can You Do with Social Media?

Even though social media is often seen as something only for twentysomethings, or a tool for socializing with friends and talking about what you had for breakfast (that's not actually what most people use it for), a lot of businesspeople are discovering that social media is a great benefit to themselves and their companies. Social media becomes very powerful when used tactically as well as strategically...when you add the world "marketing" to "social media."

You can catch or outpace the competition. Your competitors are likely already using social media to talk to *your* customers. While your sales staff is still cold calling and attending the one big trade show every year, your competitors are connecting with their customers, and yours. By joining the social media world and listening to the conversations around your company, and even your competitors, you can make those same connections.

You can grow individual or company thought leadership fast. It no longer takes years to grow a reputation in an industry through conferences, trade shows, and the trade journals or mainstream media. Now, a reputation can be grown in just a few months of purposed social media activity. By writing an industry blog, connecting with like-minded people on networks like Twitter and LinkedIn, and participating in online discussions, people can establish their expertise in short order. Social media lets people find a public forum to share their knowledge, educating and building trust along the way.

You can harvest intelligence about your industry. Some of the early social media adopters in any industry have been in trade media. They're always looking for a way to grow their readership and reduce their costs, to maintain their expertise and credibility, and to grow with the times. Even the animal production industry, an industry not known for its rapid acceptance of change, has made this move, with the biggest trade media group, Watt Agriculture, going digital in the last few years. Not only do they publish their magazines online, they blog, and they sponsor and moderate a social network for people who work in the animal industry.

The net result is that Watt Agriculture can deliver its magazine to more readers while reducing printing costs. It can not only monitor the discussions readers are having, but also participate in them. It can discover new ideas and information for future stories and further solidify its own reputation as a thought leader and expert in the industry. The ultimate payoff for Watt is more people turning to it for trusted information, largely through paid subscriptions.

You can build your network for business purposes, or tap it again. Whether it's an old friend from college or former co-workers from a job you held 15 years ago, social media makes it incredibly easy to find and reconnect with people from your past. Jason ran into an old high school friend on Twitter. It just so happened that old friend oversaw the public relations account for a major U.S. auto maker. Jason has worked with said auto maker since. Social media also facilitates a more efficient method of connecting and growing relationships with people you meet and connect with at conferences, networking events, and other business or social functions. Professional relationships blossom more readily with top-of-mind awareness. Seeing your name and status updates in that important prospect's LinkedIn stream each day positions you better for the sale.

The Ball Is in Your Court

Social media has become one of, if not the preferred method of communications for today's consumers. They're not picking up the phone as much. They're not visiting your corporate website as much. They're not paying a visit to your location as much.

They're turning to online communities, social networks, and ratings and reviews sites to learn about products and services. But they're not learning from the companies that provide them, but from other users just like them who have bought and tried them.

You can let them go there and find out about you from someone else. You can ignore the online conversation and assume that everyone on social media sites is akin to the petty, anonymous trolls who comment on the local newspaper's website.

Nothing is stopping you...yet.

But in the coming years, and perhaps even months, your market share is likely to dwindle. Your marketing will steadily become less and less effective. Public perception of your company will decline. Customer service issues will too, but not because you're doing a great job of keeping customers happy—because you're doing a bad job of keeping customers at all.

You can be a manager...risk averse and skeptical of that which you don't know.

Or you can be a leader...willing to push change, not fear it; a driver of innovation, not a passenger in someone else's ride.

You can listen to what customers—yours and your competition's—are saying about their needs and adapt to meet them. You can build relationships and trust with consumers over time, making them loyal to you and stakeholders in your success. You can focus on the lifetime value of a customer, not the short-term dollar amount of his or her next purchase.

You can join your stakeholders in conversations and even collaborate with them to create new products, services, or shared value for the greater good.

You can join social media sites *and* be social there.

But you better do it quick. Because although the world of social media marketing is relatively new, it's not right off the assembly line. Your competition is considering social media marketing as well. In fact, they may already have a head start.

Endnotes

1. http://www.facebook.com/press/info.php?statistics.

2. http://www.istrategylabs.com/2011/01/2011-facebook-demographics-and-statistics-including-federal-employees-and-gays-in-the-military/.

3. http://www.experian.com/blogs/marketing-forward/2011/01/25/americans-spend-2-hours-13-minutes-per-month-on-twitter-com/.

4. http://thenextweb.com/socialmedia/2010/09/08/the-average-twitter-user-is-how-old/.

5. http://www.comscore.com/Press_Events/Press_Releases/2010/2/comScore_Releases_2009_U.S._Digital_Year_in_Review.

6. http://discoverdigitallife.com/activating-social-media/.

7. http://www.imediaconnection.com/content/25781.asp.

8. http://www.itu.int/ITU-D/ict/statistics/at_glance/KeyTelecom.html.

9. http://www.internetworldstats.com/am/us.htm.

10. http://blog.zerista.com/2010/06/02/social-media-adoption-current-facts-stats-part-1/.

11. http://www.internetworldstats.com/stats14.htm.

12. http://www.internetworldstats.com/stats.htm.

3

Your Competition May Have Already Kicked Your Ass

Look out the window. Do you see your competitor peering in? Do you see the dozens of people chatting with their sales representatives in the streets right under your nose? Do you see the person walking up to your door only to be intercepted by a friendly passerby from your competition's support team?

If your company is not using social media for marketing purposes, this very scenario is happening under your nose right now.

You might not be blogging, chatting up fans on Facebook, or soliciting new product ideas from anyone and everyone in a public forum like MyStarbucksIdea.com, but the other guy is still peering in your window.

Using social media monitoring platforms—services like Google that crawl the Web and report back on what they find based on the keywords input—your competitors are watching your prospective customers talk. They're talking about how they're ready to buy a product like the one you sell and asking if anyone knows of a good source. They're watching your customers complain about the rude and annoying sales clerk or your please-kill-me-now hold music. And do you know what your competition is doing next?

They're saying, "You should expect more from a company than that. Perhaps we can interest you in buying from us. You know us better. We're here having conversations with you online. We're part of your world, and we understand you."

And then they're taking your customers right out from under you. But you never even saw it coming. In February of 2010, Chris Geier, the community and social media manager for Redman, Washington-based K2, a business process management software company, posed an innocuous message on Twitter. It read, "Alternatives to Telligent Community Server? Recommendations?" Michael Fraietta was watching. He wasn't actively following Geier, waiting to pounce the day he decided to shop around for a different community service. Fraietta was just performing his duties as community manager for Jive Software, an enterprise social platform and Telligent Community Server competitor. Part of those duties included checking the alerts from his social media monitoring platform, which included a search for Jive's main competitors.

When Geier's mention of "Telligent" hit the Web, Fraietta was instantly alerted to the message. He responded by posting a public Twitter message directed to Geier. (This is called an "at" message because of the @ symbol used to tag the username and notify the user who has mentioned them.) The message was viewable by any-one but notified Geier to see it because his username was mentioned. It said, "@chrisgeier Chris, check out @JiveSoftware for an external community server. Here's ours, http://bit.ly/jivespace - Mike." In Twitter vernacular, what Fraietta essentially communicated in that simple message was this:

> "Hey Chris! Look over here! I saw your tweet about alternatives to Telligent, and this is my response. You should check out Jive Software for an external community server. Here's a quick link so you can click and see the company's Twitter profile. You can click on it and go right to the prod-uct page. My name's Mike if you have any questions."

All this was packed in the message and told Chris everything Mike wanted him to know:

- The "@chrisgeier" syntax told Chris that someone had mentioned him in a tweet.

- Twitter told Chris it was a reply to a previous message and linked to it, for future reference, or even a reminder of what he had previously said.

- The "@JiveSoftware" listing appeared as a hyperlink, so Chris or anyone else could click through to the Jive company's Twitter page.

- The "http://bit.ly/jivespace" link is a shortened URL (web address) that, when clicked, takes Chris (or anyone else) to the Jive product page on the company website.

Geier told us that after seeing Mike's timely and direct response, he clicked through and investigated. He signed up for a demonstration of the Jivespace software solution and became a qualified lead.

You might think the moral of this story is how Mike Fraietta was paying attention to Twitter and was able to jump on the opportunity presented to him, but it's not. It's important, but it's not the most important one. You might think the moral of the story is how Twitter enables people like Chris Geier to ask their network for recommendations to products or services, but it's not. It's important, but it's not the most important one. You might even think it's about how Jive had an awesome product that was able to do everything someone like Chris was looking for, but it's not. It's important, but it's not the most important one.

No, the most important moral of this story was the fact that, out of all the people Telligent has working for it, none of them seemed to be watching for their company's name on Twitter, and thus may have missed the chance to fix Chris's problem, salvage the relationship, and keep the customer.

So who do you want to be? Telligent or Jive?

Your Audience Doesn't Trust You Anymore, Anyway

The problem isn't just that your competition is using social media to woo your customers. It's that your customers are also talking to people about products and services, instead of talking to you. You have an ulterior motive. The social connections they make online do not.

It's easy to think your customers should trust you—especially if you're really good at what you do. The problem is, they don't. They don't trust you because you make money when they do.

Put yourself in the role of the consumer for a moment. Let's say you're buying a car. You walk onto the lot and from the moment the salesman approaches you, you're skeptical. And you should be. Salesmen over the years have generally taught us they'll do anything to make the sale. They're in it for them, not us.

Social media and technology company Alterian conducted a survey led by Lancaster (U.K.) University professor Michael Hulme in early 2010. They asked 1,000 people in Great Britain and 1,000 people in the United States about their level of trust in a variety of brands and companies.[1]

Only 5% of those asked indicated they trusted advertising. Only 9% thought companies always act in the best interest of customers. The survey showed that 58% sampled felt that companies were only interested in selling products to them, not necessarily the product or service that was right for them. Meanwhile, 84% of the Alterian sampling said they use the Internet to find some form of comparison with people they believe to be similar to themselves who are reviewing or talking about the product.

Certainly, we could go on with stats about how word-of-mouth marketing is more effective, how chief marketing officers of companies indicate ratings and review sites as primarily important in their social media efforts, or how your customers don't trust you, but let's step back and look at how this environment of mistrust emerged in the first place.

Picture yourself in the late 1990s and early 2000s. The dot-com era is running high (too high perhaps). Enron is making loads of money (or so it seems) and Arthur Andersen is counting it for them (again, so it seems). Corporate America is on top of the world.

But consumers are angry. A movement is beginning that would result in the National Do Not Call Registry in the United States. (It was implemented in 2004.) XM Satellite Radio, which offered to clear up your radio programming of annoying advertising, was readying for a 2001 launch. Some of the crafty web developers were adding pop-up blockers to Internet browsers and digital video recorders—devices that allowed you to fast-forward through commercials—were appearing at the Consumer Electronics Show (CES) for the first time.

Notice a theme?

Shortly thereafter, the bubble burst, as did Enron, Arthur Andersen, and more. Destitute web hopefuls then realized if they were to recover from the ashes of an inflated online market's explosion, there was only one answer: Make it easier for people to get online so a market existed.

Armed with a new consumer's bill of rights, developers and programmers began exploring new ways to get people online. It was no longer about the corporate website or selling things. It was about connecting people, tearing down geographic boundaries, and (sometimes) just seeing what would happen.

August 1999 saw Pyra Labs launch Blogger.com, a publishing platform that allowed people to build and publish their own websites full of web pages in a mechanism no more difficult than filling out an email subject line and message. With the start of Ryze, a professional social networking site launched in 2001, and later Friendster (2002), online communities beyond seemingly archaic bulletin boards and forum communities began to rise. As more and more discovered the new post-dot-com-burst web, one in which you could not only control your media environment, but also discover like-minded people from around the world without leaving your home office, the new medium of social media took shape.

Today, it's not enough for a website to offer pictures of products. Now customers want to write a review, then share it with a friend. If they have a bad experience with a company, they want to tell their social networks about it. And many of them have built up large communities of followers and friends to share that review with.

Take that promise of user-generated content one step further and see how consumers like Dave Carroll can write a song and record a music video called, "United Breaks Guitars," that brings an entire international airline to its Internet knees (see Chapter 4, "Here's the Secret: There Is No Damn Secret!") and you're looking at a new landscape of customer interaction.

And so is your competition.

Go Ahead, Buy an Ad

You've seen the statistics of social media, but let's also look at the statistics of traditional media. This is probably where you feel more comfortable, but should you?

The cost of participating in social media isn't free. There will be time spent and some hard costs, regardless. But logging on and signing up for a social networking account that allows your customers to engage with you is free. And using some alerts to let you know when people mention your name online doesn't require a financial investment. Compare that to your traditional methods of communicating with your customers and you see why we're bullish on social media for your business.

- Trade show attendance has declined 38% in the last decade while the cost to exhibit has risen 50%.[2]

- Newspaper advertising revenue fell more than 28% in one quarter in 2008 according to Media post.[3] No fewer than 20 U.S. metropolitan daily newspapers have either folded or moved to a hybrid or online-only model since March of 2007.[4]

- Generator Research predicts television advertising will fall more than 75% in the next decade.[5]

- Starting in 2007, radio advertising declined for 14 consecutive quarters.[6]

- From 2008 to 2009, only cable television and online mediums showed audience growth with network television, local television, magazines, and newspapers all in decline.[7]

We're not saying traditional media is dead, or that you should ignore it completely. But you should take a long, serious look at what each channel can produce before you start your "business as usual" spending for your upcoming fiscal year. Remember: It's not always an argument of ROI, but what you get out of the activity.

So while the social media marketing skeptics spend thousands on billboards and millions on TV spots that deliver guestimates as metrics and have little long-term benefit, their competition (and perhaps yours) is building lasting relationships with customers on the social web.

But We're a B2B Company; We Don't Count

And don't think you can get away with the excuse of being a business-to-business (B2B) company. They aren't different animals.

Yes, buying cycles are longer, costs are typically higher, there's (usually) no such thing as a showroom or retail space, and people don't just walk by and consider buying. Sure, it's different in some ways, but there's one critical area where B2B marketing isn't different than business-to-consumer (B2C) or any other kind (if there is another kind).

People don't buy products from a building. They don't buy from a logo. They don't even buy from a company. People purchase products and services for their business from other people. And those other people are human. Humans engage in conversations. Humans frequent social networks. Humans enjoy finding and sharing content with their contacts. We're here to tell you there's no such thing as B2B marketing. It's P2P marketing—person to person. Social media is important for the business customer and those types of customers are using social media:

- 57% of U.S. workers use social media for business purposes at least once per week.[8]

- Social media tools are gaining a "deeper penetration into the enterprise with use by executive managers and IT."

- 59% of B2B buyers are engaged with peers online who addressed their challenges.

- 48% followed online industry conversations on topics.

- 41% followed online discussions to learn more about topics.

- 37% posted questions on social networking sites looking for suggestions or feedback.

- 20% connected directly with potential solution providers via social networking channels.

- 59% shared learning with others through individual discussions, blog posts, discussion forums, and tweets.[9]

In short, even B2B companies can approach social media with a personality. You can have relationships with the people you're selling to. And you can communicate with them in the same way your B2C counterparts are doing it. Several B2B companies have approached social media marketing with a little creativity and have been rewarded with great success.

Destroy Your Printer

Expert Laser Solutions in Southbridge, Massachusetts, is a managed print services provider. They're the people you call when you need to lease a new copier or laser printer, so you can have someone service and stock the machines to save costs and maintenance hassles. Nathan Dube, one of ELS's marketing staff, accepted the challenge of increasing awareness of his company using social media channels.

He didn't fall back on the ho-hum webinar on toner cartridge recycling or even a blog about laser printer technology. Instead, he asked readers of the company blog, followers and fans of the company and Twitter, LinkedIn, and Facebook, to make videos of themselves destroying their printers. The marketing department comes up with a fun idea that makes customers or potential customers destroy a current product that they'll likely replace by coming to you? Brilliant!

Even with a modest following on the company's respective social networks, the 2009 contest doubled ELS's website traffic and resulted in 100 new inbound links (which helps in search results). The entries were hilarious and even resulted in a recycling magazine profiling the company on a web-TV show.

One company, Telesian Technologies in nearby Worcester, reached out after seeing the contest and hired Expert Laser Services to be their print/copy management provider. The contest was so successful that they did it again in 2010. They now count $4,000 a month in recurring revenue as a direct result of the contest. For a small business, that's a nice return. The winner won free toner cartridges and a $100 donation to the charity of his or her choice, which also proves another point: You don't have to spend a lot of money to use social media marketing successfully. The point is that using social media marketing can pay off big time, even if your business is decidedly not sexy. It can pay off for small businesses and even for small investments.

All it takes is a little creativity.

The Shipping Industry Goes Social

London, England-based ShipServ is a leading e-marketplace provider for the maritime global shipping industry. Its vice-president for marketing, John Watton, set out to use social media to improve the company's image and market awareness, drive more website traffic, and attract new sales leads.

ShipServ researched its audience and online behaviors, redesigned its website to provide more customer-focused content, revamped its customer relationship management system to track leads more effectively, and established an online community in a LinkedIn group. Through its content, including blog posts, whitepapers, videos, social networking activity, and e-newsletters, ShipServ turned in the following success metrics:

- Increased web traffic 59%

- Generated more than 1,000 whitepaper downloads

- Cultivated 378 members in the ShipServ Maritime Network LinkedIn group

- Saw LinkedIn and Twitter emerge as top-20 traffic sources for the company website

- Increased contact-to-lead conversion by 150%

- Increased lead-to-opportunity conversion by 50%

- Increased sales-ready leads by 400%

In the end, Watton estimated they would have spent $150,000 to get that through traditional methods. Using social media over a three-month period, they invested a mere $30,000.[10]

But It Doesn't Have to Be That Complicated

As incredibly productive as a well-planned, measurement-driven social media marketing effort can be, there is still the random act of awesome that makes getting involved even more compelling.

A good example of this involves a small town, a remote car starter, and Jason's mom.

Sara George lives in the small town of Pikeville, which is nestled in the Appalachian Mountains in Eastern Kentucky. During the unusually cold winter in 2010, she decided she wanted a remote starter kit for her car for Christmas.

Jason explored the very few options of car stereo and customization shops in Pikeville, but only one claimed any level of competency in installing such gadgets. He wrote her a check and told her it was for her starter kit.

Fast-forward three weeks. Sara logged in to Facebook one morning to see a message from a gentleman named Greg Tackett scroll across her news stream. Small towns are small towns, so it's safe to assume Sara and Tackett had met. They were at least friends on Facebook. Greg's message on that cold, January day was, "Stay warm and get your remote starter today at Greg's Custom Audio, Video & Car Stereo!"

This blatant marketing message was posted on his personal Facebook page. Social media purists would scoff at such an abuse of their precious "community." They would scoff so hard, they'd hurt themselves.

Sara responded, "I'm in the market. I'll call you."

And she did.

One of Sara's more clever co-workers added a comment, "What kind of discount are you giving your Facebook friends?" Greg responded, "Our Facebook friends always get the best deals!" Another commenter said she wanted one too and added, "I would need three," for each of her family cars.

Greg's then-going rate for a car starter and installation was $350. If each of the commenters who said they were ordering actually did, he pulled in roughly $3,000 from posting one Facebook message.

Let's make a few assumptions about Greg's efforts and see how he did:

Let's say Greg invested about an hour setting up his Facebook page, and spends about 30 minutes a week on it, but invests no money. He doesn't follow the social media "rules" of keeping business on his brand page and his personal page for personal activity. He doesn't care if he mixes in a marketing message with his other personal interactions on the social network. He has 550+ Facebook friends, and we're pretty certain 75% of them live in Pikeville, Kentucky. He might pass them on the street and say hello personally. They trust him. They know he has to make money through his business. They don't mind the fact that he posts the occasional marketing message on Facebook.

What he performed that cold morning was marketing brilliance: He sent a relevant message to a receptive audience of people who trust him at a relevant time. And one message posted to a receptive audience at the right time grossed $3,000.

Social media marketing doesn't have to be any more difficult that that.

Do You Want to Be Greg Tackett or His Competition?

The accidental car starter sale isn't an anomaly. You have people in your social networks (online and offline) who trust you. If you were to find that relevant time to send a relevant message to them when they were receptive to it, you'd drive sales, too.

It might be that you happen to run into them the day after someone breaks into their house and they need a security system like the one you sell. Or that you see a contact on Twitter complaining about the service he or she experienced with AT&T and you work with Verizon.

But it can be more focused, calculated, and strategically orchestrated if you want it to be. You can find out where your target audience is spending time online, what content they appreciate and share, and perhaps what kind of community gap exists in their networking world. You might discover there isn't a good place for people in the maritime industry to go for online conversations about international shipping, and so you create and provide it, cornering the market and beating your competitors to the punch.

You can develop extraordinary content for your customers and fill it full of darn good reasons why they should click through and give you their email address to sign up for that webinar, or even buy something from your website. You can track it, too, by pulling some code from your analytics software and installing it on your blog or website.

You can.

Or you can be Greg Tackett's competition. They probably thought Facebook was a stupid waste of time, something only teenagers do. They figured if someone wanted a car starter on a cold day, they'd think one exists and just happen by the shop for an install. Or maybe they thought the ad they took out in the Yellow Pages (you know, the one on page 312 of that big yellow brick that props open the utility room door?) was all they needed to do.

But if they did happen to have a Facebook account on that cold January morning, if they were connected to Tackett, or even Sara George on the network, and logged in that morning, they saw one thing happen right before their eyes.

Their competition kicked their ass.

Endnotes

1. http://www.alterian.com/resource-links/campaigns/brandsatrisk/ brands-at-risk-nc.pdf/.

2. "The Rapid Decline in Conference Attendance: Why It's Happening and How a High Quality Agenda Can Help," *Tradeshow Magazine*. http://www. vscommunications.com/vsreview/ContentDownloads/VSR_SR1.pdf.

3. Eric Sass, "No Rest for the Dreary: Newspaper Revs Fall 28%," *MediaDailyNews*. http://www.mediapost.com/publications/ ?fa=Articles.showArticle&art_aid=117749.

4. http://newspaperdeathwatch.com.

5. Bruce Barton, "Television Advertising: An Irreversible Decline?" *Contacto Magazine.* http://www.contactomagazine.com/biznews/ tvadvertisingslump0309.htm.

6. Pew Project for Excellence in Journalism. http://journalism.org.

7. Arbitron (http://arbitron.com), comScore (http://comscore.com), Nielsen (http://nielsen.com), Audit Bureau of Circulations (http://accessabc.com).

8. IDC State of Social Business, January 2010. IDC Corporate USA, Framingham, Mass. (http://idc.com).

9. All stats from *Inside the Mind of the New B2B Buyer*, DemandGen Report/ Genuis.com, January and February, 2010.

10. "A Fascinating B2B Social Media Success Story," http://www.businessesgrow. com/2010/06/20/a-fascinating-hardcore-b2b-social-media-success/.

4

Here's the Secret:
There Is No Damn
Secret!

From the beginning of human communication, and the subsequent advent of communicating for a commercial purpose, people have been conditioned to accept one-way broadcast communication. Send your message out to the masses as far and as wide as you can, and hope that a few of them get it and come to you when they're ready to buy. This is how advertising works in any medium—radio, TV, print, outdoor advertising.

Thanks to interstate highways and increased time spent in vehicles over the last 60 years, our highways are plastered with billboards and advertisements blare from radio stations incessantly. Magazines and newspapers flood us with advertisements and inserts. Many television programs have done away with the opening theme song just to squeeze in one more commercial. Sporting events plaster sponsors all over the stadium. Even public radio and public television, which were once a haven from advertising, now have their "underwriter messages" two, three, and four times an hour.

Consumers are tired of being yelled at with advertising and marketing messages. Social media allows consumers to turn off the broadcasts and simplify their online experience to communicate with other people. Real communication implies each person speaks *and* listens; communication goes two ways between two parties, not one party yelling all the time with the other being forced to listen. Because technology has evolved that enables them to do so, consumers can now turn off the broadcasts and communicate with other people.

As a result, social media forces companies and organizations to be more human in how they communicate with customers.

Social Media Marketing Is Not About Technology, It's About Communication

Social media is about talking to customers in the places where they're spending their time and are willing to listen to you. In Chapter 2, "It's Not Them; It's You!" we talked about how many people were users on various social networks. Everywhere you look, businesses are pushing their Facebook and Twitter accounts in hopes that these millions of people will connect with them through social media platforms. Social media is where people are spending their time.

Many businesses get confused in their approach to social media because they don't understand that social media platforms are built on technology, but are built for communications. The technology is often intuitive and simple for the users. The communications happen naturally because the people performing the task are humans, not computers or even marketing spokespeople. Thinking social media requires some great technology skill set is like thinking you need to understand digital video transfer code to be able to watch a DVD.

Social media platforms are about technology. Social media, and thus, social media marketing, are about communications.

Instead of thinking about websites, widgets, and whiz-bang apps, you should be thinking about listening to conversations, participating in them, developing key talking points, and providing information as a resource to those you converse with.

By grounding your approach to social media marketing in communications, your efforts will bring far better results. Focusing on the technology means you'll wind up in the weeds of the shiny new object and miss the greater opportunity.

Tools Change; the Need for Messaging Won't

Think about your first exposure to social media. Was it Facebook? Mark Zuckerberg didn't invent social networking anymore than Al Gore invented the Internet. In fact, there were other "modern" social networks in use before Zuckerberg created Facebook, like Friendster and MySpace.

From Usenet groups to early chatlike functionality on computer bulletin board systems that evolved in the 1980s, social media and social networks have connected individuals online for decades. Social media didn't begin to migrate into the everyday user's life until it was easier to be online, thanks to user-friendly tools like blogger.com and early large-scale social networks like Classmates.com.

But that migration did not take place because people were looking for ads. It didn't take place because marketers were there. Sure, some sites had banner ads, but marketers weren't populating the core reason you were there: to connect and have conversations with like-minded individuals.

As marketing types saw the migration of their audiences from TV, radio, and print to this new online realm, some began exploring social networks to see if they, too, could join the online party. Some failed and some succeeded, but those who tried learned.

What they learned was that people didn't want to be yelled at with ad messages. They learned that consumers did want information from brands occasionally, but it had to be delivered differently. Walking into a community forum on a social network pushing your marketing message right out of the gates was like walking into a social gathering in a restaurant screaming your recent sale over a megaphone. You were asked to leave pretty quickly.

What they learned was that if you assimilate into the community and build relationships with community members, you eventually earn the right to discuss products, services, and business with community members. Better yet, they learn that you are the right person to talk to when they need those products and services.

So entering an online community or conversation as a marketer isn't such that you don't need messaging, goals, or objectives. It just means that you have to set your expectations of time, volume, and activity differently. You have to watch the crowd from afar, listen to their conversations, and gradually earn trust that you're not there to violate their privacy or take advantage of them. You have to get closer to the group and become a part of it day-by-day, moment-by-moment.

When you spend enough time building those relationships, you learn what the group will tolerate and will not. And you know what? They may not tolerate any marketing on your behalf. But that's okay. You're still a trusted member of that community and those people will turn to you when they're ready to buy.

Notice that in the previous few paragraphs, we didn't mention Twitter or Facebook. We didn't call out blogs or LinkedIn Groups. This is a communications strategy and philosophy. And with regard to the social web, social media, and social media marketing, the approach will remain the same, regardless of which tool is the shiny new community object.

Social Media Is Not an Advertising Medium, but Social Platforms Can Be

So we understand social media users do not want to be advertised to. They've come here to avoid advertisements and being shouted at. This is where they can find peace from commercials for cars, beer, insurance, and cleaning products. Marketers who violate this unwritten "rule" and blast out commercial messages are immediately hammered on by the network's users, until they either apologize and stop, or leave altogether. (There are a few exceptions, but they are by far the exception, and not the rule.)

However, many of these networks do allow for advertising in specific ways, such as on a sidebar. Facebook and other networks sell ads that are targeted specifically to users based on a number of factors, such as geographic location, age, and marital status. Figure 4.1 shows an example of some of these ads. For example, ads for dating sites are only shown to single people, ads for local restaurants are only shown to people who live in that city, and ads for new cars are only shown to people who are not teenagers, who typically don't buy new cars.

Finding target markets is the biggest advertising/marketing benefit of social media. Companies can directly target and reach only those people their products will appeal to. High-end luggage companies can target frequent travelers and road warriors, but ignore homebodies. Public speakers can communicate only with meeting planners. And restaurant owners can target convention goers only on the days they're in town.

Understand that the no advertising "rule" applies to your participation in social networks. But advertisements like those you can place on Facebook, as well as other networks like LinkedIn, are the types of accepted, or at least tolerated, advertising messages in social media. The general population accepts the fact that they'll see some ads in exchange for being able to use the site for free.

Figure 4.1   Facebook shows specific ads to specific users, based on their geographic location, age, and even marital and family status.

Social network advertising, such as Facebook's, is actually much more appealing to the user because of the hypertargeting. Social network users plug in information about themselves to populate their biography on the site. From birthdays to marital status to favorite books to business interests, the network has a lot of user data. By anonymizing that data (and providing users the option to allow the network to use their anonymous data in such a way), sites like Facebook and LinkedIn can allow advertisers like you to drill down your targeting.

If you want to take out a Facebook ad and only deliver it to 35- to 55-year-old men in Dallas, Texas, who list "marketing" as something they're interested in, you can do that. This microtargeting allows advertisers to enhance the efficiency of their advertising by hitting topical relevance points that are generally not possible with other advertising opportunities.

When you take out an ad in People magazine, you have a broad demographic profile. When you take out an ad on LinkedIn, you can deliver it only to CFOs. What you sacrifice in total impressions, you make up for in relevant impressions and higher click-through rates.

Facebook and LinkedIn add an interesting layer of user data, too. Because you can "like" a company on Facebook and "follow" a company on LinkedIn, your advertising can even be targeted to people who like or follow companies in certain verticals. To a degree, you can use social platform advertising to home in on your competitor's audience.

Erik recently noticed an example of hypertargeting on Facebook. An ad started appearing on his Facebook page for Audible.com, featuring A Dog's Purpose, a book written by W. Bruce Cameron (author of 8 *Simple Rules for Dating My Teenage Daughter*). Because Erik knows Bruce and is connected to him on Facebook, Audible was able to see the Facebook connection, determine that this Bruce is also one of their authors, and then feature Bruce's book in the ad. The idea is that because Erik knows Bruce, he's more likely to buy an Audible.com subscription to get Bruce's book.

Twitter's advertising opportunities are different and somewhat limited to larger companies with big budgets. You can purchase promoted tweets and be a promoted account on a certain hashtag conversation so your account and name appear at the top of any search for that hashtag. In general, Twitter advertising is interruptive and early reactions from Twitter users have been more negative than positive. But it gets your name and account in front of others, so it has some merit.

Only a few companies of any significance, out of 150 million Twitter users, have had major success by using their Twitter streams as advertising-only options. Dell is the most notable. Its @DellOutlet twitter account promotes sales and overstock items to purchase for discounted rates. Since 2008, Dell has surpassed $6.5 million in sales from the channel.

But understand that Dell created that channel with the intention of giving buyers an option. Other Dell accounts on Twitter serve as engagement and conversation points, and many Dell employees are available as company contacts as well. (@RichardatDell, @LionelatDell, and @JohnatDell are just three of many customer support and communications staff members on Twitter.)

Other companies, such as New Orleans-based Naked Pizza, mix conversation, retweets, and replies to friends and customers with weekend coupons and deals and measure significant success from doing so.

In both cases—Dell and Naked Pizza—neither company paid Twitter for the right to advertise there. They are communicating opportunities to the networks of followers they've built on the platform. But they understand that building those networks of followers is dependent on a more natural and personable use of the networks as well. They mix conversation and engagement with buying opportunities. Their audience either responds or it doesn't. They learn from experimentation and become more efficient over time.

Does Dell still advertise online? Of course. So does Naked Pizza. But they have figured out more efficient ways of driving sales by building relationships and being present in the conversation with their customers.

So while our traditional marketing training and mind-set may tell us the best way to reach consumers is to join a bunch of networks and blast advertising messages all over the place, hoping to reach a few customers, the proof is in the pudding. Social media audiences want their marketing information delivered differently. They want brands to join the conversation and engage with them, to listen to their wants and needs and become a member of their little online group.

And when you do so as a brand or company, the consumers will respond by turning to you when they're ready to buy. See Chapter 11, "It's All About the Benjamins: Social Media Marketing Drives Sales," for more information on how social media can contribute to your sales efforts.

This Ain't "Rocket Surgery"

Social media is not hard. It can be complex, but as we like to joke, "It ain't rocket surgery." If you're adept at talking with people, then you can handle social media. If you're adept at marketing, then you can handle social media marketing.

Anyone who has run a business or focused on marketing and communicating about a product or service understands strategic planning—setting goals and objectives, creating strategies and tactics, measuring results—and knows that although it's complex, it's not impossible. (If you don't understand marketing and strategic planning, hire someone who does.) Social media marketing is not about learning to use a new tool and knowing a bit of HTML code and being able to syndicate content on blogs and matching Twitter feeds with Facebook posts. Social media is about communicating with people. Knowing that will help you start off on the right foot.

Starting in Social Media Is Like Asking an Investor for Money

The right foot is counterintuitive, however. Your first inclination is to sell first. It's been conditioned in marketer's brains, even explicitly taught, in marketing and sales courses throughout the years. But because social media is grounded in relationship building, social media marketing is too. It's not something you can turn on, put your intern in charge of, and expect to work. Like a good advertising campaign, television commercial, or even successful direct mail piece, successful social media marketing takes time to develop. Think of it in terms of asking an investor for money.

You wouldn't make an appointment with an investor without a business plan and some strategies, would you? You shouldn't jump into social media without similarly arming yourself. Before you get started, you should devise a plan of action and pinpoint possible candidates for the job among your employees. Read Chapter 13, "Assign Responsibility and Be Accountable," to see our take on roles and responsibilities in your social media marketing efforts.

Before you dip your toe into the social media marketing waters, you need to first ask some telling questions:

1. **Why are you using social media?**

    If the reason is, "because everyone else is doing it," you're not ready. Remind yourself of the six things social media can do for your business and walk down the road of planning for a bit first. If you jump in without a good reason, you're not going to be able to measure or justify your time. No goals means no way to measure what you've accomplished.

2. **Are you willing to follow the accepted practices?**

    Are you comfortable with having conversations that, at first, don't seem to have a direct cause-and-effect relationship to making the sale? Can you be satisfied talking to a few hundred or thousand of the right customers rather than hundreds of thousands of those who might or might not be right? Can you step aside from the sales-first mind-set and build relationships over time? Can you participate in social networks (at least the ones you focus on) regularly? Are you willing to invest time and attention to all this?

    Can you be transparent? This means you should be honest about the things you're doing, and don't fake it. Producing fake blogs or planting good comments or reviews from anonymous accounts that don't disclose you're a company official is dishonest and, thus, not kosher here.

    Being transparent also means that when someone complains about you, let them. Solve their problem for them, tell them publicly you did it (do it in the same place where they complained, so everyone can see you're caring and responsive), and don't retaliate or try to get their comment taken down. That only makes your company look like a schmuck and a bully, and then you have two problems to deal with—your customer complaint and the public perception of you as a bullying schmuck.

3. **Who will be responsible for the social media efforts?**

    Someone needs to own this, and it can't be a committee. You need someone who will deal with all of the tasks associated with social media. Regardless of who it is, you need to know who will build your social networks, who will communicate on your behalf, who will plan the editorial calendar, and so forth. You also need to know the following:

- Who will respond to customer complaints, compliments, and questions? You need at least one employee who you can trust to speak for the company. It will most likely not be your intern or newest entry-level employee. It should be someone with experience and maturity to handle angry customers, to hold friendly conversations, and to craft persuasive messages.

- How often will you participate? Ideally, someone will be monitoring your social media networks several times a day. Your customers are on here at different times, so someone should be handling customer communication on an ongoing basis.

- Are there restricted topics? You should develop a social media policy to lay out all the rules for topics and content. (See Chapter 12, "Remedy Your Fears with Sound Policy.") A social media policy is where you discuss what you can and can't talk about, where you can and can't participate. This is where legal and compliance departments should actually have a lot of input because this is where they're going to save your bacon.

4. **How will you launch and promote your social media presence?**

   Will you use traditional marketing channels? Will you put the information on your website or send an email notice, or will you just let people trickle in? You'll answer these questions as part of the strategy you'll develop over time, rather than doing it right at the beginning. Launching social media won't be a one-time event. It will be important to let customers know about your new social media efforts on an ongoing basis.

5. **How will you define and measure success?**

   Believe it or not, this is where a lot of companies fall down. They decide, "we're going to add social media" and then quit a few months later because they didn't see any results. The problem is that they never defined what success was, and so they don't know if the results are worth anything.

   In Chapter 1, "Ignore the Hype. Believe the Facts," we talked about how it was rather silly to discuss the ROI of social media before you ever get started. But as we said, that doesn't mean you don't measure social media. You need to choose your goals and define what success looks like. For example, "a successful campaign will result in a 70% increase in web traffic, 10,000 new newsletter subscribers, and a 30% increase in web sales, within one year." And if you don't meet those campaign parameters, then you need to figure out why and whether it can be fixed.

Social Media Marketing Is About Planning and Measuring

Social media is no magic bullet to huge profits. There's no secret password or hand-shake that, if you know it, will guarantee success. But there are steps you need to take and best practices you need to follow if you want a chance at success. If you don't follow them, you might not fail, but you won't be as successful as you can be.

- **Set goals and objectives**—This is true for anything you want to accomplish, whether it's a new product or service offering, a new department, or even hiring a single person. You need goals and objectives you want to meet—the end result and how you're going to meet them. They could be increased sales and profits, higher ROI and reduced costs, or finding the best person available to manage your social media marketing. Your goals and objectives should be realistic and measurable. These could be goals like "increase web traffic by 30% in 6 months" or "reduce customer service calls by 12%."

- **Create a strategic plan**—After your goals and objectives have been established, you need to know what tools will be needed to reach them, what benchmarks you'll set along the way, and even knowing who it will take to execute the strategy.

  Although you'll probably want to create a committee to help create and execute the plan, it's more important to have someone overseeing the entire plan and making sure everyone is doing their part. Committees tend to overanalyze and overthink things like this. Erik knew a university department that spent six months debating what they should do with their social media plan. They didn't sign up to use a single tool because they debated whether it would even be effective. The obvious solution was to try just one tool and see what happened (but, then again, it was a committee...).

- **Measure the results**—You never know if something is working until you try it and measure it. Erik's university department could have more easily figured out if they were on the right track if they would have just picked one tool, tried it, and measured the results. Depending on the results they got—based on their goals and objectives—they could have poured more effort and energy into it, held steady, or even dropped it completely.

The great thing about social media is that it is easily measurable. Do you want to measure web traffic? Just check your website's measurement tools (called web analytics), and see if the number has increased by 30%. Do you want to measure customer service calls? See if the number of calls has indeed dropped by 12% and if the appropriate web traffic has gone up (check visits to the support section or FAQs of the website, visits to customer support blog articles, and so on).

Social media is often easily and accurately measurable. You can't say that about traditional marketing, whether it's TV and radio advertising, print advertising, direct mail, billboards, or even trade shows (see Chapter 5, "Make Some Noise: Social Media Marketing Aids in Branding and Awareness"). Measuring social media is the best way to figure out whether your strategy is working and whether goals are being met.

- **Commit to the process**—Many companies that are unfamiliar with social media follow a two-step process: (1) When we join it, people will show up; followed by, (2) well, we gave it a couple months, and no one showed up, so let's quit.

Social media marketing is like any other type of marketing: It's a process. It takes time. If you enter the social media realm, you should allow at least a year before you make a final decision on whether it works or not.

For example, when it comes to starting a corporate blog, it takes at least six months before you'll start seeing any demonstrable results and successes. Sometimes it will come sooner, but it usually takes about six months of consistent blogging before you see evidence that it paid off. One of Erik's clients, a manufacturing company in the Northwest, had more than $200 million in annual sales using a basic Internet sales strategy. But the company realized a 6% increase in sales after following an intensive blogging and social media strategy for an entire year.

Five Mind-Set Shifts That Make Successful Social Media Marketing Managers (and One Caveat)

The answers to these questions will point you in a direction that will inform your plan for social media marketing. But all the planning in the world won't do much good if you don't have the proper mindset to follow through with the blueprint. And it's not just your mindset, but your employees' too.

The resistance to social media is fairly common in the workplace. The companies that are not using it still outnumber the companies that do use it. But the ones that use it have shifted their mind-set about using it, what they want to do with it, and how it's going to be used.

1. If you want people to trust you, you need to trust them, namely employees and customers. Just as you need to trust your employees, you need to trust your customers to talk frankly about you on your website, as well as on any other. You need to trust that they're doing it already, and trust them to respond appropriately when they're approached by someone helpful from your company. (And if you get people who are unreasonable and refuse to be reasoned with, you need to trust that they were always going to be this much of a jerk, no matter where or how you encountered them.)

2. It's not about the sale; it's about the lifetime value of the customer. Let's say you own a coffee shop that does a fairly brisk business. One customer comes in five times a week, 50 weeks a year, and pays $4 for a large latte every day. The value of that customer is $1,000 per year, for as many years as she comes to your coffee shop. If she comes for 10 years, then she has a $10,000 lifetime value.

   What is it worth to take a little extra effort to make sure she stays happy and continues to come back? Maybe give her a free biscotti once in a while, or make her 10th coffee a free one? Would you listen seriously to her complaints if she brought them to you? Maybe you'd even consider her a trusted customer and ask her opinion on a new offering or new drink.

   Typically, unless you sell a subscription service, like cable TV, it's difficult to track your repeat customers and loyal fans. You don't know which customers come in to a local retail store and buy your brand of ketchup, shoes, or bathroom cleaner. You don't know which of your customers have sworn by your product for years and tell all their friends about you.

   Social media lets you hear from those people, find the people who love your product, and communicate with them accordingly. With some clever marketing, you can figure out how to reach your best customers, see what kind of influence they have on their friends, and even arm them with additional information or incentives to tell their friends.

3. Online is no different than offline. You already know you need to trust your employees to talk to your customers online, but what should they talk about? The same thing they would talk about offline. If salespeople learn about new opportunities via referral, they would follow up with

the new lead and see how they could help solve any problems that person may have.

Your salespeople can use the same process with social media. When it comes to finding sales opportunities, your sales staff could use Twitter or LinkedIn to listen for buying cues, provide solutions to problems, or direct users to a web page that answers a question, or even answer the question directly.

IBM takes an interesting sales and marketing approach with social media. They send "seekers" to blogs, discussion forums, and social networks in the public sector and monitor the discussions that are taking place. Whether someone is looking for a new storage device, talks about replacing a piece of hardware, or even has questions about an RFP, the seeker recognizes those as buying clues. The seeker turns that information over to a lead development rep who calls the prospect and qualifies them, and then passes that lead over to the appropriate sales department, who works with that person in helping them make a new purchase. Although IBM hasn't been specific, the company has found millions of dollars of sales leads through this program, and it is continuing to grow in this area.

That is how you use social media to find and communicate with new customers.

4. There's an audience for everything, but bigger audiences are available beyond the spray. "The spray" refers to the typical marketing and advertising "spray" we're showered with whenever we turn on the TV or radio, drive down the highway, or even read a newspaper online.

    Yes, there are people who will respond to regular advertising messages. If there weren't, no one would create them. However, these are people who buy their products based on price, not based on value or on relationships with the company. They're not going to be your loyal customers.

    The audience you want to find with social media marketing is a loyal audience of raving fans who will tell their friends about you.

    In the DirecTV case, no amount of money thrown at a marketing campaign can equal dozens of happy customers telling their entire Twitter network that they're pleased with their TV provider. The people in that network certainly wouldn't respond to tweets about "Buy 3 room receivers, get the 4th free!" or "DirecTV users can watch the Georgia Tech-Clemson game with our Sports Package for just $9.95 per month (some restrictions apply)." But they would have responded to their friends talking about how much they have enjoyed their own DirecTV.

5. **Measure what matters, not everything you can find.**

   Some marketers love numbers. They believe that the more numbers they know, the better armed they are. Want to know what day more people come to your website? That could be important. Want to know what hours more people are likely to respond to a tweet or a Facebook ad? The analytics can tell you that. Want to know which city delivered the most traffic from the Netherlands in the last year? You can even know that (but we honestly don't know when or why you would ever need to know that).

   Don't fall into the analytics traps of trying to know everything you can figure out. Holland's a great country, but knowing the city traffic sources from a country you don't serve won't do a thing for your sales.

   What you need to measure are the goals you previously set. If you said you wanted to increase web traffic by 30%, then check to see if you're hitting it. If you wanted to drop customer service calls by 12%, make sure that's happening. That's where analytics are important; the rest is meaningless, even if it is kind of cool.

6. **(The Caveat) Your social media fans are a subset of your customer base.**

   Despite everything we've said up to this point, please keep in mind that your social media fans are only a portion of your entire customer base. Not every Coke drinker is on Facebook, not every ketchup buyer has a cell phone, and not every iPhone user downloads apps.

   We may have made it sound like your entire customer base is lurking on Facebook and Twitter, waiting for you to talk to them, but they're not. Don't get us wrong, there are a bunch of them out there—probably a pretty sizable portion too, given the way social media has been growing.

   You might do something that raises hackles and causes big outbursts on social media, but that doesn't mean everyone feels that way. Although your social media fans will get loud, you do have an entire customer base to take care of.

   This is where understanding your social media customers' habits and measuring your entire marketing campaign are going to become important, as well as monitoring what people are talking about.

Social media marketing isn't different than other forms of marketing in that regard. All of your customers aren't on one channel or another. Some watch TV. Others prefer reading books. Some read the newspaper and others don't.

As you've migrated to the web to market your business, you've probably discovered that some customers will go to your website and others won't. Some want you to email them specials while some prefer to not share their email address. In this regard, social media is very much the same. Some of your customers will check in to your store on Foursquare. Some will follow you on Twitter. Others may "like" your brand on Facebook. And others won't.

The only way social media marketing really differs from traditional marketing is that it requires you to listen as well as talk, to participate in conversations, and to build relationships rather than just check off sales.

The secret of social media marketing is no damn secret. You just have to be human.

And we're pretty certain you know how to do that.

5

Make Some Noise: Social Media Marketing Aids in Branding and Awareness

One of the first groups that will lay claim to social media is the marketing department. And that might not be such a bad idea. We're both marketers by trade, so we're going to be a little biased in our support for this argument. Even though other departments in your company could own social media, we believe the responsibility for social media across the organization belongs with marketing.

After all, social media is about communication, and that's all marketing is, isn't it? Most companies communicate with their customers through the following:

- TV ads
- Radio ads
- Newspaper ads
- Billboards
- Brochures
- Trade shows
- Direct mail campaigns
- Websites

A lot of companies don't even make it as far as a website. A website was a big stretch for a lot of companies as recently as five years ago. Even now, only 44% of small businesses have an actual website. The companies that have one might not fully understand how to work it or use it effectively, and they might even outsource the management of it. But they know the world is plugged in and people are looking for websites.

We've reached that point with social media.

One reason is the speed at which social media has been accepted and carried into the mainstream. Businesspeople have a hard time accepting it as anything real because its widespread adoption took a fraction of the time traditional mediums took and they didn't have a chance to watch and learn the way they did with radio, television, or even early versions of websites.

Erik Qualman collected stats that reveal just how quickly social media has caught on. In *Socialnomics: How Social Media Transforms The Way We Live And Do Business,* he wrote about the number of years it took each medium to reach 50 million users:[1]

- Radio: 38 years
- TV: 13 years
- Internet: 4 years
- iPod: 3 years
- Facebook: Added 100 million users in less than 9 months
- iPhone applications: 1 billion downloads in 9 months

Just because it happened fast doesn't make it a fad. It makes it something to pay attention to. So what does this have to do with the marketing department controlling social media?

Everything.

Marketing is all about customer communication, but up until a few years ago, it was all about talking at the customers, through commercials, print ads, billboards, and brochures. The only time marketers talked to customers was at trade shows or in focus groups. Now the customers are able to talk back, and a lot of companies don't quite know what to do about that. It freaks them out. And they're freaking out a little more when they realize their customers are talking with each other, too. Some companies are frightened at the prospect of their customers talking to each other.

We know of one company whose sales staff nixed the idea of sponsoring a social network for its customers. It was afraid their customers would talk about the company's pricing, despite the fact that the customers were already members of an industry trade association and could communicate via email. The company's fear kept it from utilizing a closed social network that could have helped it win future customers because it was too scared of something that was a nonissue.

What that company failed to realize was that its customers weren't prevented from talking about its pricing because it decided against the social network. The customers continued to talk but through back channels and away from the company's watchful, even potentially participatory, eye. By "controlling" the message, the company missed the opportunity to have any say-so in the message at all.

Social media hasn't just wrested control of your message away from the marketing department, it shows that the marketing department never had it in the first place. Now we can see people talking about the company in public channels. Before social networks, blogs, and online forums, those water cooler conversations weren't indexed, searchable, and found by people online. Marketing never controlled your message; your customers did. Marketing was, and is, just along for the ride. The only way it can affect the message in today's socially enabled world is to participate in these conversations, defend the company when it's warranted, and even inject the company perspective if the opportunity presents itself.

Your Brand Is What the Community Says It Is

In their book, *Branding Yourself: How to Use Social Media to Invent or Reinvent Yourself*, Erik and coauthor Kyle Lacy said that a brand evokes "an emotional response to the image and/or name of a particular company, product, or person." In other words, it's how the image or name makes the person feel—anger or happiness, comfort or discomfort.

Marketing guru Seth Godin defines a brand as "the set of expectations, memories, stories, and relationships that, taken together, account for a consumer's decision to choose one product or service over another."[2] The brand is less of a physical object, logo, or even organization. It is a world of images, emotions, and intrinsic values that can only be determined by each individual the brand touches. Your marketing people are going to disagree vehemently because they believe brands are what they make. Brands, in their eyes, are the logos, symbols, color combinations, taglines, sales copy, and all the websites and marketing collateral they spent hours and hours of committee time debating and agonizing over.

But those are only identifiers for your customers, so they can recognize you in a crowd of other logos, symbols, color combinations, and taglines. It's why they should pick your box off of a shelf or how they know to go into your store and not the other guy's. It's how they know what products, services, or companies to tell their friends to try or to avoid.

And social news sites like Reddit.com provide opportunities for customers to influence their friends' buying habits. Reddit is a popular voting website where users can submit stories and then vote on them. The more votes, the higher the story appears on Reddit's pages. The site is so popular it sold to Condé Nast for an unverified amount of money, believed to be in the millions. So when users take an interest in something, it's bound to be seen by thousands of people.

One of the things Reddit readers took interest in was a Greenpeace antiwhaling campaign. In 2007, Greenpeace asked people to name a humpback whale it was tracking as part of its Great Whale Expedition. One of the suggested names was "Mister Splashy Pants," but some Greenpeace whaling advocates hated the name, saying it wasn't "beautiful enough."

Users from Reddit and other social networks thought it was awesome, so they voted heavily for Mister Splashy Pants, and moved the percentage of votes from 5% to 75% of the total in less than a day. More than 20,000 votes came from Reddit.com users. The surprise success prompted Greenpeace to extend the voting for an extra week, and that's when things really took off. Greenpeace said they had never seen traffic on their server reach such high levels. The traffic meant exposure to new audiences and better numbers in people who sign up for enewsletters, donate to their cause, and more. More traffic means more volume of everything, so Greenpeace benefitted, as could your company.

On December 10, 2007, Mister Splashy Pants was declared the winner, gaining more than 78% of the 150,000 total votes. The second-place name was Humphrey, which received 3% of the votes. The other beautiful names? Less than 1% each. Greenpeace not only responded to the loss of control of their whale naming by donning the animal, "Mister Splashy Pants," but even took a cue from its public and developed website calls-to-action labeled, "Save Splashy."

Alexis Ohanian, the founder of Reddit, pointed out that with social media, companies will lose control of their message, which is not such a bad thing. During a speech about the Greenpeace instance he said, "By giving more control and authority to your users they will surprise and impress you."

What Greenpeace did in the case of Mister Splashy Pants was watch its marketing message and connection with its audience get hijacked by an audience it wasn't anticipating to be involved in the effort. Instead of changing the rules, shutting the contest down, or even doing something to motivate the more conservative naming fans to counteract the social audience's response, it embraced the new direction. The audience wanted something the brand perhaps even wasn't sure of, but it trusted them and even allowed the audience to co-own a bit of the brand. That collaboration with fans and customers comes at a small price—the temporary comfort level of your marketing department—but reaps benefits well beyond a small marketing effort like the naming of a whale. People who participated will always feel a sense of ownership in Greenpeace they may not have before.

Co-ownership with customers is a powerful position that Moleskine now knows well. Its notebooks are considered some of the world's best and most popular notebooks. They're easily identified by the black cover, elastic band, and accordion pocket in the back (see Figure 5.1). But the brand alleged to have been used by creative greats like Pablo Picasso, Vincent Van Gogh, and Ernest Hemingway faded out of existence by the mid-1980s.

Figure 5.1 Moleskine notebooks engender a lot of passion and support from their fans. To them, the brand "Moleskine" is just as important as the notebook itself.

A small Italian company, Modo & Modo, decided to relaunch the Moleskine notebook in 1997. They ended up launching a notebook craze that has seen rapid growth and use of the little black notebooks in the last 13 years. But what's interesting about Moleskine is that they let the users define the message about the notebooks, even going so far as to adopt some of the recommendations their customers made in conversations on the site.

One Moleskine fan, Armand B. Frasco, even started a blog community at Moleskinerie.com, where fans could gather and discuss the different uses of the notebook, show off their different photos, art, and usability hacks, and even discuss the best pen to use in the classic notebooks. The company was watching. And listening. They remained responsive to ideas shared on Moleskine about the product, letting the site's community provide ideas for giveaways, promotions, and more. The community was so important to Modo & Modo's market research and even marketing efforts, it eventually bought the blog from Frasco. It continues to maintain the blog today, much in the spirit of giving fans a place to share and collaborate.

Domino's Pizza is another example of letting customers define who they are, but one that even took cues from the social media world and translated them into traditional advertising. After the company was embarrassed in early 2010 by a YouTube video of two North Carolina store employees desecrating a customer's order, it responded by changing its mainstream advertising messages to emphasize the company's responsiveness. Television advertisements featured photos sent in by customers of poorly delivered pizzas, then company executives apologizing and taking steps to correct the mistake. The ads have been a big hit among consumers, showing the pizza giant is paying attention when customers have issues with the organization. And the advertisements, while a traditional medium, were a communications response right out of a social media marketing playbook.

Ultimately, your company's brand is not what you think it is. It's not what the marketing department says it is. It's what your customers believe it to be. And the only way you're going to get their definition and your definition to match is if you meet or exceed their expectations.

It's important to remember that because your brand is what your customers believe it is, you need to make sure it's what your customers want it to be. It's not enough to give them a quality product or great service anymore. If they want a red and blue widget instead of a green and yellow one, give it to them. If you see indications your customers aren't pleased with your customer service, make your representatives kill them with friendliness, high-fives, and uber-positive responses.

Because if you do, they're going to tell their friends about how awesome you are, and do your marketing for you. And if you don't, they're going to tell their friends about how badly you suck, and do your competition's marketing for them.

Of course, traditional marketers don't have traditional metrics to measure that kind of word-of-mouth marketing, so they tend to ignore it, taking shelter in the numbers they can explain.

Traditional Marketing and Its Metrics Have Lied to You for Years

A big problem companies have with social media is that they can't measure it using old-school marketing techniques. Traditional marketers expect to see old-school numbers in social media, hoping to gain millions of viewers, tens of thousands of listeners, and thousands of readers.

They believe that, based on the numbers of TV viewers, radio listeners, and newspaper readers, they can get a pretty good estimate of how many people watched the show, listened to the station, or read the paper where their ad was placed.

Here's how the typical argument goes:

1. Ten million people watched this program.

2. Our ad was on that program two times.

3. Therefore, our ad was seen by ten million people two times.

These traditional marketers dismiss social media with a sniff of derision and a wave of their hand because their social media outposts only have a few thousand fans; this is not nearly as many viewers/listeners/readers they believe are responding to the old-school method.

But their expectations are too high. They've been lied to by traditional marketing and PR people. Here's what we mean.

Let's say a company wanted to advertise a new product on the Golf Channel. They check out the Golf Channel's website, which says the network has a global reach of more than 120 million homes, and believe that if they run an ad on the Golf Channel, their ad will be beamed into 120 million homes.

But look again at the exact wording they use. The Golf Channel is beamed into 120 million homes around the world, but that doesn't mean it's watched by 120 million people. Not even close. According to the Golf Channel, there are 26.2 million golfers in the United States alone. Although that's nowhere close to 120 million, is it safe to assume there are 26.2 million Golf Channel viewers?

Not even close.

The Golf Channel's average daily viewership is around 77,000. That's not "a global reach of more than 120 million homes." But the Golf Channel can't sell advertisers on

77,000 average daily viewers. Why? Because traditional marketers have been prom-ised millions of viewers, tens of thousands of readers, and thousands of listeners.

But the Golf Channel isn't alone in all this. Newspapers and magazines do it all the time. They like to boast about print runs, but rarely mention readership. Radio's Arbitron ratings and TV's Nielsen ratings are based on surveys and estimates, not actual numbers of viewers.

And this is the problem. There is not a completely accurate way to measure the number of viewers on a TV channel, but marketers like to think they're reaching more than 120 million homes. This is why measuring traditional marketing and PR is actually quite difficult. We're being told we need to pay attention to one set of numbers, but it turns out the numbers are not even realistic.

When those traditional marketers turn their attention to social media data—num-bers that are much more defined because in an all-digital medium, counting things is scientific, not guesswork—they're deflated. Since they're used to inflated and hypothetical numbers that have set unreasonable expectations, the real numbers of how many people interact with online content seem infinitely low. It's easy to con-vince a CEO that spending $100K on an ad buy on the Golf Channel is worth it when you can say, "It has a global reach of 120 million people." It's a challenge to make that CEO happy when talking about spending $100K on a social media initia-tive that, if successful, might drive a few hundred thousand people to sign up for your email newsletter or share a review of your product with their friends.

Why We Can't Measure Traditional Marketing and PR

Public relations, traditional marketing, and the mainstream media people like to say they can measure what they do by measuring sales, web views, column inches, and so on. They run some ads, put up some billboards, place a few stories, and look for a spike in sales.

In public relations, the common practice of "measuring" success is to count the number of column inches or airtime gained through story placement, measure the cost of the advertising costs based on the column inches or airtime (usually at the standard, nondiscounted rate), and come up with the "value" of the press they received. If sales went up after a particular block of TV ads or a placement of their product in some major newspapers, they say, "Look, we made sales go up." If sales don't go up, they say, "Well, it's a work in progress, but hey, at least we got this much 'value' in earned media."

The same is true for advertising. Commercials are produced, ad space is purchased, and Nielsen and Q-Scores are pored over. "Look!" they shout, "our show was viewed by three million people," but they can't be sure whether 2,950,000 of those viewers were in the bathroom when the ad was shown. So when you ask the advertising department to accurately measure the sales and return on investment (ROI) of the communications effort, they explain that advertising is more of a top-of-mind-brand-building exercise that's more art than science.

And don't forget trade shows. You spend anywhere from a few thousand dollars to more than $30,000 for a major trade show. You hire a booth designer, hire a display firm to put up your display, and collect dozens of business cards, which your staff forgets to follow up on or put into a customer relationship management (CRM) system. And the hundreds you spent on giveaways were a success because you gave most of them away, but you didn't track who received them. When sales don't go up (mostly because the contacts aren't in the CRM system, and no one called them after three months), you call the trade show a failure. When a few people do call your company first, and the salespeople remember them from the show, you think maybe the show was worth going to, and so you're willing to do it again.

We don't mean to pick on traditional marketing. They really do have a tough time measuring the cause and effect of their work. Did the latest block of ads cause sales to increase, or was it the end-of-summer discount? Did the newspaper articles lead to increased product sales, or did a client finally make a major purchase at the beginning of her new fiscal year? Did sales tank after the trade show, or do you typically have a long sales cycle? Traditional marketers can never be entirely sure.

Although we agree that the PR and advertising campaigns are the most likely culprits for increases in sales in the previous examples, we can't be absolutely sure. Which commercial on which station at what time was the most effective? Was it the one with the two guys in the hot air balloon airing during prime time, or was it the one with the talking lizard during the play-off game? Was it the short story in the major metro newspaper, or was it the longer story in the chain of small-town newspapers? Most marketers can't be sure which part of the campaign was the successful one and which part flopped. Knowing this would be helpful because it would help them figure out which parts they could trim to make their marketing dollars go that much further.

Traditional marketing just can't tell us that 10% of January's sales happened because of the ads and not the newspaper articles, or that the radio commercials are doing better than the billboards. And there is nothing but surveys and educated guesses that say you need to focus more attention on radio because it had the highest ROI for this particular campaign. But all is not lost. You can measure social media marketing!

Why We Can Measure Social Media

The great thing about social media is that, unlike traditional channels, there are all sorts of tools to measure its effectiveness. Although the numbers don't run in the millions, or even the hundreds of thousands, companies can see hundreds, and even thousands, of rabid fans who flock to a website and make a purchase.

We can actually demonstrate that blog post A led to a spike in sales on Monday, and a Facebook campaign launched on Friday did absolutely nothing.

But the lower numbers of people visiting or seeing the blog post—12,000 is not 120 million, after all—mean that a lot of traditional marketing people are ignoring social media. Thousands are not nearly as sexy as millions, so no one wants to spend a lot of time dealing with these numbers.

So classically trained marketers and business people write social media off, without realizing that their big expensive TV ads did not reach most of their intended audience anyway, or that most of the people came to the website because of a previous relationship with the company and not because they passed a billboard on the highway.

However, web measurement tools like Google Analytics let social media marketers not only track how many visitors came to their website, but they can also provide the following information:

- What pages they visited, such as a sales or product page.

- What pages they came from, such as blog posts, web articles, online ads, or Twitter messages.

- How long they spent on a site.

- What page-to-page path they followed. Did they take the planned-out sales path?

- What search terms brought them to your site.

- What part of the country they came from.

- What time of day they showed up.

So, imagine being able to determine the following: Customer A comes to your website and purchases three items online. By looking at the web analytics, you can see that she showed up at 11:52 a.m. from Harrisburg, Pennsylvania, 10 minutes after your marketing department posted a tweet. (You can even confirm that she clicked the particular link they sent.) She went straight to the page, looked at an FAQ page, went to the catalog page, and then placed the order.

Customer B arrives at the website because of a Google search at 12:37 p.m. from Orlando, Florida. He spends 5 1/2 minutes on a blog post that describes how to fix a common problem most potential customers face. (You can also see that it's one of your most popular blog posts.) Customer B goes straight to the order page and orders five items to help solve that problem and to prevent it from happening again.

Compare that with measuring traditional advertising and marketing methods:

You run TV ads for $80,000 in six major cities. Your sales for those cities increase, which shows that the advertising works. But you have no way of knowing which ads at which times on which stations prompted the purchase, or whether all of your new customers even saw the ad. With social media and activity online, you can spend $80,000 designing a campaign that focuses on six major cities and track how many people visit, convert, and even then advocate for your product or service. You can even divide those numbers and see how many came from each city.

Compare Costs Between Social Media and Traditional Media

Real estate giant Century 21 took a big step in 2009 when it dropped its traditional marketing channels, like TV advertising, and set up a presence on social media, focusing on YouTube, Twitter, and Facebook. More recently, the Realtor launched a blog and an iPhone app.

Century 21's CMO Bev Thorne admitted the decision was very controversial. She believed it was the right thing to do, saying in an interview that "television was no longer providing any real tangible benefit for our brand."[3] Thorne said she realized it did not make any sense to put money into a medium to build brand awareness because 94% of homebuyers start their search online. The Realtor's ultimate goal was to drive homebuyers to Century 21 brokers and agents, and social media could do a much better job of it than traditional TV advertising. Thanks to websites such as Realtor.com, Homes.com, and Zillow.com, interested homebuyers can get a look at homes for sale, see their prices, get a virtual tour of the inside of the houses, and even get questions answered about schools and local hospitals. Before these online tools were available, buyers would have to find a real estate agent to tell them about a house, let them see inside, and answer all their neighborhood questions. Now that these, and many more, online tools are available, many Realtors are being forced to embrace social media.

Although Century 21's decision was not a popular one in the traditional channel, corporate world, it was successful. In the first year of its digital strategy, the real estate giant increased sales leads by 65% and decreased the cost per lead by 50%. In the following year, the Realtor increased leads by another 40% and cut its cost per lead by another 33%. In other words, more people are interested in buying houses from Century 21, and Century 21 is spending less money to reach these buyers, but with greater success than they ever did with traditional marketing methods.

Before we go on, we want to stress that we are not suggesting you should replace traditional marketing with social media. That would be crazy. Although measures in traditional channels are not as specific or defined as they are in the digital realm, you can still reach a large audience using largely consumed media. More people will watch your television commercial than are likely to see your tweet. Social media marketing delivers a more relevant and interested audience, however. Instead of blasting a message to the masses hoping it reaches an audience that is interested, social media marketing helps you gather an audience that is interested in hearing your message.

So don't give up on traditional channels. Instead, add social media to your marketing toolbox. Remember that social media marketing is more about a two-way (or multiple-way) line of communication. It is different than traditional channels. Use those mechanisms to invite customers to connect with you on more intimate level. If you have TV ads, post them on YouTube. If you use direct mail, refer people to your website. Your radio commercials should tell people to check out your Facebook page.

But analyze the cost effectiveness of reaching audience members across your marketing efforts and optimize around what works best. Does direct mail drive more leads or sales than a radio campaign? Compare the costs and benefits and streamline your marketing efforts—including your social media marketing efforts—to ensure you're getting the best bang for your buck. Understand that not all of your customers will be reachable through all channels, so diversifying the touch points you target to reach your customers is important. But stupid is as stupid does. If one or more channels isn't proving valuable, move that money to one that is.

Although we don't want to run through a social media budget, or delve into the costs of traditional marketing channels (thousands of dollars), there are some basic considerations you should factor in when comparing social media and traditional marketing costs.

What Traditional Marketing Costs

If your company is large enough to have an in-house marketing department that can create your ads, you're paying salaries to your creative team. If you outsource everything, you're paying several thousand dollars per month or more just to have your creative team on retainer.

TV and radio commercials have production costs, billboards incur production and placement costs, and direct mail needs printing and postage. You might end up paying even more for specialty pieces, such as hiring a video production company to shoot a high-end TV ad or licensing a piece of music for a commercial.

Of course, there are media placement costs, too. TV commercials can cost anywhere from less than $100 to more than $100,000 for a single placement, depending on the market, the channel, and the time of day. (And remember, the viewing/listening/reading/open rate for traditional marketing is almost always calculated at less than 10%, and more often than not, less than 5%, of an estimated audience, not an actual audience, so you can never really be sure of the real numbers.)

And this is before you get into research and development, production, sales, or distribution of the actual product.

What Social Media Marketing Costs

Social media needs a couple of people: someone who knows web design and someone who knows marketing. (By marketing, we mean understanding message creation and how to move your target audience with those messages. We'll discuss why this person is typically not a fresh-faced college grad in Chapter 13, "Assign Responsibility and Be Accountable.")

Other than that, costs are minimal. The important social networks—Twitter, Facebook, LinkedIn, and blogging—are all free to use. Web analytics tools are free. Social media analytics tools can cost a few hundred dollars per month and are optional for smaller companies, but crucial for larger companies. You can start to spend money as you get deeper into social media, but even that is measured in hundreds, not thousands, of dollars per month.

That's it—nothing else. Throw in the standard computer costs, desk space, and salary for your employees, and you have enough to launch a social media campaign. Or, you can outsource it for anywhere from several hundred to several thousand dollars per month. That much money won't buy you 10 seconds of ad time on a national network, but it will let you reach thousands of your exact target audience directly.

In 2008, Cisco was already a major proponent of social media, with 22 blogs (each gaining 475,000 views per quarter) and accounts on Facebook (100,000 fans), Twitter (2 million followers), and video-sharing site YouTube (2,000+ videos with 4 million views). But the company had never used social media for a product launch, so the sales team decided to do it with a new piece of equipment, the Aggregated Services Router, aimed at network engineers.

In a typical product launch, more than 100 Cisco executives and journalists would fly in from 100 countries to San Jose, California, where they would be handed a paper press release. The marketing team would also place print ads in major business newspapers and magazines. Instead, Cisco decided it was going to meet its users in their online worlds, on virtual gaming sites like Second Life, where they could build an online auditorium, and invite people to "sit in" on the press conference and demonstrations. It even held a concert that featured eight bands in seven hours that users could listen to while they were on Second Life. In addition, Cisco used YouTube videos, videoconferencing, video datasheets, an online discussion forum, and a Facebook users group to tell people about the new router. All told, the launch reached 9,000 people, which was 90 times more than they have reached in past launches, and Cisco considered it one of the top five launches in its history.

The net effect was more coverage for less money and lots of audience time saved. Not only did executives save themselves a few hours of time by recording a video presentation, but print ads were replaced with industry media coverage, which netted 1,000 blog posts and 40 million online visits. Best of all? They pulled it off for one-sixth the cost of a traditional launch (and saved 42,000 gallons of gas in transportation costs).[4]

The moral of the story? Go to where your customers are, rather than making them come to you. Speak to them in their language instead of yours. Do the things they like to do instead of making them do what you like.

Social media won't reach millions of TV viewers in 30 seconds. But, social media will let you reach your audience directly and influence their buying behavior directly—by letting your people connect with other people online, joining them where they already are, speaking to them in their own environments, and not interrupting their day.

The 500 Million Water Coolers Are Now One Big One

Since when did the customer become so knowledgeable about your product or service? Most executives ask that very question when seeing what customers are saying about their brand online. What makes them an authority on your product, let alone able to tell other people about it?

The answer is their honesty and willingness to talk about their experiences. Friends trust their opinions because they know the person in question doesn't have a financial stake in whether someone buys the digital camera they recommend. These friends also have knowledge of the customers' expectations and requirements. In contrast, the customers might have a general lack of trust in the marketing departments of the world's companies.

In *Socialnomics: How Social Media Transforms The Way We Live And Do Business*, Erik Qualman shows marketers why trust in companies and brands is so important:

- 25% of search results for the world's top 20 largest brands are links to user-generated content. User-generated content includes consumer comments and reviews on websites.

- 34% of bloggers post opinions about products and brands. Their readers are usually people who trust them or are looking for an unbiased source of information.

- 78% of consumers trust peer recommendations. More than three-fourths of the people trust recommendations from people like them, not professionals.

- Only 14% trust advertisements. The thousands you spent on creating the ad, which will only be seen by a fraction of the audience, is only trusted by a fraction of those viewers.

- Only 18% of traditional TV campaigns generate a positive ROI. In other words, you spent tens of thousands of dollars and only made part of that back.

- 90% of people who can TiVo do. People then watch the recorded shows and skip the ads you spent tens of thousands of dollars on.

Basically, companies are spending thousands of dollars to reach customers through traditional advertising, but consumers are trying to avoid those advertisements, and only a fraction of the consumers who actually see the ads trust those ads.

This may go a long way in explaining the 18% ROI on those traditional TV campaigns.

Meanwhile, consumers trust their friends' recommendations more, and they're communicating with them. More importantly, they're communicating with them publicly on social media. A woman tells her friends on Facebook that she and her family had a great time at a restaurant. A friend responds that he had a lousy time the last time she was there, and 30 people all chime in to the discussion talking about the last time they each visited that restaurant. Some people say they'll try it because of the woman's message; others promise never to go because of the friend's bad experience. But none of them will try it because of the TV ad, because most of them skipped it, and the rest don't trust it.

Other social media tools exist for customers to share their experiences as well. Social sites focused on restaurants, stores, hotels, coffee shops, vacation resorts, and more exist. And other tools exist to pull them all into one convenient location.

For example, Google Local will not only give turn-by-turn directions to a new restaurant on a mobile phone, it will also collect and share reviews on different reviewer websites like Yelp.com and Urbanspoon. The customer can decide whether to visit the restaurant based on the feedback she finds, and after her visit, leave feedback of her own for the next customer to read. Because the social consumer trusts third-party recommendations over brand marketing copy, these reviews on niche networks are critical to your branding and awareness. Keeping an eye on them and ensuring dissatisfied customers have their issues addressed is a must-do for local and review-driven businesses.

But even for larger businesses, the reviews and ratings sites—even niche sites only have a small number of people frequent them—are important to know, watch, and perhaps even be active on. The social consumer is watching your every move as a brand or company. While not all of them can damage your brand or fan the flames of negative awareness, not knowing what's out there can certainly prove detrimental to your branding and awareness efforts.

Putting Metrics Around Branding and Awareness

Like we discussed earlier, it's possible to measure social media success and failure, showing which social networks and messages are resulting in increased sales and market share and which ones are not very effective. The tools range from subscription-based platforms that require a monthly fee to free sites that provide a minimal level of data collection from your social efforts. With these tools, you can glean a lot of valuable information about your social media marketing program:

- Social media monitoring tools like Radian6, Alterian SM2, and Sysomos can not only find the different things your customers are saying about you, but they can also measure the sentiment and the mood of those messages. For example, if a customer complains—"My hamburger from Big Bob's sucked!"—these tools can flag this as a negative sentiment so the appropriate people will see it and can hopefully rectify the situation.

- Influence measurement tools like Klout and Twitalyzer show marketers who the influencers in their industry are. When a blogger or Twitter user with a high Klout score, which roughly translates to having high influence, says something positive about a company, the marketing team will certainly want to know about that. They can take further steps to help turn the blogger into a raving fan. Providing free products for review, inviting the blogger to be a part of a focus group, or even just a thank-you note from the company can go a long way in cementing that relationship.

Here's how this works: A luggage company begins a social media campaign and uses Radian6 as a way to monitor the social media chatter. A frequent traveler and owner of the luggage company's product sends out a tweet or asks a question on a travelers' forum. "How do I change the wheels on my Lift-n-Tote rolling suitcase? Do I need a special tool?"

A representative from the luggage company sees the message via Radian6, even if he has never been on the forum or is not following the customer on Twitter. The representative jumps over to the forum or sends a responding tweet, answers the question, includes a link to buying the wheel replacement kit online, and makes the customer happy. Not only did she get her question answered, but she feels like the company listened to her.

The same company is also monitoring their competitors' name brands in Radian6. Someone sends out a tweet that says, "My new Duffel Drag sucks! The handle snapped off after only three days, and I need a replacement quick."

The luggage company representative has a couple of choices he can make: Send a response that says, "That's too bad. If you stop by the Lift-n-Tote store in your area, I'll arrange a 20% discount for you," or he could send a brochure and coupon to the Duffel Drag owner's home.

By monitoring the social media conversation, a company can keep abreast of what people are saying about its brand and even its competitors, rather than being caught off guard. It lets a company determine what kind of response its marketing team should give and which one would be the most effective.

But the one thing that should never happen is measuring whether a customer is "worth" responding to.

Klout is a way to measure the influence score of customers who are on Twitter. Some companies have begun using this to see whether a customer has enough influence to warrant a response or whether he or she is safe to ignore. The problem with this approach is that influence scores are only a measurement of how influential someone is online, and not in real life.

Erik's wife, Toni, has a relatively low Klout score, about a 21 out of 100. It's enough to earn her the rank of "Explorer," which is only slightly higher than someone who just signed up for Twitter two weeks ago. If she lodged a complaint on Twitter, and a customer service representative checked out her Klout score before responding to the complaint, he might dismiss her out of hand as someone who is not very influential. After all, Toni only has a few hundred followers, and she doesn't tweet that often, so she must not have a lot of sway with her network, right? But actually, Toni carries a high amount of influence among her family and friends.

Six years ago, Toni and Erik bought a new Scion xB as a family car. She was so impressed with the car, she gushed about it to her family. Within three months, she referred her parents to her Scion dealer, and they bought an xB and an xA. She also referred her sister and husband to the same dealer, and they bought two xAs.

Now, according to Toni's Klout score, she is someone a numbers-focused rep would immediately ignore. But she is also someone who directly influenced the purchase of four new cars within a three-month period, all with the same dealer, and even with the same salesperson.

The moral of the story is this: Just because someone has a high Klout score doesn't mean she is necessarily influential. And just because she has a low score doesn't mean she isn't influential at all. Although someone with a high Klout score might reach a lot of people, that doesn't mean she can get those people to make major buying decisions. It sometimes just means she can get people in her network to click a link to a new blog post or to see a new picture or video, not buy a new car.

It also means that someone with a low Klout score still has people in her life who love and trust her. And if that person recommends her family or friends buy a product or service, chances are, they'll buy it. And if she recommends her family or friends avoid a company or brand, chances are, they'll avoid it.

Analytics tools are a great way to measure the influence of people in a social network, but they shouldn't be used to pick and choose who you're going to be nice to or help. If nothing else, these people might know someone who does have a high influence and enlist her help in making their situation public. Reaching out to influencers in a community is a great way to build your network. (We'll discuss this more in Chapter 8, "The Kumbaya Effect: Social Media Marketing Builds Community.")

Although we could devote an entire chapter to the flawed thinking and metrics behind many social media influence scores as well, we won't. Suffice to say that each measurement tool, especially those that claim to rank and deliver influencers for your outreach and targeting efforts, has different ways of looking at influence. Klout earned due criticism when it first appeared because it only measured Twitter. Influential people not signed up for the service, like noted author Malcolm Gladwell for instance, didn't have much clout, according to the site's rankings. This is a ridiculous notion.

What these tools do provide is a layer of measure and statistics to add to your decision-making for social media marketing efforts. Influencer ratings like Klout, measurement aggregators like SWIXhq, and even the measures you can pull out of Facebook Insights or monitoring platforms like SocialMention.com or Sysomos, add context and depth to your branding and awareness efforts. Sure, some of them can provide a neat nugget statistic your CEO will enjoy telling his or her friends, but none of these platforms alone should drive your thinking.

What should is focusing on your objectives and measuring activity that proves or disproves you're moving the needle on them. That is true for measuring your branding and awareness efforts. It is perhaps more true for social media marketing efforts focused on building community.

Endnotes

1. Erik Qualman, *Socialnomics: How Social Media Transforms The Way We Live And Do Business*, Wiley, 2009.

2. http://sethgodin.typepad.com/seths_blog/2009/12/define-brand.html.

3. http://smartblogs.com/socialmedia/2011/03/01/walking-the-social-media-territory-with-century-21s-bev-thorne/.

4. Casey Hibbard, "How Social Media Helped Cisco Shave $100,000+ Off a Product Launch," *Social Media Examiner*. http://www.socialmediaexaminer.com/cisco-social-media-product-launch/.

It's Your House: Social Media Marketing Protects Your Reputation

In March 2010, candy giant Nestlé received a crash course on social media, when it was pummeled on its Facebook page by protestors and critics who were loudly complaining about Nestlé's use of palm oil from deforested areas in Indonesia.

And in one, fell swoop, the chocolate giant learned what every company needs to know: Social media presents a need for a different type of crisis communications. The company created the fan page on Facebook so its fans could talk about their favorite Nestlé products and see announcements about new candies. Waking up one day to see a bombardment of complaints about unethical practices wasn't what the company had in mind for its social media efforts. They weren't prepared.[1]

The comments were part of a Greenpeace campaign against Nestlé that launched that same week, following a report that said the candy giant was buying palm oil from a supplier that was responsible for deforestation in Indonesia and the deaths of thousands of orangutans.[2] Comments from page visitors ranged from why they quit buying Nestlé products to displaying altered Nestlé logos, such as retooling the Kit Kat logo into Killer (see Figure 6.1) or stamping bloody orangutan prints on the traditional corporate logo.

Figure 6.1   Protesters on the Internet had a field day using their graphics skills to retool the different Nestlé logos to draw attention to their campaigns.

Pop Quiz: If you're a large multinational brand that is being hammered by thousands of activists and protesters from around the world, what would you do?

A.   Have an open dialog with the protesters and organizers about their concerns.

B.   Launch a full-out attack with attorneys and sternly written cease-and-desist letters.

C.   Nothing.

    D. Turn the response over to a junior-level person who was tasked to handle a community page on the world's biggest social network.

Not too surprisingly, choices B and C are the ones most companies follow, which only makes the problem worse. But Nestlé chose option D. It's most memorable response, and one that is often cited as a big "Don't" in crisis communication seminars, was "...we welcome your comments, but please don't post using an altered version of any of our logos as your profile pic—they will be deleted."

This set off a huge thunderstorm of responses. The Nestlé spokesperson got into an argument with fans who were upset that Nestlé focused on the nitpicky details of an altered logo, rather than discussing the more important issue of Indonesian deforestation and animal slaughter. Here's what some of the comments and responses started to descend into:

> **A Facebook Fan:** "Not sure you're going to win friends in the social media space with this sort of dogmatic approach. I understand that you're on your back-foot due to various issues not excluding palm oil but social media is about embracing your market, engaging and having a conversation rather than preaching!"
>
> **Nestlé:** "Thanks for the lesson in manners. Consider yourself embraced. But it's our page, we set the rules, it was ever thus."
>
> **Another Facebook Fan:** "Freedom of speech and expression."
>
> **Nestlé:** "You have freedom of speech and expression. Here, there are some rules we set. As in almost any other forum. It's to keep things clear."
>
> **A Third Facebook Fan:** "Your page, your rules, true, and you just lost a customer, won the battle and lost the war. Happy?"
>
> **Nestlé:** "Oh please...it's like we're censoring everything to allow only positive comments."

And it only got worse. After hundreds of people expressed their outrage about the extinction of orangutans, the page administrator responded, "Get it off your chest—we'll pass it on." Messages were deleted, both from commenters and the administrator, if they were argumentative, contained altered logos, or were generally negative and nasty.

Finally, for whatever reason, the administrator realized the company was being snowed under with comments, and his own vitriol was not only adding fuel to the fire, it was also bringing in more attention as people who were leaving comments went to their own social networks and asked their friends to get involved. It finally reached its peak when the national and international media started paying attention to the Facebook fight (see Figure 6.2).

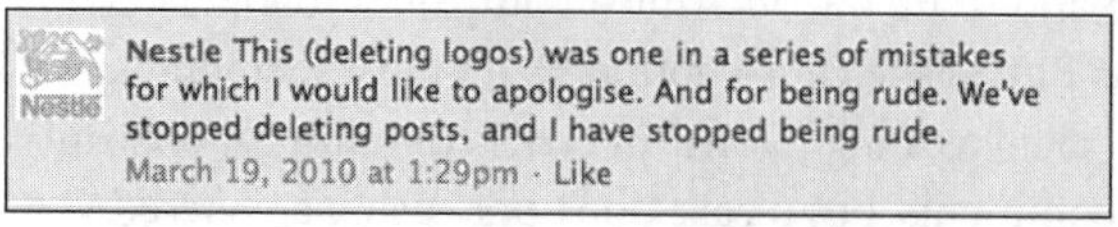

> Nestle This (deleting logos) was one in a series of mistakes for which I would like to apologise. And for being rude. We've stopped deleting posts, and I have stopped being rude.
> March 19, 2010 at 1:29pm · Like

Figure 6.2   The Nestlé Facebook administrator realized he was not winning any friends and was creating more problems than he was solving. The commenters didn't necessarily stop being rude, but the administrator did stop adding fuel to the fire.

Eventually, after two months of constant onslaught and global attention, Nestlé announced it was no longer buying palm oil from companies that destroyed rain forests, and Greenpeace declared its campaign a success.[3]

But the concession did not come without a price. Nestlé's reputation was tarnished online, and the company completely lost whatever control it thought it had over its social media network. A year later, the page has more than 180,000 fans, and the activism has not stopped. Although people have stopped talking about the campaign, Nestlé only seems to use the page for announcements and not for interacting with fans. Meanwhile, every announcement the company makes is met with more statements of outrage about how Nestlé supports slavery and genocide in Africa, calling on them to cease doing trade with the Ivory Coast, and any other controversial issues Nestlé might be associated with, even on the periphery.

However, Nestlé employees are taking matters into their own hands, sort of. Some employees will post messages saying they work at a Nestlé plant in a particular city or country, but that's it—nothing more than "I work at Nestlé in El Salvador" or "I work 4 Nestle Kenya." Although this might attempt to counter the negative comments, it doesn't make much of an impact. But the corporation refuses to engage with the complainers directly on any issue.

Although this is not a dumb choice, given the furor that arose in 2010, it's also not a smart choice. It means they're not really participating in conversations on their Facebook page at all, and they are giving people the chance to hit it with more negative comments. It means they have given protesters a chance to air their grievances without responding to them, which only tells the protesters this is a safe place to attack the company without any concerns about rebuttals or being contradicted.

This brand attack can—or at least should—elicit a crisis communication response from a PR professional who works to contain the negative publicity about their employer and the brand they've spent years creating and building.

Obviously, we don't want your company to be a mini version of Nestlé. By anticipating negative comments, even public outcries about your company, product, or service, you can avoid much of this type of negative interaction. By understanding the nature of social conversations, their viral potential, and what it takes to inject your position into a firestorm of detractors in an effective way, you can be a savvy crisis communicator for the twenty-first century.

What Is "Crisis Communication"?

Crisis communication means different things to different people. To former crisis communicators like Erik, who was once the risk communication director for the Indiana State Department of Health, it means communication during a public emergency. More commonly known as Crisis and Emergency Risk Communication (CERC; that's government speak for you. Why use two words when four will suffice?), it means communicating as much information as possible to fully inform the citizens of an affected area. To PR professionals, crisis communication means communication during a company crisis with the media—and increasingly, the public—through social media. This corporate crisis communication becomes necessary during product recalls, brand attacks like the one Nestlé experienced, or political crises, like a politician or business CEO-lebrity caught in a compromising position with someone who is not his spouse.

CERC and corporate crisis communication require different approaches, different ideas, and two completely different types of plans. But its qualities are important to understand because they can better inform your business's crisis communications measures. When you boil it down, CERC is basically regular public relations at a lightning-fast pace. It means dealing with the media and the public and working to put people at ease:

- In corporate communication, the first instinct is to hunker down and contain the bad news. In CERC, the first instinct is to flood everyone with as much information as possible. Neither of these is always the best choice, but they usually are the first instinct of their respective practitioners.

- In corporate communication, the negative end result is a loss of money. In CERC, it could be a loss of life. Of course, some instances of corporate communication may also be about a loss of life, such as a tainted food or drug recall, or safety problems related to an automobile. Similarly, a CERC situation could be related to a loss of money, such as during a fire or chemical spill.

- Corporate communication is often about containment, keeping as much information in house as possible to mitigate damage to the company's reputation and avoid a possible lawsuit. CERC is often about widespread communication, trying to reach as many people as possible, so nothing is hidden from the public.

- Many times, corporate communication is the most visible response from the company with other actions happening behind the scenes, like the legal response, brand management, and the product recall team. In CERC, the communication team is there for support, communicating with the public about everything else that is going on: incident response, medical response, and cleanup. That's because corporate communication is more about guiding the public perception, trying to manage the message people are receiving. CERC is about informing the public, keeping them up to date with what the first responders are doing, and managing the message so people can take the appropriate actions.

Both CERC and corporate communication need social media as a way to monitor what people are saying about the incident and even to respond to the public to correct misinformation and relay correct information. But you need to monitor what the public is saying and respond immediately when appropriate. You can't rely on traditional media to deliver your message because those channels don't operate as quickly as the Internet. Besides, traditional media is going to be a filter on your message anyway, delivering select pieces of it on their own schedules.

You Just Can't Wait for Traditional Media to Catch Up or Get It Right

Natural and man-made disasters move so quickly that developments leave traditional media in the dust. Stories are held until the evening news and the morning paper, unless it's big enough to warrant breaking into regular programming or one of the 24-hour news networks picks it up. The media outlets that have evolved with the times have done so using social media platforms like Twitter and content RSS feeds first popularized by bloggers to post breaking news to digitally connected audiences.

So social media is quickly becoming an alternative to traditional media—even an alternative used by traditional media—letting citizen journalists report on what's happening around them, reaching people in their networks immediately, often before the mainstream media or the outlet's main reporters even show up.

On January 15, 2009, Janis Krums was on a ferry on the Hudson River, when US Airways flight 1549 made an emergency landing on the river. His tweet (Figure 6.3) was the very first communication about the landing, and it had been read and retweeted by thousands of people 15 minutes before the first news reports hit the airwaves. In fact, nearly 35 minutes after Krums sent his tweet, he was on MSNBC being interviewed as a witness.

http://twitpic.com/135xa - There's a plane in the Hudson. I'm on the ferry going to pick up the people. Crazy.

3:36 PM Jan 15th, 2009 from TwitPic
Retweeted by 1 person   Reply Retweet

RT

jkrums
Janis Krums

Figure 6.3 Janis Krums's historic tweet was read and retweeted by thousands of people 15 minutes before the mainstream media reported the river landing.

Social media sites, even personal Twitter accounts like Krums's, are breaking news before the news does. Mainstream media often has a printing and broadcasting schedule it has to follow, and they're going to stick to it. People depend on the news being on their TV or their front porch at the same time and the same amount of time/paper every day. And unless the news is truly catastrophic, they'll stick to that schedule without fail.

That breaking news mentality extends to companies and brands as well. Remember the Domino's Pizza story we touched on in Chapter 5, "Make Some Noise: Social Media Marketing Aids in Branding and Awareness"? The pizza giant faced a serious crisis of credibility and cleanliness, thanks to the two employees and their disgusting video desecrating a customer's order. The video was passed around the Internet at lightning speed—almost as fast breaking news of celebrity deaths or arrests—and the company had no time to think before the public outcry was at a fever pitch. One Domino's Pizza spokesman said that people who had been loyal customers for as many as 20 years were "second-guessing their relationship with Domino's."[4]

Domino's Pizza executives decided to do nothing, hoping the furor would die down, but it only grew. They stayed away from social media for two days before finally taking action, creating a Twitter account to respond to any comments and questions. They also created a YouTube video with their CEO addressing the concerns their customers had raised. Although they had been talking about their commitment to customer health and safety in the traditional media, no one on Twitter seemed to notice. The company hadn't already been participating on the network, building relationships with customers and proving they were interested in their audience's feedback or input to that point. The company's traditional mindset meant it was bound by traditional media's schedule and filter, and couldn't reach the social media users who were making the loudest noise.

Although some social media practitioners said this 48 hours of unanswered questions and discussions hurt its brand, the fact that Domino's Pizza took to the same networks where people were questioning the company's commitment to customer care shows some forward thinking and a willingness to address problems head on. After almost two years of active participation on the social web through these channels, Domino's Pizza has a noticeably better online reputation among fans and followers. They have used social media marketing since the incident. And if they've only used it for the one purpose—to be present in the conversation so they can better communicate with the social audience when a crisis arises—that's a significant improvement.

While the crisis communicators are waiting for their stories to hit the media, the public is already talking about what's happening on Twitter and Facebook. By the time the TV news talks about the story, it's been on social media for several hours. By the time it appears in the newspaper the following morning, the events are already in their second day of discussion on social media.

The public isn't waiting for the media anymore. They're using social media to create and consume their own news. Anyone who wants to reach his audience, especially in times of crisis, needs to incorporate social media into a reputation management plan. This type of plan includes choosing traditional and social channels with which to communicate, monitoring mentions and brand pages on multitudes of socially driven websites to ensure accuracy and protect against detraction by disgruntled customers and building a consistent presence to offset any sudden claims or news that is detrimental to the company.

The question facing companies now is whether they will respond to the social media news or will they only wait for traditional media? The biggest mistake they can make is not to respond at all. Social media—if not the mood of the country—makes it necessary for companies to respond to crises as they occur.

When You Don't Listen or Respond, You Get Chi-Chi'd

By now, we've probably scared the hell out of you, and you'd just as soon never get involved with social media. We don't blame you; thousands of pissed-off bloggers and Facebook fans can intimidate anyone. But you can't stay away from social media—because your customers are already expecting you to be on there. Remember Gary Vaynerchuk's statement from Chapter 2, "It's Not Them; It's You!"?

> It doesn't matter if you think it's stupid (or scary). It's free communication, and there's a crapload of users.

Social media users have come to expect their favorite brands to be on social media. This expectation of response and interaction has gotten so pervasive that people get upset when they don't hear back from a company about their complaints, so they tell their friends about it, telling them about how they were ignored and their problems went unanswered.

The story of Chi-Chi's Mexican restaurant is a cautionary tale often told to executives about what could happen to companies that don't respond well, if at all, and take their customers for granted. Although the story of its demise begins in 2003—long before much of the movement we now know as social media took root—it still shows how crisis communications and responding to customer's concerns are critical components of a company's marketing and communications efforts.

Chi-Chi's was a sit-down Mexican restaurant chain with headquarters in Louisville, Kentucky. In November 2003, a Chi-Chi's restaurant in suburban Pittsburgh was hit with the largest hepatitis A outbreak in U.S. history, resulting in four deaths and 660 more people getting ill. But rather than deal with the problem, respond to media inquiries, or communicate with the public, Chi-Chi's top executives avoided any contact with the news media. Instead, they issued very dry, factual one-page statements. Two weeks after the outbreak was confirmed, Chi-Chi's COO, Bill Zavertnik, visited the site of the outbreak, read a brief statement to reporters, refused to take any questions, and took the corporate jet back to corporate HQ.

Subsequent media statements came from Chi-Chi's parent company, having obviously been written by lawyers who were looking to avoid a class-action lawsuit. The problem is, their reactions made people extremely angry because they felt ignored and unheard, so they filed their class-action lawsuits anyway. Ten months after the initial outbreak, when it was already in bankruptcy, Chi-Chi's was forced to close all U.S. locations and pay $2 million to settle the 60 biggest lawsuits it faced.

Who knows what could have happened if the company had been more transparent in its communication with the media and the public? Would it have kept Chi-Chi's in business? Would it have avoided the class-action lawsuits that ultimately killed it? No one can be sure. But we do know that despite their best efforts to avoid media scrutiny, the company failed and died anyway. However, straightforward communication might have gone a long way to saving them.

Before we go on a huge rant against corporate lawyers being prevented from going anywhere near the communication office, let us first say we understand the need for corporate lawyers. But although they do important work, they should not be in charge of the actual wordsmithing, or even the response. Legalese is signal one to the public that the company doesn't understand them, or that they don't want the public to understand the company. The response needs to be decided on by executive management and created by the crisis communicators, who will hopefully have their finger on the pulse of the public. If you yourself don't know what the public is thinking or wants, ask the people who do.

Talk to the salespeople and the marketing department. Let PR manage the response, give sales and marketing some input, and let the legal department keep people out of jail or from violating any laws or regulations. But don't let them take over the public response, or you could run into the same outrage that Chi-Chi's faced, after it offered up a sanitized, half-hearted written statement, without actually engaging their customers. Remember, you're not going to avoid making people mad during a corporate crisis. You will make them even angrier if you look like you don't care.

Of course, responding poorly is only slightly better than not responding at all, because it only adds to the mess. The story about Nestlé's response to its non-fans created a bigger problem than not responding at all. And now that Nestlé has adopted a nonresponse as its strategy, you can see how well that's working out for them now. (Hint: It's not.)

Six Steps for Dealing with Detractors

Because dealing with detractors, even those who have every right to be talking negatively about your company, is intimidating and stressful, you can handle them with grace, humor, and honesty. We've told you stories of how not to handle crises in social media communications. Now let's look at how your company should handle incidents when people talk bad about your organization online.

1. Acknowledge their right to complain.

    Free speech may not be a founding principle of every country, but it certainly presides in communications online. If a customer has a run-in with your brand at any point and isn't satisfied, she can, and often should, tell someone with the company, or even just a friend.

2. Apologize for their situation or your mistake, if warranted.

    The two most powerful words in diffusing a tense situation are, "I'm sorry." But you don't have to claim responsibility for the situation by doing so, especially if you don't have all the information to make that determination. Apologize for the detractors' trouble, the situation, or their experience and ask for more information on how you can help them or make the situation better. If it turns out your company did something wrong, you can say you're sorry for that, too. Even if your lawyers tell you not to.

3. Assert clarity in your policy or reasons, if warranted.

    Sometimes people are upset about a return policy or some rule you follow that can't be changed. It's perfectly fine to assert yourself to someone who is being negative about your brand, but do it politely, with compassion and by supplying the reasons your policy exists. Don't make the reasons about the detractors; make it about the betterment of every customer's experience.

4. Assess what will help them feel better.

    Comcast's Frank Eliason answered upset customers on Twitter in 2007 by asking the question, "How can I help?" What those four simple words do is turn the power of the conversation over to the customer and let him, if just for a moment, dictate the terms of what would help. When the customer feels listened to and empowered, the company often earns credibility in his mind.

5. Act accordingly.

    If you can, within your company's policies and within reason, do what the customer says will make her happy, do it. We understand there will be instances when a customer request is either beyond your individual power to enact or is just unreasonable. But if it's within the parameters of appropriateness, do it. Putting out the flames of a detractor's fire quickly and sufficiently is the best way to turn that detractor into a fan. Or at least someone who isn't flaming you anymore.

6. Abdicate.

    If you've exhausted all reasonable means of addressing the customer's issue and he still insists on unreasonable responses or refuses to quiet his claims, it's okay to step away. By politely offering the solution again and informing the customer that this is truly all you can do and you are happy to do so, but you have to move on to other customer issues, the decision is on him. The great news is that if you and your team decide you've been fair, honest, and reasonable with the customer, but they're being unreasonable, the rest of the audience watching the conversation will think they're being unreasonable, too. Jason likes to say, "Sometimes a turd is a turd." And no one will fault you from walking away.

But It's Not Always About the Negative

We would be remiss if we spent this entire chapter talking about the negative side of the reputation equation. Protecting your reputation can take on a proactive spin as well.

Using your monitoring solution to search for mentions of your product or service will certainly help you identify the harmful conversations in which you need to participate. But it will also show you many more positive or even neutral mentions of your brand. Just because these conversations don't have the big red flag sticking out of them doesn't mean they should be ignored.

If putting out fires is one execution of reputation protection on the social web, then fanning the flames of good fires is another. Whether it's dropping in to say, "Thanks! Appreciate the support!" or just answering a question someone posed related to your brand or the industry, at a minimum you will appear present and accounted for in the conversation.

Your presence in online conversations alone will cut down on a ton of potential negative conversations or complaints about your company. Socially enabled companies see a customer in need and fix the issue almost instantly. It's not because these companies only respond to the bad. It's because they're present in the conversation. Company representatives chitchat with folks as well as address customer service issues. They drop in and say thank you or retweet a Twitter message that compliments the company.

They're participating in the conversation.

If the only thing you do in protecting your reputation through social media marketing is finding a handful of positive mentions each week and reaching out to say, "Thank you," you're protecting your reputation just a bit.

Protecting Your Reputation Has a Technology Side, Too

Let's say you own the best doughnut shop in Philadelphia. The local newspaper says so, and the general consensus of the public agrees. Even your competition might say, "Yep. They're darn good." But if you aren't using the web and social media much, Google won't think you're the best doughnut shop in Philadelphia. So protecting your reputation applies to search results as well.

This is where social media and search engine optimization overlap to create a golden opportunity for your business. Two of the primary factors that help a particular piece of content rank well in search engines were how recent the content was and how many people linked to it. Recency and third-party endorsement still go a long way in capturing search engine rankings. Recency is most readily won by blogging. Blog platforms are made to help you publish content frequently, so one of those two big factors is addressed when your company publishes blog posts. Promoting those posts to attract links from other bloggers and websites helps the other big factor.

With the evolution of social search, however, Google (which accounts for 80% of the search market) is beginning to use a wider net for capturing those third-party endorsements, while delivering more customized results for each user at the same time.

Social search is another layer of information the search engines take into account when producing results, based on your social connections. These connections—your social graph—produce what Google considers more relevant results for your search query. When you type in "best bakery in Philadelphia," instead of seeing what *Google* thinks are the best websites that answer that question, you now see results that include what *your friends* think is the best bakery in Philly. That is, if Jason is talking about your doughnut shop, it could show up in Erik's search results.

Jason has many friends in Philadelphia, so if he searches for the best bakery, his results will be influenced by his friends' activity on social media sites. In early 2011, Google's top result for the query, "best bakery Philadelphia" was a shop called Imagicakes. But Jason's top result was Termini's Italian Bakery, thanks to his friend Bill Lublin's review on Yelp.com.

Google search results can be further influenced by the number of "likes" a company collects on its Facebook fan page or mentions it gets in Facebook conversations. If even casual social media participation can affect where you rank in search results for certain people, then protecting your electronic reputation in the search engines is helped by social media activity.

Affecting the search engine results extends beyond using Twitter and Facebook to ratings and review sites as well. By using social media monitoring services to be aware of new reviews on sites like Yelp, Urbanspoon, MerchantCircle, or even Google Places, companies can immediately address negative reviews and even amplify positive ones to capitalize on what customers are saying about them online.

All this activity helps your company move up in the search engine results. It also helps ensure that if a blogger or online audience member gets upset and takes his or her frustration out on you online, that piece of content doesn't rank high for a search result for your brand or company. Remember Jeff Jarvis's blog post we talked about in Chapter 2? His Dell experience beat out the company for search engine results for "Dell" for quite some time.

You don't want the bad outranking the good any more than you want your competition outranking you for certain keywords. Social media activity adds to the all-important factor of prominence in the search engine's rankings. In a video about Google's Local Search rankings,[5] Google product manager Jeremy Sussmann explained prominence was determined by how well known or prominent certain business are based on sources across the web. Those sources include blogs, review sites, social networks, and more.

Putting Metrics Around Protecting Your Reputation

Protecting your reputation is just as much a function of marketing as it is of public relations. As PR cleans up a mess, the marketing department has to work that much harder to overcome it in the future. A major misstep means marketing has to go to extra lengths to convince people that whatever the earlier problem was is no longer.

This means that a tarnished reputation could become so cumbersome that the only thing that's going to overcome it is millions of dollars. If you're a small company with a huge problem, you don't have millions to blow on fixing it. Chi-Chi's had such a big problem that the only thing that solved it was selling most of their restaurants and closing down the rest, leaving only a few overseas restaurants and a packaged food division.

Obviously, protecting your reputation is worth something. At the very least, it's worth thousands, hundreds of thousands, or even millions of dollars; at most, it's worth your company's very existence.

Although social media activities can be easier to measure than other mediums because of the digital nature of the Web, reputation management is much more difficult. This is because you're using hindsight to look back at incidents and opportunities. You can tabulate the total losses by adding up all the customers who left, adding up their projected sales, and coming up with a pretty good idea of what you lost. But you can't put math behind potential losses you avoided by being on top of the online conversation.

Let's say you discover a serious security flaw in your software that could allow someone's financial information to be stolen. You discover the problem, fix it, address it in the media, distribute the fixes, and weather the storm of complaints, even though no one lost any of their information. For the most part, people are annoyed, but remain customers.

How do you measure what could have been? Would you have lost 2% of your customers or 60%? Would you have been sued and for how much? You can get a rough estimate of what the disaster could have cost, but short of actually letting it run its course, you'll never know what the end results would have been.

That doesn't mean you shouldn't try, though. You can use the different social media monitoring tools to not only find mentions of your company or certain industry keywords, but also to measure the sentiment of those comments, and tell you whether people like, are neutral about, or dislike the name in the mentions. Figure 6.4 is a screenshot from a social media monitoring service.

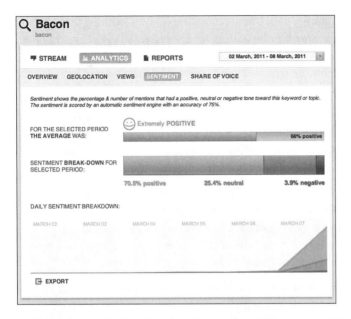

Figure 6.4   Frankly, we were rather surprised to see that 3.9% of the sentiment was negative about bacon. Who doesn't like bacon?

But with tools like Radian6, Sysomos, and AlterianSM2, the people in charge of reputation monitoring can use software to identify problems and complaints and begin addressing them immediately, rather than being caught by surprise. Some of the metrics your company should measure for your reputation management efforts include the following:

- Positive online mentions and sentiment using social media monitoring or online clipping services and data analysis

- Negative online mentions and sentiment using social media monitoring or online clipping services and data analysis

- Search engine result rankings using a search marketing rank checking tool or service

Any of these results can show you a measure of your company's reputation. Comparing your reputation today with a year ago, or even a looking back on today a year from now, gives you benchmarks and even potential goals to improve upon or maintain.

Keep in mind that monitoring your brand reputation is not something that can be handled on a wing and a prayer, or by waiting for the perfect storm of angry consumers and consumer activists to air your dirty laundry. Savvy social media practitioners constantly monitor the sentiment and analytics of their brands and related industry terms.

In 2009, Jason wrote an industry report called "Customer Twervice: Exploring Case Studies & Best Practices in Customer Service Efforts Using Twitter."[6] He looked at the customer service efforts of eight different companies, including Network Solutions, an Internet domain and web hosting company.

Just two years earlier, Network Solutions had very low positive sentiment scores in online conversations. That is, no one liked them; customers disparaged them, complained about them, and, for the most part, had nothing nice to say. But two years later, they were, as Jason called them, "one of the best examples of reputation management via customer service out there."

"The four things we look at in terms of our social media strategy are brand and reputation management, connecting with our customers, connecting with our community, and driving new business," said Shash Bellamkonda, Network Solutions social media director. "The social media team is trained as customer service representatives."

Although Network Solutions uses social media as a customer service tool (product managers will jump in and answer questions from time to time), it ultimately protects their reputation as well. NetSol is unusual, but not unique, in that the company views reputation management as a customer service function, rather than public relations. Even though the customer service department would probably not typically be called on to manage a company crisis, by responding to customer service crises, customer service representatives have managed to improve Network Solution's online reputation in two years with one simple tool that lets people communicate 140 characters at a time.

"Our long-term goal is to have more customer support front-line people there," Bellamkonda said. "We have 40 people on Twitter from customer support right now, but they don't do regular monitoring. We have Twitter volunteers who engage with customers to help the social media team, but our philosophy is to train everyone else to engage in it."

As more people use social media, whether it's Facebook, Twitter, or any of the other thousands of social networks out there, it's important to monitor what's being said about your brand. If you do something wrong, be prepared for people to blast you for it. But don't get defensive because that will become the story.

If an employee behaves badly, be prepared for news to go viral, but don't sit quietly and wait for it to go away because the story will grow even bigger. If your reputation is already poor, start using social media as a way to improve it by listening, responding to complaints, and demonstrating your commitment to your customers.

And look at your search engine results. Do you deserve better? Are you the best, or at least in the top 5 or 10 at what you do in your area? Do you rank there? Start employing search engine optimization tactics to protect your technological reputation as well.

Protecting your reputation using social media lays a great foundation for the next benefit of social media marketing for your business: good public relations.

Endnotes

1. Elliott Fox, "Nestlé Hit by Facebook 'Anti-Social' Media Surge," *Guardian*, March 19, 2010. http://www.guardian.co.uk/sustainable-business/nestle-facebook.

2. "Sweet Success for Kit Kat Campaign," http://www.greenpeace.org/international/en/news/features/Sweet-success-for-Kit-Kat-campaign/.

3. "Sweet Success for Kit Kat Campaign,"http://www.greenpeace.org/international/en/news/features/Sweet-success-for-Kit-Kat-campaign/.

4. Stephanie Clifford, "Video Prank at Domino's Taints Brand," *The New York Times*, April 15, 2009. http://www.nytimes.com/2009/04/16/business/media/16dominos.html.

5. http://www.youtube.com/watch?v=L1ONMavPX2o&feature=player_embedded.

6. Jason Falls, "Customer Twervice." http://www.socialmediaexplorer.com/customertwervice/.

Relating to Your Public: Social Media Marketing and Public Relations

Say the words public relations, and your first thought is probably about press releases, TV news interviews, and newspaper stories. PR flacks—a slang term for PR pros—are paid professionals whose job it is to get your company or your product into the mainstream media. They have relationships with journalists and can call them up to get a story placed. Or they have an email list of journalists a mile long they send press releases to on an alarming basis, hoping one of them will stick.

But public relations is no longer just a matter of dealing with the mainstream media. The mainstream media is still important, but it's not the only game in town anymore. In fact, the mainstream media has suffered a serious blow in viewership, readership, and listenership thanks to social media. Today, public relations professionals must be aware that easy-access online publishing platforms like blogs and social networking tools make everyone a publisher. Thus everyone is the media.

According to the Pew Internet & American Life's 2011 State of the Media Report, more people got their news online in 2010 than they did from a physical newspaper. This is the first time in the Internet's history that this has ever happened. The only media source that beat the Internet was television news, and the Pew Center says this gap is closing.[1] In fact, according to the report, the audience dropped for every form of news media, except for online (see Figure 7.1). The online audience grew by 17.1%, while newspapers dropped 5%, and network and cable news dropped 3.4% and 13.7%, respectively. This last figure is especially surprising, given the fact that cable TV was once considered a major growth sector in mainstream media.

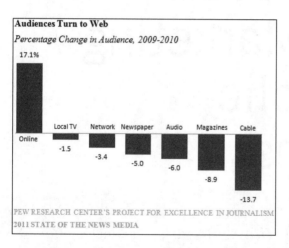

Figure 7.1 American news gathering habits have all shifted in favor of online news sources. Cable TV news—once a major growth sector—had the biggest drop in viewership.

This has spelled trouble for the mainstream media, which is losing its revenue to online ad revenue. This causes the media outlets to lay off staff, which affects the quality of their news coverage, which means people desert their favorite media outlets to get their news elsewhere, which reduces readership and viewership, which causes the media outlets to lose revenue, and the whole thing becomes a vicious cycle. No one is sure where this cycle will end, but it has caused a spike in popularity of online alternative news outlets and programs, citizen journalism, blogs, and even video news programs.

Remember in Chapter 2, "It's Not Them; It's You!," when we talked about how Target had a policy of not dealing with nontraditional media sources? What happens if your company has a similar policy and you ignore blogs because you think they're written by angry people sitting in their underwear in their parents' basements? What will happen to your public relations efforts if the mainstream media in a city drops off so much that the city's newspaper shifts its content online or shuts down completely?

It happened to the *Seattle Post-Intelligencer*, which was the first major metropolitan newspaper to go online-only in March 2009, followed by the *INDenverTimes* in April 2009, which replaced the shuttered *Rocky Mountain News*. Because several newspapers and even more trade publications around the U.S. have folded, gone online, or significantly cut back, traditional mainstream media is being stretched thin. There are fewer local news stories, fewer opportunities for businesses to make a major announcement, and fewer reporters to cover these stories. The Pew Center estimated that 1,000 to 1,500 newsrooms were lost in 2010, making newsrooms 30% smaller than they were in 2000.

That doesn't mean local news gathering is lost, it's just moving online. In 2010, Yahoo! hired several dozen reporters to cover news, sports, and finance for their Yahoo! Local News coverage. AOL hired 900 journalists, 500 of who are working in their local Patch news outlet. But it's not just the big online companies that are covering local news. Ordinary citizens are taking matters into their own hands as well.

The Southeast Indianapolis Communities (SIC) blog (see Figure 7.2) focuses strictly on news around the southeast quadrant of Indianapolis. It is able to provide more in-depth information than the city's newspaper, the *Indianapolis Star*, publishing hyperlocal news stories about upcoming events, high school sports, and issues of concern to Southeast Indianapolis residents, such as bike lane development plans, local trash schedules, and new businesses in area neighborhoods.

Because most of these events won't appeal directly to all of the *Indianapolis Star* readers, the blog is able to reach exactly the audience its editors want to reach: people who live in that section of Indianapolis. As a result, readers may turn to the SIC blog, rather than the *Star*, which could cut into readership and ad revenues. And as papers like the *Star* turn more and more to national news and wire reports in an attempt to save money, these local blogs become more important to local readers.

This means they are going to become important to you as they replace the traditional media. Companies like Target and their PR professionals will be forced to either deal with the nontraditional media on a continuing basis or fight harder for smaller spaces in fewer media outlets.

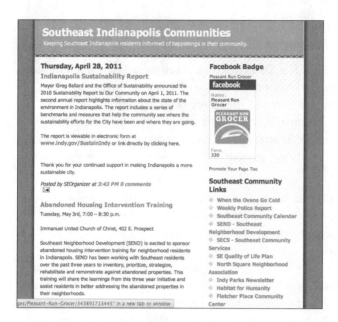

Figure 7.2   Local news blogs and websites are filling in the gaping holes left by decreasing coverage by local newspapers, which are relying more on wire services and national news, and less on local news, for their news coverage.

So although we're not telling you to ignore mainstream media, we do want to get you thinking more positively about online media, whether it's the large Internet companies like Yahoo! and AOL providing local news coverage or the local bloggers covering their own little corner of the world that the mainstream media won't even talk about unless someone got shot or a house burned down.

Public Relations Is Not Only About the Mainstream Media Anymore

This massive change in the media landscape also means that PR professionals have to change their tactics as well. Gone are the days of press releases, publicity stunts, and fabricated events that trick an unsuspecting public. It's no longer acceptable to blanket a city's local media or an industry's trade media with press releases. This strategy might have been the standard practice years ago—and still is, for many PR pros—but it is almost completely frowned upon by online journalists and bloggers these days.

However, social media is making it much easier for PR professionals to continue to provide media relations services to their clients. As we discussed in Chapter 5, "Make Some Noise: Social Media Marketing Aids in Branding and Awareness," (and discuss in greater detail in Chapter 11, "It's All About the Benjamins: Social Media

Marketing Drives Sales"), sales and marketing are now about relationships and trust. If your customers trust you and feel like they have a relationship with your employees and your company, they're more likely to buy from you. The same is true for PR professionals. Social media allows them to have relationships with journalists, both citizen and professional, and to earn their trust. If their "customers" trust them, they're more likely to buy from them, paying them with the currency of airtime, column inches, and blog posts. So although PR professionals still have to pay attention to traditional media, they need to recognize it's not the only game in town. Now they also have to play nice with the social media, industry media, and even the general public.

In fact, it's this last group that requires PR professionals to pay attention to what the general public is saying about their clients and employers. That's because with free blogging platforms and cell phones with video and still cameras, every citizen is a journalist. It means that anyone is a publisher, and can report or break news before the mainstream media ever catches hold of a story.

While we were writing this chapter, we heard news that Osama bin Laden was killed. Only we read about it on Twitter, where it had been announced before it ever reached the airwaves. Keith Urbahn, the chief of staff for the former defense secretary Donald Rumsfeld, tweeted out the news (see Figure 7.3). It was immediately picked up by the people in his Twitter network, who retweeted it to their own Twitter networks. The news reached thousands of people in mere minutes.

Figure 7.3 It turns out Urbahn's source was a TV news producer, which means Urbahn didn't really break the news, although he scooped traditional media. Almost.

Urbahn's tweet might have been the catalyst that told the country, and even the world, about the dramatic news. But he said in interviews that he did not break it because he actually heard it from a TV news producer. But someone sure did break it.

Sohaib Athar, a computer programmer in Abbottabad inadvertently live-tweeted the attack on bin Laden's compound as it happened (see Figure 7.4), making him the first person to give any kind of public update about what was happening in the compound. He said it was completely unintentional because he didn't know bin Laden was there.

Figure 7.4   Sohaib Athar's series of tweets unwittingly reported the bin Laden mission as it happened. "Something nasty" indeed.

The point of this story is to demonstrate the idea that it's not always the mainstream media that makes or breaks the news. In some cases, it's not even the citizen journalists and news bloggers who do it. Occasionally, it's someone who gets a little tidbit of news from a friend and passes it on or happens to be in his apartment when a helicopter convoy attacks a nearby fortified mansion.

This means public relations professionals can't ignore social media. They can't limit their focus to the mainstream media or even the new media bloggers and video bloggers. It means they need to consider everyone as a possible news maker and monitor social media as a whole to see who is talking about their clients and employers. Finally, they need to reach out to the professionals, the semiprofessionals, and the accidental amateurs equally.

Journalists Are Using Social Media, Too

But social media isn't just limited to the enthusiastic amateur who is looking to become the next Woodward and Bernstein. Journalists are jumping on the social media bandwagon as well, using Twitter, LinkedIn, and even Facebook both to engage their audiences and to gather information and get story ideas.

According to a Spring 2011 report by Brunswick Research, 90% of journalists they surveyed have been at least influenced by social media, whether by a story that originated on social media or by investigating or even writing a story.[2] We have both been contacted by journalists to give expert comments about social media through quotes in newspaper articles and appearances on TV news programs.

According to this same report, 43% of journalists around the world said blogs and microblogs (namely Twitter) have become important sources of information, and 32% of them said social networking sites are important. Looking to the future, 72% of business journalists said social media would have a positive impact on the quality of their reporting.

What this means for PR professionals and the PR department is that business journalists are increasingly more open to being contacted via social media, finding their stories on blogs, and using social media to research their stories. PR professionals should be using the corporate blog as their newsroom, posting press releases to the blog, keeping in contact with industry journalists via Twitter and LinkedIn, and even pitching the occasional story idea to journalists they have become friendly with on social media sites.

The PR department should keep regular contact with journalists through as many social media outlets as possible. This means that the IT department shouldn't block access to all the social networks (see Chapter 2 for our thoughts on why IT shouldn't be making any calls about who gets on social media and who doesn't).

Journalists are becoming a lot like your customers, thanks to social media. They no longer want to be yelled at, receiving the same press release that every other schmo on the media list received. Just like consumers want to be heard by their favorite brands, journalists want to think they're being treated respectfully by their sources.

PR flacks need to stop carpet bombing journalists with generic press releases, hoping one or two of them will stick. Instead, they need to tailor individual emails to journalists, reach out to them via Twitter, or make a phone call, pitching a story and explaining why they think it would be a good fit for that journalist.

Some journalists have become so disgusted with the laziness of PR pros who still insist on using the old-school press release carpet bomb method that some of them have taken to publicly posting a list of the offending flacks, including their emails, so they will be picked up by spammers. In 2007, Chris Anderson, the editor-in-chief of *Wired* magazine, grew so disgusted by the generic emails he was receiving from PR practitioners, he took a stand. Because none of the practitioners would even do a modicum of research to find out the appropriate magazine staffer to receive the pitch, he compiled a blacklist and published it on his website, causing a huge storm of controversy in the PR industry.

This attitude has carried over, and many journalists have begun creating their own blacklists, lumping in entire agencies and companies who spam journalists. There is even a growing idea that unsolicited press releases may violate the CAN-SPAM Act, which makes it easier to prosecute spammers who send unsolicited, unwanted emails. This means your PR people have to treat journalists like you want your marketing and customer service people to treat your customers.

Social Media Lets PR Skip the Gatekeepers and Editors

One of the things that has surprised us about public relations in the Internet age is that journalism has changed but a lot of PR people still use the same old tactics. This is where social media can be a boon to a company's public relations efforts.

In the "old" days, press releases were faxed to an editor, who looked through the day's releases, assigned a story, and swept the rest into a trash can at the end of the day. Nowadays, releases are emailed to editors, which are either assigned and forwarded to a particular journalist, or they're deleted, and the janitor doesn't even have to bother with them.

The Internet has made most of this unnecessary, yet it's surprising how many PR professionals still use these old methods to reach journalists. For one thing, PR professionals are now expected to call or email and individually pitch a particular journalist. It's easy enough to find out who that is—PR professionals can pick up past copies of the magazine or newspaper, watch the program they're trying to pitch, or just look it up on the website. Every media outlet has a phone number, and most of them have a website. Just some basic research will reveal the journalist they need to contact.

What's more important is that social media lets PR professionals skip the gatekeepers and editors completely. There's no need to send an editor anything. Instead, a PR professional send it directly to the journalist with the customized pitch and create the relationship at that level.

Why more PR pros aren't embracing social media as an effective way to do media relations is beyond us. Social media has made media relations one of the easiest tasks they'll do all day. The use of blogs and Twitter conversations means that PR professionals can more easily converse with journalists and get their story placed.

Quit Waiting for Traditional Media to Catch Up

In Chapter 6, "It's Your House: Social Media Marketing Protects Your Reputation," we talked about how social media has grown to the point where it's sometimes breaking the news before the mainstream media does. The Osama bin Laden story is just the latest example of social media's instantaneous transmission of information. Before that, it was the US Airways flight that landed in the Hudson River in New York in 2009 or the first images to come out of Port-au-Prince, Haiti, after the 2010 earthquake.

Despite the 24/7 fountain of information on cable news, traditional media is often behind the news cycle. TV news, radio news, newspapers, and magazines are not reporting new information as it happens, but rather on their own publishing schedule. The problem is that you're dealing with tradition, publication schedules, and an entire city filled with other people who think their news stories are equally as important. This is where social media can make a huge difference.

Let's say your company wants to announce a new government contract that will lead to a facility expansion and 75 new jobs in the next nine months. You organize a press conference, and the mayor will be there to help announce the new jobs initiative. Rather than waiting for the TV news to carry your news announcement at 5:00 (when everyone is driving home), 6:00 (when everyone is eating dinner), and 11:00 (when people are getting ready for bed), you can use social media to make your own announcement. Rather than waiting for the newspaper to carry your story the next day, you can use a blog to run your own story. And rather than waiting for your industry's trade journals to run your story in a month or two, and only if you buy a half-page ad in their magazine, you can use your Twitter feed and email newsletter to notify your customers about your big news.

This is where social media tools like a blog, video stream, and Twitter are going to make a big difference.

For example, when the mainstream media shows up to the press conference, have an intern with a digital video camera stand with the reporters and record the CEO making the big announcement. Later, interview the CEO and the mayor to get exclusive footage that the news channels didn't get. Upload the videos to the company blog and have a full-length video that visitors can watch, rather than the 10-second clip the news channels showed. (As an added bonus, track the number of people who watched the video and how long they watched it. The news stations can't even do that.)

Publish the press release—complete with statements from the CEO and mayor—the text of the CEO's and mayor's speeches, and a description and timeline of the expansion to the company blog. Next, promote them to the media outlets that could not make it.

Send all of this information to the citizen journalists and industry bloggers who would be interested in this sort of news. You will reach a bigger audience of people who (1) didn't watch the TV news that night, (2) don't read the newspaper, (3) don't live in your local community, and (4) are in your industry, but won't read the story until the next time the trade magazine comes out. By using social media to promote your news, you're not only able to stay ahead of the mainstream media, but you can also avoid their filters and time constraints.

Avoiding the Filter of the Traditional Media

Time and space: It's the biggest problem with mainstream media, but it's the same problem that everyone faces. In a 30-minute news broadcast, at least 8 to 10 of those minutes are commercials. Then you have sports and weather, which are another 6 to 8 minutes. That leaves 12 to 14 minutes to cover all the news for the entire city—fires, murders, accidents, politics, disasters, world politics, and world disasters. Oh, and your story, which has been reduced to a 20-second segment about how your company is going to add 75 new jobs in nine months.

Newspapers are a little more forgiving. They have more space—measured in column inches, or how many inches of text appears in a news article—than TV stations have time. Your news article could be more than 1,000 words, but it could end up getting cut down to 650 words to make room for a new ad from that new car dealership on the west side.

Trade magazines may give you more space, but you're limited to their publication schedule, which can be monthly, bimonthly, or even quarterly. And a few trade journals will press you hard to buy ad space in their journal as a *quid pro quo*. Buy the ad, and they'll run your story. Don't buy it, and they'll drop it in if they have the space.

Never mind that you spent three weeks planning the press conference, coordinating the schedule with the mayor's office, writing the speech, writing the press release, rewriting the speech, and making sure all the media outlets were there. Three weeks of work have been boiled down to 20 seconds, 650 words, and a slightly modified version of your press release (with the mayor's name spelled wrong) sitting next to the half-page ad you bought, thus destroying any credibility the journal article was supposed to bring.

From a public relations point of view, this is one of the most inefficient uses of time: three weeks of work for 20 seconds of coverage. Although the 20 seconds is extremely valuable, it still doesn't give a full picture of what the announcement will mean for your company, what the new jobs will mean for your community, and most important, what it is your company actually does and what it will do as part of the new contract.

This is where social media is going to make a difference. All the information you published to the company blog—press releases, written statements, videos of the press conference, video interviews with the CEO and mayor, a description of the contract, and the timeline for expansion—is far more accessible to more people. People can read it, comment on it, find out more information about your company, and learn where they can apply for jobs. Potential customers will find all this information via search engines, see what a great job your company is doing, and contact your business development people so you can do a great job for their company. And the information is potentially there forever. A television commercial is gone in 30 or 60 seconds.

Even though the mainstream media coverage you got won't tell the whole story, you do need to be grateful for getting it. But also know that many people who saw or read the story are also more likely to visit your website to find out more information. If you give them more information than they expected, it gives them a chance to become more interested in your company and the products you offer. Now public relations has become a marketing channel, and PR pros are doing their part to get customers to learn more about you. All of this PR work will also help gain the attention of some of the influencers in your industry, and that's where your PR efforts are really going to pay off.

The New Media Relations Landscape

Robert Scoble (@Scobleizer) is a superblogger (see Figure 7.5 for a screenshot of his blog). He's considered an influencer in the tech community and has the network to prove it. With more than 178,000 followers on Twitter, he has the potential reach of the total audience of CNBC, which gets about 200,000 viewers per day. Author and social media consultant Chris Brogan (@ChrisBrogan) has nearly 182,000 followers. And Heather Armstrong (@Dooce), who we discussed in Chapter 2, has 1.5 million followers.

These individuals are superbloggers, people who wield a lot of power and influence. Companies fall all over themselves to get their products mentioned on their blogs and on the blogs of anyone who reaches tens of thousands of people a month with their pronouncements. Technology companies and publishers will send products and books to Scoble and Brogan in the hopes of getting a positive review. Consumer companies will send Armstrong products asking her for a brief mention in one of her blog posts. Companies know they can reach a targeted audience of people who are likely to be interested in their news, rather than reaching a general audience, most of whom aren't that interested.

Figure 7.5   Robert Scoble's reach and popularity get him into places most people can't go, like Facebook's data center in Prineville, Oregon. Source: www.scobleizer.com

Of course, you have to have something big and splashy if you want to catch their attention. When we asked Scoble for permission to use his screenshot, this was the automated reply we received. And with his level of reach and influence, he can get away with it.

> To PR people, if you want me to cover your product you've got to give me more than one day warning. I do videos and I'm already scheduling out July.

> I don't do press-release rewrites like other tech bloggers. It's best to get in touch with me at LEAST A MONTH before you launch (right now my calendar is totally booked until late-June — you can get on that at http://tungle.me/scobleizer!). To see a successful pitch, see how Flipboard pitched me (it is my favorite startup of 2010): http://www.google.com/buzz/scobleizer/EsMhJvooEWv/Its-interesting-because-I-get-dozens-of-pitches (Flipboard showed me what they were doing THREE MONTHS before they shipped!)

> I specifically am looking for world-changing technology and startups, if you have one, please be persistent. I am often out shooting and miss cool stuff once in a while.

A mention from these kinds of superbloggers—and there are hundreds of them, each commanding different niches and industries—can make an entire sales quarter with a quick video blog or mention. It pays to make this part of your social media PR strategy.

But you'll never reach these people with a canned press release or typical corporate approach. If you think it's hard reaching the daily newspaper in your city, imagine what it's going to be like to reach someone who believes he's an honest-to-God celebrity. It's not enough to just have a compelling story or a really cool idea. You have to show these new media luminaries that you have what it takes to play on their level. Basically, your company has to have a superblogger too—or at least a pretty damn good blogger.

This is where getting your employees involved as bloggers is going to make a difference. Superbloggers love to be in the know; they love to be connected. This is how they've built their reputation and their networks to become these superbloggers: They get all the good stuff first and share it with their networks. The people who read them have come to rely on people like Robert Scoble for the latest news in the technology world, interviews with the thought leaders, and an inside look at what's happening at the companies like Facebook, Google, and Twitter.

There are even superbloggers in your own industry. There is someone who owns your particular industry, in your particular niche, and is widely read by your employees, your competitors, and your customers. If you want to catch his or her attention, you have to be a content-generating machine. You won't get it by just posting your press releases or some legal-approved, marketing jargon–filled sterilized dead fish. You need engaging content that will catch the attention of your superblogger's readers. If your superblogger is going to be the first in your industry, you need to be the second, so your employees, your competitors, and your customers are also reading.

So, you have to think of your company as a publisher and a media outlet, not as a follower and a reader. You're not just putting out press releases that you hope the local or trade media will pick up. Rather, you want to put out stories, videos, and interviews that get your readers excited. And even though this piece of advice is appearing in the public relations chapter of this book, this is not going to be your PR department. It's going to be your internal employees who excel at whatever it is your company does. If you build cars, it's going to be the engineers and designers. If you make baby food, it's going to be the nutritionist. If you run a sports team, it's going to be the players and coaches.

This doesn't mean you or your employees need to stop doing what you're doing and start focusing on blogging. But you need to refresh the company blog at least once a week, whether it's shooting a quick video on a digital video camera, dictating a blog post for the PR or marketing folks to write, or at least outsourcing content to a freelance ghost blogger to make blog-ready.

Talk about the hot-button issues in the industry. Talk about what concerns your customers. Talk about what awesome new projects you're working on (without violating any trade secrets or governmental regulations) or the newest acquisition of the company. Avoid the corporate speak and the legalese (let the lawyers review it, but they shouldn't have a say in the actual writing of the piece). Let a senior executive who is intimately familiar with a particular project do a video interview about what the next three months are going to look like. Have the CEO discuss what the next fiscal year is going to hold for the company. Get the sales team to talk about their time at the latest trade show and who they ran into.

Blogging needs to be a major part of your new media relations, but it can't just be the typical corporate bullshit. Remember, this is the "no bullshit" book, and your approach to blogging and new media has to be no bullshit too.

Crisis Communication Starts Months Before You Have a Crisis

Although we like to joke that crisis communication is just public relations speeded up, it's more than that. Given people's expectations of the quickness of a response during non-crisis times, it's hard to get much faster than that and still be effective.

The Center for Disease Control and Prevention's (CDC) Crisis and Emergency Risk Communication (CERC) mantra to crisis communications is "Be First. Be Right. Be Credible." The best way for you to be credible is by being seen as the authority right now, so people know who to turn to when there really is a crisis. The best way to be first is to start right now. And being right? Just make sure you have the experts in your company talking about their areas so they're the ones the media calls when there's really a crisis, and you can get the right information out immediately.

Crisis communication starts now, while you're still talking about public relations. It means you're laying the groundwork by building relationships with your local and trade media, industry bloggers, and superbloggers. It also means you're building those journalist relationships with your customers who are the ones most likely to alert everyone else to the problems with your company.

In a lot of cases, your fans can leap to your defense and help alleviate the drama of the crisis you're mired in at the moment. If your company is dealing with a serious problem and you've been laying the groundwork for a solid relationship with a lot of your customers, they'll be in the same spaces as your detractors. If someone complains, a lot of times, your customers will respond on your behalf, before you ever even hear about the complaint.

The best way to build this kind of loyalty is to work with your marketing department and determine who your best customers are on social media. Give those customers additional access and information that your average customers don't get. Include them in announcements before they hit your website, invite them to VIP-only events, give them a sneak peek at a new product rollout or service offering, make them beta testers on your new product, and publicly thank them whenever they sing your praises or recommend you to a friend. By encouraging this loyalty, you'll not only keep them as returning customers (your sales department will thank you for this), but they'll also be on your side when something bad finally does happen.

On a smaller scale, you need to consider who is going to respond to people who are saying something negative or nasty about your company, especially when they're a small fry and won't do much damage. They can't be ignored, but they don't call for a full-scale response either.

Dealing with Detractors

It's the thing a lot of social media naysayers fear most. "What do we do when someone says something negative about us?" It's what keeps most businesspeople off social media in the first place, failing to realize that people are already saying negative stuff about them right now. Believing people aren't talking about you when you're not on social media is like believing people aren't gossiping about you when you're not around.

And if they can get past their initial hesitation, what usually hangs them up is what they should do if it ever happens. Do they put out a press release? Do they delete the comment? Do they send a cease-and-desist letter to the complainer?

(**Note:** Never, *ever* send a cease-and-desist letter to a complainer. Not only is it going to be met with derision, but you'll immediately blow up the story and become known as the thin-skinned company that couldn't stand one negative complaint from one individual. On the other hand, you'll get more traditional and new media coverage than your PR department could have ever hoped for. It just won't be the kind they wanted.)

Here's the answer: You don't need a policy; you need a commitment: *We will respond to all complaints.* Whether it's a complaint about the product quality (customer service), the pricing (sales or marketing), or a corporate practice (PR), you need to commit to responding to any and all complaints that people have. But it doesn't have to be a full-blown response, complete with strategy meetings and position statements. It just needs to be one response from one person in the company and a promise either to make things right or to investigate and make sure it doesn't happen again.

In July 2010, Jason formulated his Six Steps for Dealing with Detractors. It serves as a step-by-step system for handing disgruntled audience members. The steps are

- Acknowledge their right to complain.

- Apologize for the situation or your mistake, if warranted.

- Assert clarity in your policy or reasons, if warranted.

- Assess what will help them feel better.

- Act accordingly.

- Abdicate if they persist.

By acknowledging their right to complain, even with "I'd be upset if that happened to me," or "You should be upset about that," you empower the customer and make him feel as if you've elevated his issue to a level of importance and priority. Apologizing for the situation is not an admission of guilt and often makes him feel better. "I'm sorry that happened to you," is very different than "I'm sorry we messed up." But be ready to apologize for messing up if you did.

Asserting yourself is tricky, but it has to be done. If a customer is complaining that your store wouldn't accept a return on an opened package, you have to assert your policy on the matter. You may also want to encourage her to provide feedback to the appropriate channels within your company to change the policy, but diverting the frustrations to a policy statement and not the store manager in question depersonalizes the anger.

Now it's time to assess what will make the customers feel better. Do they want a refund? Do they just need some acknowledgement of their frustration? They wouldn't be complaining if they didn't want some sort of restitution or response. Find out what it is they're looking for. And, yes, sometimes it *is* as easy as asking. When you know the answer, if it is within reason, do it. If it's not, then explain why the response isn't feasible and ask for alternative solutions from the customer.

And if you have done all you can do to accommodate and placate the person in question, but he still insists on being a detractor, then abdicate. The powerful thing about conducting these types of conversations in the social media space is that you aren't the only people watching the responses. That person's network and often your network online are watching, too. If you've exhausted all reasonable methods of resolution and the person is still being problematic, the audience can see that as well. Apologize that your solutions aren't satisfying the customer, and state that you've offered reasonable approaches to the situation and have exhausted your options. If the customer can find one of your suggestions that satisfies his need for resolution, great. If not, you'll have to move on.

The truth of the situation online is that sometimes a turd is a turd. There are people who complain just to complain and will never be satisfied. You need to respond to new complaints and address them accordingly, but know that occasional detractors just like being detractors. Walk away as respectfully as you can and leave the offer open for them to accept a resolution you're comfortable with. Then ignore them unless or until they decide your solutions are acceptable.

What's magical about doing this is that the audience watching is probably about to jump in and tell the detractor he's being a jerk, if they haven't already. They want you to walk away as much as you do. And if the detractor continues his assault, the community will typically come to your defense, making the individual feel less comfortable with venting publicly.

All fires, in the end, sputter out.

Ultimately, having a solid social media PR practice and plan of attack will save you and your company a lot of money, can help increase sales, and can even improve customer service, saving you money there as well. That's a nice metric to add to the list of what strong social media PR can do for your company.

Putting Metrics Around Public Relations

One difficulty with measuring public relations is that it's hard to assign a monetary figure to what the media coverage is worth. A common practice is to count the number of column inches in a newspaper or seconds of coverage on a TV station, figure out the equivalent cost of buying an ad for the same size or time, and arrive at the amount. So a story that takes 30 seconds on the evening news would be worth the cost of a TV commercial on that same station. Get it on all four major networks, and you have two minutes worth of "free" advertising.

The problem with this approach is that the measurement does not accurately reflect the value of the media attention you got. For one thing, a short front page story is worth a lot more than a 12-inch story on page D18. For another, the tone and the subject of the story may affect the attention you're getting. A positive announcement about a new product rollout will trump a management shake-up story in the business section.

Third, and this is the most important, *you don't know which stories led to the increase in sales.* Although you may get the occasional customer who says she saw your story on TV or in a trade magazine, you'll have a tough time tracking each and every customer to see if he was influenced by the story.

Still, that doesn't mean you shouldn't try.

Social media can also make a big difference in the measurement and effectiveness of your public relations efforts. For example, a story about your new iPad app appears on Robert Scoble's Scobleizer blog and sales for the app increase by 30% for the week afterward. By checking your website's analytics, you can determine that the entire increase came from Scoble's blog post and video interview, as people clicked through the hyperlink to your website in the blog post.

You can also use tools like Radian6, Vocus, and uberVu—tools we mentioned in Chapters 5 and 6—to monitor the sentiment of what people say about your brand. You can see whether people are singing your praises or complaining, and then you can react accordingly. By catching a few complaints early on, you can pinpoint problem areas and fix them before they become a big story.

Boeing had recently just joined social media in June 2010, hoping to learn how to use it properly and interact with customers. The aerospace company got more than it bargained for, learning by having their feet held to the fire.

Harry Winsor, an 8-year-old boy from Boulder, Colorado, loved airplanes. He loved drawing them, talking about them, and reading about them, so he drew a picture about his idea for an airplane that he thought Boeing should create. Boeing responded the same way it responds any time someone sends in a recommendation or idea: They sent a canned letter from the legal department saying the idea had been shredded and no copies had been kept.

Harry's dad, John, just happened to be the owner of an advertising agency and an avid blogger and Twitter user (he's @jtwinsor). He blogged about Boeing's cold response, asking *"Do I show the letter to Harry and kill his dream of being an airplane designer or throw it away and tell him I didn't receive anything so he keeps his artistic passion alive?"*[3] Winsor said that as a business owner, he understood the need for companies like Boeing to protect itself from intellectual property threats. But he thought the company representatives should have been a little more personal and caring because they were basically crushing the dreams of an 8-year-old boy.

What was surprising about this is that, despite only having been on social media for a couple of weeks, Boeing actually responded. Todd Blecher, one of Boeing's communications directors, sent out a tweet: "The letter Mr. Winsor posted is, as he said, a required response. For kids, we can do better. We'll work on it." Blecher also posted a comment on Winsor's blog addressing him directly.

> I'm a Boeing communications director. I think I can address your comments. As you state, we have to respond to the thousands of unsolicited ideas we receive in a way that protects us against possible infringement claims. Having said that, we can do better when the idea clearly comes from a child as enthusiastic as your son. We will work on this. I hope Harry remains fascinated by airplanes and grows up to be an airplane designer. To help him and others like him we maintain the following

website: http://www.boeing.com/companyoffices/aboutus/wond... I
hope he enjoys it.

Afterward, Boeing flew Harry, his brother Charlie, and his parents out to the company's Washington facility and showed them around. The story was so intriguing to
a lot of people that Boeing's previous slipup turned into a feel-good story, and it
showed that the aerospace giant actually does care about people's feelings toward
the company. Rather than hide behind the legal department, the communications
director made sure that his side of the story was told and that his company wasn't
completely presented as heartless automatons.

In this case, social media monitoring and a human PR response helped Boeing
avoid a lot of negative feelings directed their way. Although it might not have
affected their bottom line, it would not have helped their reputation in a time when
large corporations are often viewed with some suspicion and distrust by the general
public.

Public relations professionals have to deal with this kind of attitude toward their
employers on a regular basis. But social media makes it much easier for them to
respond and show the human side of their company, as well as help show the media
and general public the cool stuff they're doing as well.

Endnotes

1. "State of the News Media 2011," http://pewresearch.org/pubs/1924/
   state-of-the-news-media-2011.

2. Brunswich, "Use of Social Media Among Business Journalists," http://
   www.brunswickgroup.com/Libraries/Reports/Social_Media_-_among_
   busmedia_web_version_zls_3.sflb.ashx.

3. John Winsor, "Is Your Customer Service Ready for the New World of
   Openness?" http://www.johnwinsor.com/my_weblog/2010/04/is-your-
   customer-service-ready-for-the-new-world-of-openness.html.

The Kumbaya Effect: Social Media Marketing Builds Community

So, you've heard that social media marketing can be used to build a community of rabid fans ready to run out and market your product for you, completely free of charge, right? If that scenario is possible at all, it is limited to the handful of products and brands that probably already have it anyway. Apple doesn't need social media. If it added elements of social media marketing, it would be an instant case study, but not because of social media marketing. It would be because Apple makes great products and has rabid fans already.

But participating in social media marketing can help your business cultivate a community of people who like you and are willing to tell others about you. The scale of success might be different than the promised, unreasonable expectation, but it is possible. And it's not a concept that is beyond your grasp.

Think back to the communications and information hubs of the early twentieth and late nineteenth centuries, particularly in rural areas. Where did people come together as a community for information other than religion? The general store.

These former icons of small-town life often served up everything from hardware to fresh pie and served as a small community's newspaper, post office, and even bank all in one location. Was there community around those businesses? You bet there was.

You might think that the general store concept would never work in today's world of big-box retailers and chain grocery stores. Add a little flavor and some community building through social media marketing, however, and you'd be wrong. Any business can cultivate and build community around its brand using social media marketing, and community building can be done in a number of ways. The process of building community is also not nearly as rigid and formal as you might think.

One example of a small business that quickly built community around its new, and all but unknown, brand is FAIT ICI. This local-focused, urban general store sits nestled in the not-so-small hamlet of Montreal, Quebec. It opened its doors in the summer of 2010 under the notion that products made in Quebec (the store's name is French for "made here") that promote an environmentally friendly and healthy food lifestyle would excite the local foodie set and beyond. But, like many small businesses, FAIT ICI didn't start with investors, a financial backer, or even a marketing budget.

"We didn't have a budget for paid media," admitted Jackson Wightman, who we interviewed in March 2011. "So given some of the factors we were facing—being new, not having a perfect retail location, etc.—we needed to use some of the digital tools out there to get people to know about us and use our business."

Wightman, who opened the store with his wife Lindsay Davis, used his experiences in marketing and public relations (his day job) to lay out a digital marketing strategy to launch FAIT ICI, well before the doors ever opened.

"I'd say 3 to 4 months out, we started actively listening on Twitter, looking at blogs in our space...ones that were talking about food, the environment, organic products...we were listening to people in those spaces well before our opening. We figured out who those people are. We tried to engage them by commenting on their blogs, retweeting their content, conversing with them on Twitter, giving them Follow Friday shout-outs, and so on. And we did that well in advance of the opening," explained Wightman.

"When we finally did open and do our media event, a lot of these people covered us. And some people thought, 'How is this little, new business getting this coverage from traditional media and bloggers?' Our engagement with them helped us get attention and coverage when it came time to ask for those favors."

Wightman's insight into social media marketing falls squarely in line with the No Bullshit line of thinking. He recognized that one major hang-up small businesses have with digital tools is they mistakenly think they'll pay dividends quickly. By focusing on relationship building and thinking long term, Wightman sidestepped a typical small business bump in the road.

He also approached social media tools realistically and strategically.

"All of our digital activity was a strategy...Absolutely," he said. "We decided before opening the store to ask, 'What are the spaces and tools we would want to be in? Are we going to have a Facebook page, and if we are, then why? What would we use a Twitter account for? What would we use a company blog for?'

"But we asked how they would fit into an overall digital strategy that would add value to people's lives and build a community that would add value to our bottom line," said Wightman.

So after nurturing relationships to help announce the launch of the business, Wightman used the FAIT ICI blog to enrich and expand the relationships, thus the community. He reached out to five Montreal area bloggers, inviting them to participate in a mini series of posts about food and the foodie culture in Montreal. The bloggers were so delighted to be asked that the sense of community began to evolve, even among a relatively small group of people.

"Then we took that idea a bit farther and thought, 'Instead of doing guest posts two to three times per year, why don't we create a group blog with a fixed life span and an explicit topic...52 posts by 52 people over 52 weeks?' We approached more people—bloggers, journalists, chefs, big dogs in the community, friends, my mother and father—and said, 'Look, write anything you want as long as it has a food and a Montreal angle,'" he said.

The resulting group blog, "ici et here," which mixes the languages to say "here and here" has become a conversation point for the foodie and healthy lifestyle subculture in Montreal and Quebec. The effort is a separate and standalone website from FAIT ICI, but "brought to you by" the general store, which has created such a positive online home for the offline community to gather.

"We love Montreal and it's a great food city," Wightman explained with a passion typically offered by 12-year-olds talking about sports heroes. "We were providing a platform that not only engages influential people in our community, but one that tells the culinary story of our city in 52 weeks. It's a cool thing. We're the curators of the content, but that has generated a lot of earned media and a way to curry favor with industry and local influencers. But at the end of the day, it has brought us a lot of intrinsic benefit because we're foodies who love Montreal."

But here's where Wightman differs from many hip and trendy digital marketers. Intrinsic benefit isn't enough. This is where he becomes a true, No Bullshit kinda guy.

"PR folks often separate new and old media," Wightman said. "But that belies the power of platforms like Twitter, which is one of the best platforms you can use to get traditional press coverage. It's an unobtrusive way to communicate with many of the reporters who are covering your area or industry. We've had in the neighborhood of 30–40 articles and a couple of pieces of TV on us in the space of 8 months. An inordinate amount of that traditional coverage has come via a relationship we initially built and nurtured on Twitter."

Notice the simplicity of how FAIT ICI launched? You, too, could identify influencers within your industry and reach out. You, too, could leverage a blog in creative ways to drive interest and engagement around your brand, which—at a minimum—produces a community of readers. In your case, it could potentially also bring an inordinate amount of traditional media coverage and foot traffic to your store.

Like Wightman, you can build community around your company with little more investment than your time. There was no complex social networking platform purchased and implemented here. FAIT ICI had no marketing budget. What Wightman and Davis had was an understanding that by being social as a business—by talking to like-minded people, media members, bloggers, and more—in interesting and relevant ways, they were building community around their new company.

One of our favorite bloggers on community, Richard Millington, captured the essence of why a company would want to put time and energy into building community in a blog post in December of 2009.[1] In it, he wrote:

> *Imagine you own a high-end bicycle. The brand invites you to join a community of people who buy their bicycles. Through that community you make friends, share advice/tips for getting the most from the bike, and meet up several times a year.*
>
> *Two things have happened. First, you're locked into that brand. To leave the brand would be to leave the group. We don't like leaving our friends behind. Second, your interest in the brand has been intensified. Your interest in a bike has become a passion for cycling.*

Building community allows you ... yes, even the boring mortgage broker ... to create something that draws in people and makes them invested so much they can't leave you. It won't be about mortgages, but it might be about your expertise in real estate, home improvement, financial planning, or tangential topics that a reasonable person might trust a mortgage broker for an opinion about.

For FAIT ICI, it was a genuine interest in connecting with locals interested in locally grown and produced goods. For others, it can be more complex, both from the purpose and construct of the offline community and the technology driving their connecting point online.

Understanding Different Types of Communities

In Chapter 1, "Ignore the Hype. Believe the Facts," we talked about the social media purists—the hippies and tree huggers—and how they do a great job of preaching community. The Kumbaya Factor was probably the only thing you heard coming from social media evangelists spouting from the first inklings of advocacy through most of 2010.

But 10 years after *The Cluetrain Manifesto* and 4 to 5 years into the social media marketing world's life span, business owners started calling B.S. They wanted to see something for their efforts, but the community-for-community's sake approach of early evangelists left that to be desired. But the purists were only half wrong, remember. The "conversation," "engagement," and "community" things were working. They just hadn't yet added a focus on measuring and proving the value of each.

Several companies experienced large market share growth and even resurgence as pop-culture trends, thanks to efforts around building community. In his 2005 book *Brand Hijack*, Alex Wipperfurth chronicled the rise of Red Bull, the reemergence of Pabst Blue Ribbon as an underground cultural phenomenon, and the seemingly inexplicable evolution of Saturn vehicles, among other case studies. He explained how each of these brands earned market share and icon status by having their customers—their communities—hijack the brand.[2] Also, Malcolm Gladwell's *The Tipping Point* explained the "epidemic" nature of Hush Puppies' return to chic status in the mid-1990s.[3] Whether manufactured or, in Gladwell's terms, "tipped," by a seemingly insignificant event or person, none of these hijacks or epidemics happened without the presence of a community around the brands.

Granted, there are varying degrees of community. Some are formal online community platforms with registrations, logins, and passwords, like Verizon's Thinkfinity, an educational content resource for teachers. Others are just an informal network of people, like Pabst Blue Ribbon fans who dug the PBR. But the brand caught on, and now a fairly active forum community exists at www.pabst.com that features discussions on beer, supporting firefighters, and art.

The formal and informal examples of community building only scratch the surface of the possibilities, however. Maker's Mark Bourbon, a former client of Jason's, has a vibrant online and offline community called the Maker's Mark Ambassadors. Each ambassador is officially registered with the brand as a member of the loyalty club, gets his name on a barrel of bourbon, and receives official, insider brand communiqués. Each spring, the members are invited to a special Ambassador's weekend in Kentucky to visit the distillery, buy special bottles from their barrel's batch when it matures, and mix and mingle with other Ambassadors, distillery staff, and more. And the Ambassadors are such raving fans of Maker's Mark that they serve as brand evangelists for the product, even going so far as to buy drinks for complete strangers who might have considered buying a different drink.

Sea World San Antonio has a very different type of community. It mostly revolves around a 20,000-plus member Facebook Fan page. When fringe animal rights zealots stop by to post complaining messages on the company's wall, its fans spring into action, inviting the person to go play on someone else's Facebook page (see Figure 8.1). There's no login and password or official company connection. These are just people who hit the "Like" button on the Sea World San Antonio Facebook page. (Compare this with what happens on Nestlé's fan page, as we discussed in Chapter 5, "Make Some Noise: Social Media Marketing Aids in Branding and Awareness.")

Figure 8.1 Sea World San Antonio's fans leap to the defense of Sea World whenever animal rights activists complain on the park's Facebook page.

The point is that the definition of *community* is fluid. Don't think building community around your brand or company is about signing up for a community network-building platform, like Ning, and having a formalized, online community. In fact, your company already has a community. You just don't know it.

To prove it, answer these questions:

- Do you have employees?

- Do you have current customers?

- Do you have vendors or other businesses you work with?

- Do the people involved in the three preceding items have spouses, children, or friends?

There's your community. All you have to do is give them a reason, and perhaps the tools, to tell other people how cool you are.

There's More to Building Community Than Just Making Friends

Don't worry! We're not lapsing into a raging fit of hugging trees here. It's not enough to just find people who like you and make them tell their friends. Remember: If you add the word *marketing* to the term *social media* it's about business.

To tap into the business side of communities, you need to approach community building strategically. You need to set goals, objectives, and measures for success. This enables you to put metrics around community building that make sense for your business.

The reason you might want to build community around your brand or organization is pretty self-explanatory: The more people you have who like you, the more people you have to (a) talk to and (b) ask to talk to others for you. Building community is basically a social media purist's way of saying "building customers" to distract you from the sales part of the equation.

But in building this community of customers, you have to listen to that first half of the social media equation where the hippies were right. You have to be human. You have to engage in conversations. You have to be customer-centric, not brand-centric.

The fundamental key to being a successful community builder in the social media space is to change your marketing focus, ever so slightly, from focusing on sales to focusing on customers. Think about that for a second. It's not about sales; it's about customers. And no, they're not the same thing.

To focus on the sale is to have all eyes on the dollar. You're worried about the short-term transaction, making budget, hitting your numbers, driving the bottom line, one sale at a time. But to focus on the customer is to step across the line from transactional marketing to relationship marketing. You're not worried about the sale that day, but rather on the lifetime value of that customer to your company. It's okay if she walks out the door because you're focused on the relationship ... the customer. She'll sense that and come back.

If you're focused on the transaction alone, she won't.

This is the approach that separates Joe, the guy Jason buys his cars from, from other car salesmen.

Measuring Community

Salesmen like Joe can track their relationship marketing success versus their transactional marketing success. Good salesmen can say, "That's Jason. He's bought four cars from me over the course of the last 15 years. With his payments, service visits, and repair work over the years, he's probably meant about $95,000 to us."

The transactional guy says, "Just made an $18,000 sale!"

Although we wish it were that simple in the social media space, it's not impossible to measure community building and even to tie some (but not all) of that activity to your bottom line. Looking at our potential strategic goals for community building in Chapter 1, we listed the following:

- Increase your number of fans, followers, friends, or readers.
- Grow your opt-in email marketing list.
- Increase the number of your affinity or loyalty club members.
- Increase fan-generated advocacy and promotion of your brand initiatives.
- Increase fan-generated defense of your brand in negative conversations.

None of these goals points directly to a financial outcome because the purpose is to build community. But you can focus on community building and weave in financial measures that support the justification for your efforts.

CareOne Financial Solutions, a debt consolidation and counseling service, did just that. The social media team there, led by Nichole Kelly, decided to compare its prospective customers who came to its online community from traditional methods (such as a television ad, direct mail piece, and so on) with those their social media marketing team contacted and cultivated as prospects. The team found prospects on the social media side of the aisle had a 179% better chance of signing up for a debt-relief plan than regular customers. They also found the social media prospects made their first payment at a 217% higher average than the traditional customer counterparts.[4]

Taking that analysis a step further, CareOne determined that when the social media team saw customers who had abandoned the sign-up process, then interacted with the social media team, the customers returned and completed the sign-up process at a conversion rate some 680% higher than those the social media team did not follow up with. Those customers also paid their first payment at a 732% improvement.

So the community here was measured in the value of the customer contact, not the amount of money the customer paid. Customers who were engaged by the brand were simply more valuable customers than the ones the company was typically focused on.

The more informal the community, the further from revenue measuring you'll get. But website analytics packages can even delineate where traffic comes from and whether those specific users buy or convert on your site. Even though you might think it's tough to measure the value of your Facebook page or Twitter following, you can use analytics software to measure how many people came, clicked, and bought from purchase point links you post to Facebook.com, Twitter.com, and other domains. This delivers you a value from your activity there.

You can even go ninja and use social share tracking solutions like Argyle Social (see Figure 8.2). By sharing links on your social networks using Argyle Social (or similar software), you can track clicks and traffic divided by site or source as well as assign dollar values to conversion points to prove a social revenue metric.

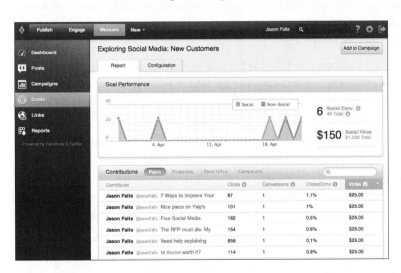

Figure 8.2   Argyle Social tracks the clicks on content you share via social networks and blogs using unique shortened URLs and then measures the number of people converting after clicking through to your website.

If you sell items on your site, place Argyle's embed code on the "thank you" page after purchase, then tell the software how much the customer would spend to get to that purchase point. Then, in your reporting, you can see you made $10,000, but

$6,000 came from typical sales, $2,500 came from sales generated by Facebook.com visitors, and the rest from Twitter.com visitors.

Of course, you have to present your Twitter or Facebook communities with clear calls to action and links to these purchase points for it to work, but as you can see, measuring community can be more than just how many followers you have. You can compare the value of your community members with noncommunity customers, measure purchase behaviors, and even purchase recommendations and referrals. As you will see in the chapters that follow, you can combine two or more of the main areas where social media benefits your brand and measure the cost savings or resulting profits from utilizing your community for research and development.

The key to placing value on what your company gets out of building community is in the planning: Set goals for the community you build and develop activities that persuade the community to deliver on those goals.

You Can Even Build Community Around Scissors!

No brand on the planet has changed more, or perhaps benefited more, thanks to its embracing of community, than Fiskars. The orange-handled scissors are just that: orange-handled scissors. Even Fiskars's own brand managers didn't see much sexiness in scissors in 2005 when the company started working with word-of-mouth marketing agency Brains on Fire.

We talked to Geno Church, who holds the title of word of mouth inspiration officer at Brains on Fire to find out more about how community can happen around scissors. What we discovered was that the scissor company was simply the common thread that tied a certain group of people together.

"They didn't see that what they were doing meant that much to customers," explained Church. "When we first got to their facility where the scissors were developed, there was white butcher paper over the windows to keep people from seeing the company secrets. Now, they give prototypes to members of their online community to use, break, critique, and offer suggestions around. It's pretty amazing."

How did Fiskars make such a stark evolution? Strategically, that's how.

First, Fiskars's marketing team did online market research to find out who, if anyone, was talking about scissors. They didn't find a whole lot of scissor chatter, but they did discover pockets of communities around scrapbooking—people who use scissors. But when the team looked a bit closer, they realized the scrapbooking forums and message boards that existed in the mid-2000s were full of snark and venom.

The insight Brains on Fire turned over to Fiskars was that scrapbookers didn't have a safe haven to create and communicate in a positive environment. There were already communities around scrapbooking that could prove valuable to a scissor company, somehow. But the social insight into the communities showed Fiskars they needed to actually create a new community with different rules. (See the Fiskars community in Figure 8.3, which shows a user's dashboard view and his connections to other scrapbookers.)

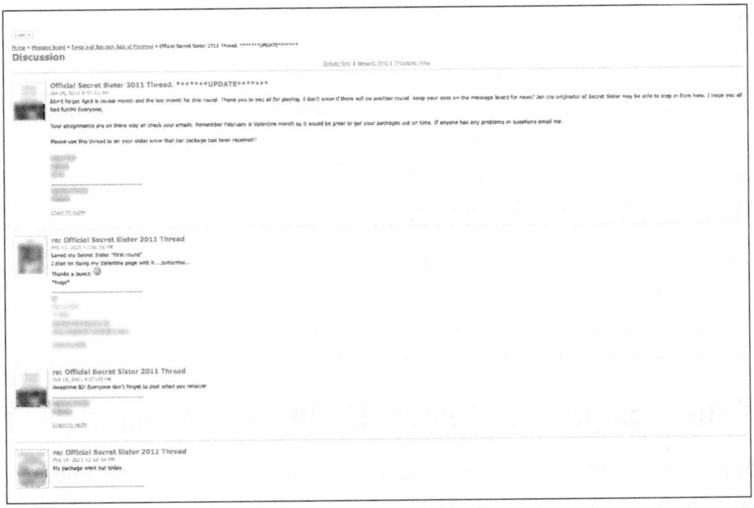

Figure 8.3   Fiskars sponsors a community for scrapbookers to talk about scrapbooking, instead of scissors, and has amassed more than 8,000 community members who connect, engage, and collaborate with one another.

The Fiskateers website launched in 2006 with four scrapbook leaders and brand ambassadors chosen by the company, which had identified influential scrapbookers online and approached them with the idea of helping build a positive collaboration environment. The goal was to drive scrapbookers to the site to enjoy the arts-and-crafts hobby in a friendly environment, establish a relationship with these members as a brand to harvest feedback, help test and launch new products, and build a sense of passion around the brand.

The goal was to attract 200 people in 6 months.

"We met our goal in 24 hours," Church laughed. By the 6-month mark, there were 1,800 members. As of early 2011, the community is 8,000-plus strong.

"We have a 500% value in return on community," Church said. "We have incredibly loyal, passionate Fiskars customers who are not just fans of the brand, but invested in the brand."

(We'll dive a bit deeper in the value of the Fiskars community in Chapter 10, "Get Smarter: Social Media Marketing Drives Research and Development," and illustrate how one strategy can accomplish multiple goals for your business.)

Think about how you can engage your customers and build community. If a scissor company can discover that its customers have a need to be filled in their online experience (a safe haven to discuss scrapbooking), perhaps you can discover a similar need for your audience.

This need is something we refer to as a social insight. Whereas advertising, marketing, and branding agencies conduct market research and surveys hoping to find a consumer insight that informs a marketing effort, social media marketers look through online information hoping to find this social insight: What can we provide our customers online that will make their digital experience better?

If your customers tell you they need a place to gather, whether for safety from negativity, access to information, or just a place to connect with other customers or fans, you have the insight you need to walk down the path of building community.

But What If Our Competition Shows Up in Our Community?

When building a community for the first time, it's natural to wonder what could happen if your competition joins in. Honestly? Nothing. If they're spending all their time in your community, they're probably far behind the curve and wouldn't be able to catch up for some time.

But beyond the reality of the scenario, let's back up and remember the ethos of what we're doing in social media. We're trying to be honest, transparent, and customer-centric. What better way to accomplish all three but to openly engage with your competition along with everyone else?

We're not advocating uncivil behavior. Not at all. But if your competition shows up, welcome them, encourage their (civil) discourse in the community, and embrace their input. Customers will translate that behavior into confirmation that you are the market leader and the more trustworthy of the lot.

Don't see it? Meet Rand Fishkin. He was running what he called, "a half-assed web design, development, and user-experience" shop in 2002 when he started learning about search engine optimization, or SEO. He started a blog to share what he was learning about the art and craft of winning search rankings.

The blog was called SEOmoz (see Figure 8.4).

We interviewed Fishkin, who told us the main reason SEOmoz took off was the lack of blogs focused on SEO at the time. In his SEOmoz posts, he would mention new blogs coming on to the scene and comment on the topics the few others were writing about in his SEOmoz posts.

Figure 8.4 SEOmoz started out as an industry blog for search engine optimization specialists. It's now recognized as the leading community of practitioners in the SEO industry. Source: www.seomoz.org.

"I would show off the work of others," Fishkin told us. "Eventually, SEOmoz became a place where people went to see what everyone in the industry was doing or talking about."

That community of blog commenters was a gold mine for Fishkin. In 2006, he wanted to diversify the opinions on his blog and began inviting commenters to guest post. He even intentionally invited the site's biggest critics to show that the blog really was about offering a platform for opinions and insights, not just promoting Fishkin's company, which by that time had evolved into an SEO consulting firm.

Fishkin added thumbs-up and thumbs-down buttons to the site so users could rate and potentially elevate the best content to be more prominently displayed and get more traffic. But Fishkin insisted users behave.

"When they would thumbs down something or leave a negative comment, I would jump in and suggest they reword it or be more positive and empathetic," he said. "Our mantra is to be transparent, authentic, generous, fun, empathetic, and exceptional. If we can't be those things, we're not being the best we can be. We insisted that the community hold itself to a high standard and over time we weeded the less-attractive elements out of SEOmoz." What's really amazing about the evolution of SEOmoz as a community and as a business is twofold. First, the audience Fishkin was first speaking to in 2004 and 2005 was his competition. The only people who want to talk about SEO all the time are other search engine nerds. True to his nature, Fishkin didn't mind.

"Because of who I am and what I like to do...being transparent and sharing the resources I've learned from...I never hesitated to talk to the competition," he explained. "I've never felt like SEO was a zero-sum game. Building up the SEO industry is going to have positive effects on everyone who plays in that marketplace."

As a result of the Fishkin ethos, SEOmoz gradually emerged as one of, if not *the* leading authority on search engine optimization in the United States. Its site boasts it's the "world's largest SEO community," and seldom does news break in the SEO world that Fishkin isn't either in the middle of it, or at least quoted.

But even more compelling is that the evolution of SEOmoz as a community also drove the evolution of SEOmoz as a company. Beginning in 2007, Fishkin's troops began offering SEO products (tools and resources, plus premium content) to their growing community. By 2009, the company actually ceased direct client consulting.

And to think, it all started out with Fishkin writing a blog that was essentially read by his competition. Think about your industry. Is there a dearth of online content available for people wanting to get smart about it? Is anyone watching the industry as a thought leader, highlighting other people's work, evangelizing best practices, or commenting on the topics of the day you face? Perhaps you can.

Yes, your competition will notice, and yes, they may even join in the discussion. But in most industries and markets, there is not a zero-sum game. Elevating the industry can make you and your business stronger, make you more widely known and respected, and even give you a leg up on the competition. You can, after all, show they come to your site for learning and conversation.

Okay, So How Do You Do This and How Much Will It Cost?

Yes, it would be easy for us to say, "Okay! Go build a community now!" But it's never that simple. You probably won't start a blog that really serves your competition. You might not need to build an actual online community platform like Fiskars did because your customers might not need one. And CareOne turned on the lights and said, "Who needs some help with debt?"—which is like shooting fish in a barrel.

Building a community starts with relationships. Assuming you didn't marry your spouse 6 minutes after meeting him or her, you should understand these things take time.

Because your community is made up of human beings—the most emotionally inconsistent of all mammals—you're going to have to read and react a lot. Humans aren't predictable. What works today will get a resounding, "That's it?!" next month.

And yes, you're going to have to engage in conversations with them. Community is built on the backs of human beings but with the wires of communications. Those wires are now two-way streets. If you're not willing to listen and respond, you'll never get community out of the transaction.

Still, you have to build communities with business in mind. If you don't, you're just playing in the sandbox. So you set goals for your communities:

- Increase online recommendations and referrals for your company.

- Drive higher frequency of purchase from your existing customers.

- Increase the lifetime value of your customer base.

- Drive X amount in revenue from your community membership fees and purchases.

- Reduce product launch costs by growing a community of first-in-line buyers to serve directly.

And then you build strategies and creative concepts to deliver on those goals.

Entrepreneur and author Guy Kawasaki offered up some savory tips on building communities in a February 2006 blog post[5] in which he listed the following (among others) as "how-to" steps:

- Create something worth building a community around. Sure, it could be your product or service, but don't forget that it could be an activity, a need, or an idea.

- Identify and recruit advocates immediately. They'll stand out when you nail down the focus of your community. In fact, they'll likely be some of the very customers you talked to in order to determine what that community focus is.

- Give people something concrete to chew on. For Fiskars, it was activities around scrapbooking. For your company, it might be tying in a new product, using it in creative ways, or even sharing experiences around the company.

- Welcome criticism. This is where you get valuable feedback from your customers. What they find wrong—or perhaps not so right—about you is helpful information, not complaining.

One of the last things Kawasaki adds is as important as all the rest, though. You have to publicize the existence of your community. Often, companies treat social media and web-based efforts as if they're a virtual *Field of Dreams*. If you build it, they will come, right? Not necessarily, and often, not at all.

Sea World San Antonio told everyone they could to like them on Facebook. CareOne advertises their support community through multiple mediums, including television. Every community takes a bit of critical mass to take on a life of its own. And if you're not telling people it's there, that critical mass is almost impossible to achieve.

Kawasaki's advice is sound. Unfortunately, the classically trained marketers and traditional business folks typically do some disappointing things with those instructions. The typical flaws we see in client approaches to these recommendations include companies that build their focal point around the product or service. They will plant paid employees or advocates and try to hide the fact they've rigged the system. When the community members discover the frauds, and they inevitably will, the company will suffer from mistrust and even an exodus away from the community.

Traditional business owners and marketers typically insist on delivering a steady diet of coupons and product pitches to their community, which most of them won't chew on but choke on. They'll respond to criticism by censoring it, fearful it will breed more criticism rather than responding with empathy, which typically builds a higher degree of trust from the audience.

And, finally, they typically announce the community by purchasing advertising online that few people see, fewer people actually click on, and, if they're lucky, a handful will convert and become members.

The misguided actions of the traditional marketer and business owner quickly remind us to remember the purist point of view in the social media marketing world: Make it about the consumer, not about you.

So, you can start to see the cost: time. If your research and understanding of your customers proves you might need to build a place where the community connects—like Fiskars did with the Fiskateers—there will be more financial commitment. If you feel the need to hire a social media marketing consultant or even an agency to help you develop a website, strategy, or community building campaign, that activity isn't free.

But you can, like Sea World San Antonio, just invest the time to build a Facebook presence, encourage fans to engage with you there, and not invest a lot up front to build something. You can just write really compelling blog posts or even record a weekly 2-minute video with your CEO that is interesting, revealing, or even silly and put it on YouTube and invite your customers and employees to share it with their networks.

Community will be different for different companies, so there's no turnkey answer to how you do this and how much it will cost. But there are some constants you'll need to keep in mind:

- You already have community. You just have to give them a reason to talk about you and invite others into the community.

- What you give them has to be really compelling ... share worthy.

- You'll build that community a lot faster if you and your employees are engaged with it and as part of that community, too.

- Your community will never be worth anything to you if you don't start out by establishing clear goals for building it.

Revisiting a prevailing idea in this book: If you're not doing it for a business reason and not measuring your success, it's just a hobby. Don't "play" with community building. Take the No Bullshit approach: Define goals. Establish measurable objectives. Enact strategies and tactics to accomplish them. Then measure what you've done to show what you've gotten out of it.

Endnotes

1. Richard Millington, "How Do Online Communities Generate Money?" http://www.feverbee.com/2009/12/how-do-online-communities-generate-money.html.

2. Alex Wipperfurth, *Brand Hijack*. Portfolio, 2005.

3. Malcolm Gladwell, *The Tipping Point*. Back Bay Books, 2000.

4. CareOneCredit.com—http://community.careonecredit.com/blogger-resources/w/wiki/defaultwikipage/revision/10.aspx, 2010.

5. GuyKawasaki.com—http://blog.guykawasaki.com/2006/02/the_art_of_crea.html#axzz1FVUjIO00, February 2006.

It's About Them: Social Media Marketing Drives Customer Service

Customer service has changed a lot in the last decade. Before the mid-1990s, you needed to make a phone call to lodge complaints, solve problems, and fix errors, usually to a customer service representative at the company's call center located at the company's headquarters. Some software companies charged for customer service, which outraged customers and sent many of them online as a way to find different solutions.

With the advent of company websites and early social media tools like message boards, company-sanctioned forums arose as problem-solving places for customers. Even though many were poorly designed and confusing, the company got by with the response, "Just search our support forums." The answer to most problems could be found there, even though for many customers the finding was as frustrating as the problem itself. If companies had a customer service hotline, economies of scale often dictated the person who answered it was someone in a foreign country rather than down the street.

But social media marketing has changed what online consumers do when they have a problem with a company. Instead of spending an hour pilfering through not-exactly answers on company forums or trying to struggle through call center communications with nonnative language speakers, customers are venting their frustrations on blogs, Twitter, Facebook, and more.

One of the most notable stories of social media as customer service is that of cable giant Comcast. Its customer service issues, like many of its industry, could fill a book. These issues did fill an entire blog when *On The Media* host Bob Garfield launched ComcastMustDie.com in 2007. As the company's employees began to take note of the growing dissension online, one of its customer service professionals, Frank Eliason, wanted to help. He began experimenting with Twitter in 2008 to see if he could help route issues and solve customer problems. He found that Twitter was not a replacement for traditional customer service help, but it was letting people get an immediate response, which improved their mood considerably—as opposed to spending several minutes waiting on the phone for help—and more important, it let them do it publicly.

Eliason sent tweets, using the @ComcastCares Twitter account, with "How can I help?" the minute he saw a complaint or a criticism about Comcast (see Figure 9.1). "Comcast sucks!" was, and sometimes still is, a common message. But Eliason still managed to respond with "How can I help?" He then followed up the message with another one about how to fix a problem, sent a Direct Message (a private tweet between the sender and the receiver), or even looked up the person's phone number and called him to offer assistance.

Whether it was a billing problem, a cable outage, or even a problem with a service technician, Eliason and his team, which eventually grew to eight people after the company saw such positive traction due to the proactive customer service approach, were always on the case, managing the Twitter traffic and solving complaints, often faster than the phone and email service departments could.

An interesting thing happened with @ComcastCares' customer service efforts: Not only did Eliason's social media efforts make national news, including a spread in *BusinessWeek* magazine, but it began to show customers who were undecided about Comcast that the company was being responsive, responsible, and concerned about

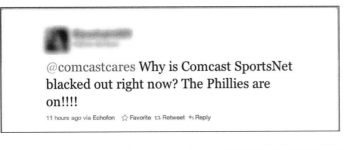

@comcastcares Why is Comcast SportsNet
blacked out right now? The Phillies are
on!!!!

11 hours ago via Echofon   ☆ Favorite ⇄ Retweet ↩ Reply

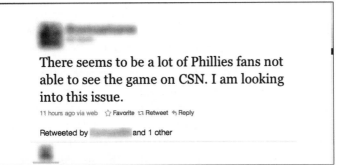

There seems to be a lot of Phillies fans not
able to see the game on CSN. I am looking
into this issue.

11 hours ago via web   ☆ Favorite ⇄ Retweet ↩ Reply

Retweeted by ▓▓▓▓▓ and 1 other

Figure 9.1 Although Comcast's original Twitter customer service pro Frank Eliason has left Comcast, the cable giant still responds to customer complaints with the same dedication as when Eliason started @ComcastCares.

its customers. In short, Eliason's customer service efforts became a marketing and PR function. All the stories about Eliason gave the company plenty of "free press" (read Chapter 7, "Relating to Your Public: Social Media Marketing and Public Relations," about measuring public relations efforts), and it also showed customers that Comcast was on the ball and solving people's problems. That helped change their minds about the cable company.

In his book, *Customer Service: New Rules for a Social Media World* (Pearson), Peter Shankman says that customer service in the social media world has to drive revenue, whether it "saves money, earns money, brings in new clients who will spend money, or cuts costs to let you keep more of the money you're already earning."

This makes sense. An American Express Global Customer Service Barometer released in February 2011 reported that 70% of Americans said they're willing to spend more money—as much as 13% more—at businesses that provide good customer service; only 58% said the same thing in 2010.[1]

In other words, you earn repeat business by making sure customers are happy. But it's not enough just to make them happy. You also need to show other people you can make them happy as well. That's what social media can do for your customer service efforts. The important thing is to remember to take care of your customers when they need you.

Why Do You Want to Hear from Your Customers?

"Our business would be great if it wasn't for the customers."

How many times have you thought that or even said that in jest? We know we have heard clients say it a few times. Customers can be annoying, demanding, and sometimes just a real piece of work. On those days, it's easy to think life would be much easier if you didn't have to deal with them. But then you sigh, rub your forehead for a few seconds, and remember where your revenue comes from.

Every customer counts and makes a difference. Customers contribute to your bottom line through sales, to your marketing effort through word of mouth, and even to your reputation. Whether you want to admit it, you need every customer. Well, almost every customer. There are those customers who are such a drain on resources and energy that you truly are better off in both the short term and long term not having them as customers. Despite them, you need to adopt the attitude that every customer counts. Your goal should be to make your customers feel well taken care of, happy, and satisfied. Happy, satisfied customers are returning customers, and returning customers means returning revenues. We learned that a long time ago.

As Pollyanna-ish as it sounds, every customer counts, and every customer affects your bottom line. (Even the energy draining, resource-sucking ones. They have an effect on your bottom line, too, just not in the way you had hoped.) And if you're willing to shrug off one customer who is underserved, angry, or even disappointed in you, then why not shrug off all the customers who are underserved, angry, or disappointed? Why not save yourself the hassles and the headaches—and the customer service costs—by letting all of them go?

You know the answer to that already. Your company will upset each of them at least once in their life cycle as your customer, or maybe one day the majority of your customers will be angry at your company all at once. If you ignore them completely, they're going to leave you, and they're going to tell their friends. Worst of all, your profitability will plummet because you constantly have to find new customers to fill up the slowly emptying bucket. And any business consultant, advisor, or professor will tell you that it costs more to find new customers than it does to keep old customers. As your cost of customer acquisition increases, your profit per customer decreases.

So it makes sense to take care of the old customers.

You do this by listening to people and their complaints and then solving their problems to the best of your ability. You serve your customers as best you can, and you apologize when you screw up. Because you know that one day you're going to need that person as a customer, and you don't want your apathy or unwillingness to answer customer calls at 4:50 on a Friday afternoon to be the reason your company is now in the toilet and circling the drain.

The point of this little sermon is this: If you leave one customer underserved, unhappy, or disappointed, haven't you failed in what you were trying to do? Isn't your mission statement about being the best in your industry? This isn't about making *every* customer happy because that's impossible. But that doesn't mean you shouldn't *try* to make every customer happy as often as possible. If you're not doing that, or that's not your primary goal, go do something else because your competition is more than happy to do it. Your competition will show your customers how they'll be treated with respect, listened to, and given great service and a lot of value. You'll be left wondering where everyone went and why they're so angry.

Putting Your People Where Your Mouth Is

Eric Eicher is an account manager with Momentum Group, a marketing and advertising agency in Indianapolis. He's also a Forum Credit Union member and had a chance to learn firsthand how his credit union uses social media after he had a serious problem and received a pleasant surprise in Forum's customer service's response to him. Forum Credit Union is one of the largest credit unions in Indiana. Eric was making a cash deposit one Saturday evening at Forum's drive-through ATM; the machine took his money, but did not acknowledge that it had received it. When he checked a second time, the money was gone, and he did not have a receipt to prove it.

Before he even left the parking lot, Eric sent a Twitter Direct Message to the Forum customer service department and explained what had happened. Sunday morning, Eric received a DM *apologizing for the delay* in getting back to him. Less than 18 hours later, and they were apologizing for not getting back to him. By Monday morning, Eric and his wife had received numerous calls from Forum explaining that they had audited the machine, it had his money, and it was already in his account. Eric said it was all resolved before 10:00 on Monday morning.

Jacki Teachnor, one of Forum's customer service representatives, said the credit union wasn't new to social media, although they were careful when they got into it. They started with Facebook and Twitter, but service reps also created seven different blogs to educate people on financial issues. She is especially pleased with social media as a customer service tool because the service reps can check complaints immediately. Whenever someone expresses his frustration with an issue, service reps can see it in real time and respond quickly.

Jacki said she had even salvaged a customer's business and earned some new business because of Twitter. Someone had tweeted a message asking if anyone knew of any good credit unions because this person had had a bad experience with Forum. She replied back, much like Comcast's Eliason, and asked how she could help. It turned out the customer had a valid complaint, which she resolved. Because of her prompt response and her willingness to talk with him on Twitter, he then asked to meet with Jacki about opening new business accounts with Forum.

"Social media fits in very well with what our customer service reps do," said Jacki. "Because we are committed to listening to our members. Twitter is one more channel where we can do it.

"We have even done special social media promotions, giving people a good rate on a loan or CD promoted only on Facebook or Twitter. We have even done Facebook polls, which is almost like having a focus group on Facebook."

You Can't Help Everyone

Sadly, a time will come when you have a customer you just can't help, no matter how hard you try. He wants you to honor a warranty that expired 10 years ago. She thinks you should replace the phone she dropped from 30 feet up. He wants you to return a channel to your lineup after it moved to a different package. How do you disappoint these customers and do it in such a way that you don't come out on the losing end in the public's eye?

Start with the same basics we discussed: You need to apologize, even if it's not your fault, and explain why you cannot do it and what you can do instead. Try, "I'm really sorry, but we aren't able to do a warranty repair on a digital camera that is 10 years old. I don't even know if the parts are available anymore. But what I can do is give you 20% off a new digital camera if you would like to come in."

Or, "I'm sorry. Our phones just aren't made to be dropped from three stories up, and our replacement guarantee doesn't cover that sort of breakage. But if you come in, we're running a special on new mobile phones, and I think we can help you find a new one. We may even have a coupon around. Stop in and ask for Cheryl."

Or, "I'm very sorry, but the channel has been moved to a different channel package as part of our programming restructuring. If you'd like, I can let you have a free one-month trial for that new package so you can try it out and see if you like it."

Although these attempts might not completely satisfy the situation or the customer, you've done everything you can. These efforts certainly beat one of those cold responses that covers your own ass but does absolutely nothing for the customer. These types of responses are not only insulting, but they also make angry customers even angrier and more willing to put energy into telling as many people as they can about your unwillingness to help. By showing even a little courtesy and concern, you might be able to defuse the situation, even if you can't help them completely.

Of course, some people complain just to complain. Some might have complained because they're angry at you and they want the world to know it, but they don't actually expect you to do anything about it. So it's always a good idea to investigate the complaint before you react.

Erik's company manages social media, including responding to complaints, for several clients. One of them sometimes receives complaints from people who started a Twitter or Facebook account just to complain. When his client offered to help, often these people never responded, so their complaint went unresolved. One complainer finally answered after three weeks, saying he never checked the account because he assumed no one would respond. He just started it so he could make his gripe public, but really didn't want to go to the effort of getting a repair.

But when Erik's client offered to help him, it wasn't that big a deal to him. Sometimes you'll receive complaints from people who have a higher sense of moral outrage and self-entitlement than most. But they don't expect you to deal with them, and you certainly don't have to. It's also good form to not respond to anyone who is clearly incensed, using foul language, or obviously on some sort of personal vendetta against your company. While some initial, "Is there something I can do to help," type responses to gauge the level of their anger are fine, and even expected, the ones you shouldn't respond to should be very clear very quickly. Raving lunatics are not worth engaging. However, you should look beyond the vitriol to see if there might be some validity to their complaints before judging them as such.

You're Not the "Jackass Whisperer"

Scott Stratten, Canadian social media expert and author of *Unmarketing*, once said during a talk, "I'm not the jackass whisperer. I don't have time to deal with every troll who wants to give me a hard time or say nasty things about me."

You're going to have to deal with your share of jackasses, the people who complain just for the sake of complaining, once in a while. They'll tweet out messages, usually with the hashtag #FAIL as part of the message. (A hashtag is a term preceded by a #. It means that term is the subject of conversation. It tells everyone else what that tweet is about and that they should use it if they want to be included in that conversation.)

The #FAIL tag should be used for truly momentous problems, like "The new TV I bought had a crack in the screen. #FAIL" or "Took my car in for service, and they forgot to put in new oil. Engine is ruined. #FAIL." But you'll still get the occasional jackass who wants to tell the world his life lies in tattered ruins in the mud because of a heinous wrong done by your company. "Ordered large Coke for lunch. Was given Diet Coke instead. #FAIL!" and "Pizza place forgot to put black olives on my pizza. #FAIL."

Despite such histrionics, you do have to deal with people like these for a few reasons:

- They *are* paying customers. If you want them to remain paying customers, you need to deal with them. Fix the problem if it's not too expensive and see if they stay happy.

- If you ignore them, they could make a bigger stink that might accidentally catch on and go viral.

- If you insult them or make them feel stupid, you'll look like a bully. That absolutely will go viral, even if the other person *is* a total jackass. Everyone loves the little guy and hates the big bad corporations. Anything that looks like you've insulted them will come back to you a thousandfold.

- If you make them happy, they could become raving fans who not only never gripe, but actually become evangelists for you. Sure, they'll go be a jackass to someone else, but your biggest concern is about getting this thorn out of your paw, and if that means making them happy, so be it. You're not in the business of behavioral change—unless you really *are* a practicing psychologist. You're in the business of selling products and making customers happy.

But you don't have to bend over backward and treat them with special care. If you want to prioritize customers with larger than average social connections or the potential to do some damage, look them up on Twitter, Facebook, Yelp, and any other place where you found their complaints. Check out their complaint history, and see if they have made it a habit of making a mountain out of a molehill.

If they do, you'll know you have a serial complainer on your hands. Fix the problem and be done with them. If they continue to gripe, state publicly that you have fixed their original problem, but if they would like to discuss it further, they're free to contact you personally. This will at least show people who read the complaint that the person is being unreasonable, while you made an honest effort to help them.

If they're not serial complainers, then maybe they do have real concerns, even if it is a Coke/Diet Coke mix-up. Apologize for the problem and promise you'll do better next time. If the problem was truly a problem—their food was too cold or the new TV was broken—provide them with a solution, like buying them lunch the next time they're in or replacing the TV and absorbing the delivery costs. And be public about it. Again, if they still complain, point out that you have solved the original problem and invite them to contact you.

But—and this is important—customer service never means you have to put up with rude or insulting behavior. If you have a complaint from someone who is insulting or makes threats or overly aggressive comments, make sure to record or copy the offending messages, then cut off all contact. Don't respond, don't try to talk them down, don't try to defuse the situation. This is clearly someone who has boundary issues, and a rational discussion is not going to solve the problem.

Customer service professionals are going to tell you that this kind of behavior is typical and something they have to deal with constantly. It's going to be the same in social media. The people who can be helped on the phone can be helped on social media. The people who are angry can be calmed down and then helped. And the jackasses are just jackasses and will never be satisfied. If you know you've done everything you can, then that's all you can do.

Sometimes It's Just Two Little Words

The words "I'm sorry" or "I apologize" can go a long way in solving a lot of problems, especially publicly. Don't be afraid to say them to people who are complaining. A lot of executives are hesitant to say they're sorry, either because they haven't been trained to do so or the lawyers have said to never, ever say you're sorry because it could be taken as an admission of guilt. Either that, or the customer service people are just so apathetic, they truly aren't sorry.

The best way to use social media to solve most of your customers' problems is if you just apologize once for their bad experience. It doesn't mean you're going to fix something. It doesn't mean you're going to accept the blame so they can sue you. It means you have some empathy for your customers and wish they didn't have this problem.

Try, "I'm sorry our product didn't work."

Or, "I apologize for your delivery being late."

Or, "I'm sorry your food was cold."

The service team behind @ComcastCares apologizes quite a bit for problems created by other people in their organization. Why? It's not the individual customer service Twitter operator's fault that billing screwed up a customer's account, that the technician didn't have the right parts in his van, or that he didn't show up at all. It's not his fault that a channel got dropped or a game was interrupted by technical delay (see Figure 9.2).

Figure 9.2   Comcast's service agents apologize a lot because they know this can go a long way toward salvaging a relationship that can be worth as much as $1,200 per year. Isn't one apology worth $1,200?

Comcast's service agents apologize a lot because they know that it's worth a lot of money to them if they don't. If a single customer spends only $30 per month for basic cable or upwards of $99 per month for cable, Internet, and phone service, she has an annual value of between $360 and $1,200. If she's a Comcast customer for 10 years, her value is between $3,600 and $12,000.

But one unresolved problem, unanswered complaint, or even the slightest hint of indifference and uncaring can cut those funds off immediately and lose that source of revenue forever. Because more people are dropping their expanded cable and switching to web-based television programs, Comcast needs to keep its customers happy for as long as possible. So service agents do it by apologizing. Two little words can mean the difference between getting $1,200 and, well, *not* getting $1,200.

There will be additional follow-up to the apology, of course, but you get the idea. Just be sorry about your customer's experience, and that will generally soften the mood and tone of the person making the complaint. It can turn an angry customer into an annoyed customer, or even a surprised and humbled one. Few disgruntled customers expect a response from customer service, especially a nice, positive response.

Another of Erik's clients is in the travel business, and when Erik's company interacts on social media on behalf of this client, each conversation begins with either "thank you" or "I'm sorry." So when a customer complains that a piece of equipment broke or he couldn't get anyone on the phone when he called, the first response is, "I'm sorry that happened to you. How can I help you?"

It's almost funny to see. If people could stammer and backtrack on Twitter, we think you could actually see people backpedaling furiously after their initial shouts of frustration. Of course, it's important to actually fix customers' complaints and answer their questions, but those two little words change the tone of the entire conversation. An apology actually lets things get done, rather than getting stuck in an argument or pointing fingers.

Make sure you're solving customer problems in a real, human way, but if you can't, explain why. Don't hide behind PR language, corporate policy, or legal department dictums. That may be the actual reason, but responses should generally never include "company policy says..." or "our legal department won't..."

"Never try to solve customer service issues with PR bullet points," said Amber Naslund in Jason's 2009 *Customer Twervice*. She's the director of community for Radian6 and coauthor of *The Now Revolution*. "The Twitter community is hypersensitive about scripted, corporate-like interactions. You have to engage people in a conversational tone or, in most cases, they won't listen to you at all."

Although we discussed it in Chapter 5, "Make Some Noise: Social Media Marketing Aids in Branding and Awareness," on branding and marketing, the lesson applies here as well: Your customers are looking for a relationship with your company and your employees. They want to feel respected and heard and any response that includes PR bullet points, corporate policy, or lawyer's CYA (cover your ass) language will only make your customers hate you and tell all their friends about the rotten treatment they received at your hands.

This is why, even if your final answer is "no," you have to deliver your "no" with an "I'm sorry." It won't fix the problem or make the customer deliriously happy. But it will make your company look like it actually cares about its customers. (Of course, it's better if you actually *do* care about your customers, but that's a different book.)

Putting Metrics Around Customer Service

Anyone with a grasp of the big picture begins to realize that PR, marketing, sales, and even customer service are not four distinct silos that compete for dollars and face time with senior executives. They're four sides of the same square. What one side does affects the other side.

Focus a lot of attention on marketing, and sales go up. As sales go up, customer service gets busy. As more people complain about problems, the PR department has to monitor the social media landscape to keep track of any problems that threaten to damage the image the marketing department has worked so hard to develop.

On the other hand, if marketing screws up, the PR department is going to pay for it. When the customer service department screws up, the sales department suffers through a loss of repeat business. So, a strong link exists between these four departments, and when one of them sneezes, the others get the flu.

What most companies fail to grasp is that a dissatisfied customer isn't just one less customer. It's a dip in sales, a loss of revenue, and a direct impact to the company's bottom line. When one customer leaves because of bad customer service, it means the sales department has to work that much harder. When the sales department signs another client, they didn't improve sales, they just brought sales back to its original number. Every lost client means the salespeople have to work that much harder to grow. Each dissatisfied customer means a blow to the reputation, which marketing has to work to overcome.

Erik's travel industry client once put his finger on the problem with bad customer service: "I'd hate to think how much business this would cost us if we weren't on here listening to people."

Of course, he identified another problem as well: You can't easily measure the effectiveness of good customer service. You can get a good estimate and figure out how much you might have lost, but even then it's not completely accurate. If you could calculate the lifetime value of a customer—we discussed it in Chapter 4, "Here's the Secret: There Is No Damn Secret!"—you could keep track of which customers your customer service department saved. You could total up the lifetime value of them and conclude, "We saved the company this much money." But that completely ignores a lot of other factors, such as the following:

- Would the customers really have left?

- Would they have taken other customers with them?

- How many people didn't buy from you because they saw the tweets and blog posts of the complaining customer?

- How extensively did these public complaints damage your reputation so that negative word-of-mouth marketing reduced sales even further?

That's not to say that you shouldn't try to measure your social media customer service efforts. You can easily measure some aspects of customer service and determine whether you're saving any money or not.

Measuring Customer Service Savings

Measuring your company's customer service savings starts with the goals you set for the department. And those goals aren't limited to simply customer satisfaction. They are often varied and even tied to the bottom line. Some examples of strong customer service goals include the following:

- Reduce call center costs by X% or $X.

- Increase customer satisfaction by X%.

- Increase positive online mentions/sentiment of the brand by X%.

- Decrease negative mentions/sentiment of the brand by X%.

We'll dispense with the easy ones first, goals three and four. Your social media team, or at least your marketing or PR department, can tell you whether you are accomplishing those goals. They can use any of the social media monitoring tools to look at the sentiment people use when they talk about your company and your products. If positive mentions go up—say, "I love my new electric pancake maker from Pat's Pancakes"—and negative mentions go down—like, "Burned my pancakes again on my new Pat's pancake maker"—then you're accomplishing those goals. Although it will be harder to measure these, you can at least be assured that you're meeting these goals.

Goal number two is similarly dealt with. Customer satisfaction surveys, referrals of friends, participation in special offers, and the amount of repeat business all go toward determining whether a customer is satisfied with your products or services. If you can count these—and anyone with a good market research bend or background should be able to—then you can see if customer satisfaction is increasing.

Customer satisfaction is also a little easier to assign a dollar figure to. Referrals of friends can be easily tracked as sales. Participation in special offers, such as the redemption of coupons, number of purchases on special days, and people using promo codes or claiming special prizes, all have a monetary value. Because these are all typically marketing functions, your marketing team should be able to tell you whether you achieved a positive ROI on your efforts.

Goal number one is the most important one. This is how you can determine whether your social media marketing is paying off. You could measure the reduction of call center costs in a few ways:

- **Measure your typical number of calls per hour.** Also measure the average number of hourly calls per customer service rep. Have they gone down? By how much? Are you receiving fewer calls per hour during a normal day? If the number of calls has gone down, but you're seeing an increase in social media complaints, does that translate into savings? Typically, a social media complaint can be handled in a few minutes, not several. If a customer service representative (CSR) can only handle six calls in an hour, but a social media rep can handle 8 to 10, there's an increase in productivity right there.

- **Measure your number of calls per hour during peak times.** If you run a cable company and your service goes down, how many calls do you get? How many calls could you eliminate if you could send out tweets and Facebook notifications that say, "We're sorry about the outage in #Cleveland right now. We're working on it and hope to have it up and running within the hour"? If you can reduce the average number of peak calls, that also translates as a savings for your company because it means you're able to save CSR resources for regular calls as well.

- **Measure the total number of issues your customer service department handles as a whole.** That includes phone *and* online issues. Has that number gone up because of the use of social media? Then that means a lot of those customer complaints were already out there, but you were able to identify them and solve the problem. It might mean you're handling more issues on the whole, but it also means you're increasing customer satisfaction.

- **Compare the cost of handling a single customer issue with the cost of handling an issue online.** Let's assume a single issue costs $10 to handle in the call center, but only $8 online (these numbers are not a real indication of how much this would actually cost). A $2 savings per issue is going to have a dramatic effect by the end of the day when looking at the cost of helping your customers. If each service agent handled 50 incidents in a day, the cost for an agent to handle 50 calls is $500; the cost for an agent to handle the same number of issues online is only $400. What if you could retrain a couple of your phone agents to handle social media customer issues instead?

We're not suggesting that you should either fire your entire customer service staff or do away with the phones and only deal with customer issues online. Rather, you need to pay attention to your customers who are talking to you through social media channels. Those customers are critical to your organization. And what they say about you online, good or bad, is both powerful when used against you, but also when you can use it for you. This is what happens when you mine those conversations and mentions for research and development opportunities.

Endnotes

1. "Good Service Is Good Business," May 2011. http://www.businesswire.
   com/news/home/20110503005753/en/Good-Service-Good-Business-
   American-Consumers-Spend.

Get Smarter: Social Media Marketing Drives Research and Development

According to Battele's 2011 Global Research and Development Funding Forecast, American companies will spend more than $400 billion on research and development (R&D) in the calendar year.[1] That's 3% of the gross domestic product! The average company spends anywhere from 3.5% to 15% of its total budget on research and development with high technology and pharmaceuticals spending in the 10s and 20s of their total budgets to develop new products and features.

Add the cost factor of market research and you're looking at a fair investment in activities that have little short-term or direct financial impact on the bottom line.

Social media can lower the cost of research and development, sometimes even eliminating it. These activities can also provide short-term and direct financial impact on your company's bottom line.

Using social media for research and development takes customer service listening to new and different heights and drives innovation and product development, which has longer-lasting and farther-reaching effects on customers.

It all revolves around your company's ability to collaborate with its customers or prospective customers in the online space. Whether using collaborative software or simply engaging your audience and watching closely what they are saying about you, your product, or even your competitors, you now have direct access to the largest focus group ever assembled: the Internet.

Collaboration Is the New Black

Do you remember the first conference call you participated in? What about the first videoconference? Even though meetings are still the bane of most businesspeople's existence, the fact that you can use technology to bring together any number of people from any number of disparate locations in the world has changed how many of our organizations operate.

Now think about that sales or travel & expense report that four or five people had to update before it was submitted. The poor office admin had to collect everyone's spreadsheets and compile them together into a document. Or, somewhat more efficiently, you would email the Excel file to person one, who would update and send to person two, and so on.

Today, collaborative technologies save thousands of man-hours, not to mention energy by eliminating duplicative file space and bandwidth on your company's computer system, by allowing dozens of people to update one document at the same time. A sales spreadsheet that 20 people must contribute to can be updated in a matter of minutes because each person can log in concurrently to revise it.

But it grows beyond the departmental level. The evolution of the social web and its accompanying technologies has made it not only possible, but even preferable for some companies to extend collaboration beyond their internal silos. Now, marketing can easily communicate with the product team, which can easily transmit messages to and from the compliance and legal staff, which can coordinate with HR, which can then circle back with marketing. And it doesn't take 12 days, six meetings, and typed and printed memos.

By using collaborative software—such as Microsoft's SharePoint, SocialCast, or Yammer—internally, companies are finding that these social media tools can be turned inward as well. As a result, companies are getting faster, smarter, and more efficient.

And we're not just citing this anecdotally from tech companies. McKinsey's Global Survey of 1,700 executives from around the globe in 2009 offered a strong validation for social software.[2] Some 69% of those surveyed reported that their organizations gained "measurable business benefits" that include better access to knowledge, more innovative products and services, lower cost of doing business, and higher revenues.

Collaborating with Customers Breeds Customers

What happens when you turn that collaboration around and invite external audiences, specifically your customers, to the table to collaborate with you? Pretty amazing things it turns out.

Prior to the last 5 to 10 years, collaborating with customers was limited to special focus groups, website comment forms, and the occasional silly slogan naming contest. But with the advent of technologies like social networks, blogs, and even video platforms, customer collaboration and feedback is on its way to becoming standard operating procedure for many companies.

Collaboration is booming. In 2009, Dorito's Super Bowl ad was created by two unemployed brothers from Indiana (whose commercial, picked from user submissions in a Dorito's contest, was voted the favorite overall commercial of the entire list of entries for that year). The Pepsi Refresh Project allows the public to submit and vote on cause- and nonprofit-related ideas with winners getting funding (more than $1 million per month.)

And it makes perfect sense. How do you acknowledge someone? Ask his opinion. How do you empower him? Listen to the opinion. We realize this is really hard for many marketers and business owners to do, but put yourself in the role of the customer. Don't you like it when companies ask your opinion, listen to it, and make changes or take your suggestions to heart? What would happen if you did the same with your customers?

Empowered customers feel that they have a stake in the success of the business. They're vested to a degree and they're proud of that. The more listening you do, the more they're vested and the more passionate they are for your brand. And customers who are worked into a passionate lather because they're empowered and vested do one thing better than any other type of person in the world: They tell everyone they know how freakin' cool you are!

Collaboration can extend beyond empowering customers. It can also captivate their passion to the point they feel an ownership or even responsibility to improve your company. Sharing ownership in your brand by collaborating with your most passionate fans builds community. It can even engender them to contribute new product and feature ideas for free.

Was Windows 7 really your idea, like the commercials indicated? No, but the marketing message was that Microsoft listened to its customers and used their changes to make the new version of the operating system their version of the operating system.

Have you ever been mad at a company and called to complain, knowing you would be satisfied if the service representative would only do X, Y, or Z and were pleasantly surprised when he resolved the situation by doing X, Y, or Z? If you know what that feels like, then you know what it feels like to be heard.

Let's Collaborate About Scissors...Yes, Scissors

Remember the Fiskars community we discussed in Chapter 8, "The Kumbaya Effect: Social Media Marketing Builds Community"? The Fiskateers website has also proven beneficial for the scissor company in the R&D category. The company's results from using community members, focus groups, and product testers have actually allowed the company to save money for research and development expenses.

"We have a 500 percent value in return on community with Fiskars," Geno Church from Fiskars's agency Brains on Fire explained. "Fiskars doesn't have to pay for R&D groups, focus groups, or certain types of market research. They've even been able to reduce the PR budget because the community is so gung ho about the brand and being so intimately involved with it. They don't need to manufacture buzz around new products or news. The community members create that buzz for them."

And how's this for R&D benefit: Fiskars engineers sent an email to the 8,000 community members—passionate fans of the brand who know a thing or two about using the product—that was packed full of technical, engineer speak. The basic premise of the survey and email was to ask the Fiskateers.com site users how they would design a pair of scissors. The email saw a total response rate of 30%. Most email marketing efforts result in just an 11% open rate.[3] Not response rate—open rate. Better yet, the brand got 997 responses to the email in 24 hours.

"It has changed the way they do business," said Church.

Fiskars has combined two goals of social media marketing: building community and facilitating research and development. It's gone from an R&D department that taped butcher paper on the windows of its Madison, Wisconsin, laboratory to keep inquiring eyeballs away from its research to one that openly sends technical specs to 8,000 people who do not work for the company for feedback. It's gone from a company that had to spend thousands of dollars per year on public relations to one that has a built-in, buzz-making army to light the fire of conversation around new products and features.

It's not that Fiskars made scissors sexy. It's that Fiskars embraced its most ardent customers as an extension of the company. The R&D team collaborates regularly with the Fiskateers community, giving each member a sense of entitlement and ownership in the brand.

When those 30% of folks responded to the technical email, Fiskars got dozens of ideas for new products and feature improvements. The company takes those suggestions seriously and has implemented some of them.

Think about how you would react if you said, "Make the thumb hole bigger and have the blades taper more," and then Fiskars sent you a new pair with a bigger thumb hole and more tapered blades. You would tell everyone on the planet that was your idea.

Including customers as stakeholders makes customers breed like rabbits. Everyone in the club wants to tell other people they should be in the club.

All it took for Fiskars to make using scissors sexy is a little bit of collaboration with its customers. And that collaboration can happen with your customers. Maybe the research and insights lead you down the road of building an actual online community. Or perhaps your customers prefer a less formal environment like offering you ideas through organized product chats on Twitter or in a Facebook Group.

The platform and technology are less significant than your desire to find a way to listen to your customers' ideas and wishes for improvements to the product, its features, or your services.

People already purchasing from you probably have ideas that can help you. All that's left is for you to give them a place to share them. And, believe us, they will surprise you with what they know about your product and how they use it.

Your Customers Know Your Product Better Than You

Why? Because, believe it or not, your customers are smarter than you. They might not know your secret recipe or the 15 steps to get your gizmo to match the thingamabob so the whatchamacallit glides just right, but they use your product. They know what it does and doesn't do and how it feels or doesn't feel. They're the first people to tell you when you screw up because they know your product inside and out. Sometimes they know what is best for your brand better than you do, right New Coke?

The traditional, closed way of thinking is that the brand knows best. But remember the nuggets of good we recommended taking from the purists? Social media is about being open and transparent. That can mean being open to ideas as well.

As we write this book, Domino's Pizza has a national television campaign promoting its new boneless chicken meal. It is delivered in a box that has a customer rating for the product printed right on the lid. Customers check boxes describing whether or not the chicken was good and return it to the company for consideration. Domino's Pizza has tapped into the ethos of the social world it operates in and is winning points from consumers by advertising the fact that it is soliciting feedback so openly.

Will Domino's Pizza make changes based on that feedback? Perhaps. But even if it doesn't, the notion that customer opinions are that important is helping Domino's Pizza in the ultracompetitive pizza business.

But they aren't the only pizza shop tapping consumers for research and development.

Papa's R&D Is in the House

Trade secrets with the big pie makers are probably protected like they were made at the Pentagon. So turning to a public forum to perform a little R&D just isn't likely. Unless you're Papa John's. The "better ingredients, better pizza" folks didn't turn to their executive chef or even product development teams for a new specialty pizza recipe in the spring of 2010. They turned to Facebook.

The Specialty Pizza Challenge called on Papa John's Facebook fans, as well as visitors to the company's website, to submit their ideas for an original pizza recipe, including a clever name and story of what makes the pie unique, to be judged in a contest. Semifinalists and finalists would be chosen, then a celebrity panel featuring "Papa John" Schnatter, Food Network star Ted Allen, Adam Kuban of the Serious Eats blog, and Rich Eisen of the NFL Network would judge the winner. The criteria included the uniqueness of the pizza, but also the story behind its creation, as well as other online activities to promote each entry.

Barbara Hyman of Los Angeles won with her Cheesy Chicken Cordon Blue recipe, which was in stores by late 2010 and driving sales for the Louisville-based company. Hyman won a stake of the sales of her recipe plus Papa John's pizza for life.

So, the company sold pizzas based on a fan's idea. Case closed?

But wait, there's more.

"The stories behind the recipes were probably more valuable than the different ways people could put together 15 different ingredients," said Jim Ensign, Papa John's vice president for digital marketing when he spoke with us in February of

2011. "Those stories helped us understand the customers better. It was the 'why' that was so fascinating."

Ensign did offer a bit of lessons learned after the effort as well.

"It being social media, we asked for one thing and got something totally different," he said. "That made it fun, though. We asked them to put together a pizza from the list of our 15 ingredients. What we got back was, 'Yeah, but if you add this ingredient, we could make it so much better.' We got information above and beyond what we asked for and even some information as to why people would combine certain ingredients, so it was pretty cool to get that level of involvement to pass on to our R&D team."

Therein lies another lesson. Just because you have access to social media for research and development doesn't mean you do away with traditional R&D. But even Ensign admitted that social media can change your approach a bit.

"It's a nice supplement to our R&D efforts," he explained. "It helps you be more effective and efficient with your R&D if you use social media to start broadly and work to narrow down your focus with the public input. Then you can turn that information over to the traditional R&D folks and go into deeper dives through some of the more traditional research. It augments, if not sometimes replaces, some of the broad, early stuff you would do in a typical R&D process."

The Specialty Pizza Challenge wasn't Papa John's first foray into R&D through social media, either. For the 2010 NCAA Men's Basketball Tournament, the company was trying to decide what would be a better prize to give away during a March Madness promotion: a trip to the Men's Basketball Final Four, a year's supply of Papa John's Pizza, or a big-screen television.

"So our social media manager just asked people on Facebook and Twitter one day," Ensign reported. "We thought the trip would be the thing everyone wanted. What we got back was that they wanted a year's supply of Papa John's and the television so they could eat their pizza while they watched the games. So we ramped up that as the prize."

Guess how much that market insight cost 'em? Not even as much as a single large Papa John's pizza.

Measuring Research and Development

To those who need to show return on investment (ROI), it's simple to see that Papa John's had a pretty easy time quantifying the success of the Specialty Pizza Challenge. You take the new pizza products generated from the contest and track their sales. Add them up and there's your neat little number.

Despite the money Papa John's made thanks to this campaign, the pizza company was even more interested in the "why" of its customer's stories. Learning more about your customers, their needs, wants, uses for your products...that's a goldmine of information that leads you to be better at delivering satisfied customers. You don't measure that in dollars. You measure that in insight, intelligence, and ideas.

Maybe collaborating with your customers doesn't lead a product feature that sells more. Maybe it leads to a product feature that makes it safer. How do you put numbers around that?

The point is that although dollars and cents certainly need to be reported, the return is not always measured in them. Still, we must measure R&D if we're going to make our social media marketing efforts facilitate that activity. Looking at our potential strategic goals for research and development in Chapter 1, "Ignore the Hype. Believe the Facts," we listed the following:

- Generate new product ideas for your company

- Improve your product features

- Improve your service lines

- Generate market research for your company

- Generate sales for your company from R&D activities

Building metrics for these types of goals can be very simple. You can actually count the number of new product ideas generated through your social media efforts and mark that first one off your list.

But to really quantify and qualify what using social media for R&D can give you, your metrics need to be more comprehensive. To measure R&D, you can track things such as

- New product ideas

- Increased sales from new product ideas

- Expanded audience for new product ideas

- Publicity/exposure from new product launch

- New product features

- Increased sales from new product feature additions

- Customer satisfaction levels after new feature implementation

- Increased safety ratings after new feature implementation

- Increased overall customer satisfaction

- Cost savings in product focus groups

- Cost savings in market research focus groups

And you can get ninja, too. We're sure that at least on an anecdotal level, Fiskar's R&D team's morale shifted when they realized they could engage and harvest information directly from customers. When you open the door to collaboration with your audiences, internal communications can improve, employee satisfaction can go up, and more.

When you think about it, what opening the doors and collaborating with your customers does is gives you and your customers more information. You get more data about how they use products, for what reasons, and in what circumstances. They get insight into what you're thinking as a company about the product or user experience.

More information makes for smarter R&D and smarter customers. That alone is a value-add to their experience with your company. Besides, getting the product and R&D teams out of the lab communicating with other human beings can't be a bad thing, right? When this happens, your traditional R&D gets a boost in the arm with even more data and consumer insight to consider.

It's Adding R&D to Your R&D

Like Ensign at Papa John's, Richard Binhammer from Dell asserts that you can't get rid of traditional R&D.

"Your traditional R&D is still there," Binhammer acknowledged when we talked about the penultimate R&D case study in social media: Dell's IdeaStorm. "IdeaStorm is a great validator and a great place for whittling in on some customer needs and demands so that you are producing the types of products the customer wants. It doesn't mean you aren't doing traditional R&D work as well—especially the nuts-and-bolts work on technology."

But Binhammer knows IdeaStorm has been a boon for the company, not just on the social capital front, but on the financial one as well. As of early 2011, IdeaStorm has harvested 15,000-plus consumer ideas, more than 430 of which have actually been implemented. That's a clip of about 100 ideas per year. Although the company won't disclose specific financials, this represents an entire product line—(PRODUCT)RED—that is associated with U2 singer Bono's (Red) effort to help fight AIDS in Africa, delivering incremental revenue to the company and contributions to a worthwhile cause.

When we probed Binhammer about IdeaStorm being a great market research tool, potentially saving the company that expense, he took the research component well beyond the walls of IdeaStorm.

"IdeaStorm is a great community, but the Web...the social web...is even better from a market research standpoint because it is real-time, unaided conversation," he said. "That tells you a whole bunch of things." Like how two people might debate or discuss the products and how they use them, which is a discussion often not found in traditional market research using focus groups.

Binhammer's point is that although market research forces you to ask certain questions a certain way and with or without the presence of certain people, influences, and so on, listening to the social web eliminates the need.

"If you're just listening and not asking the questions, then the information and research you're getting is unaided and more rich," he said. "That goes beyond IdeaStorm. That's why the aggregation of data across the social web is so very important to us."

That importance manifested itself perfectly in the second version of Dell's Netbook computers. After version one was released, a litany of bloggers and other online voices told Dell, both within IdeaStorm and around the Web, that the placement of the apostrophe key was bothersome. It was positioned too near the Enter key compared with traditional keyboard layouts, so users were hitting apostrophes instead of Enter. Someone submitted the idea to change it on IdeaStorm. Version two of the Netbook had a different keyboard as a result.

"IdeaStorm isn't about people who would go build a product giving the idea to us," Binhammer said. "It's about people who want something fixed or want something better from a company they love. They want us to do those things for them or with them."

And it works for them, and for Dell. So you're not Dell. We aren't, either. Maybe you are a small enough business that research and development just isn't in your vocabulary. Well, we've got good news: Social media means it can be.

But We're a Small Business; We Don't Do R&D

Seriously, have you ever wished you could conduct a focus group on your product or service offerings? No, you can't just open a Twitter account and say, "Hey, what do you think of our new recipe for pie?" But you can approach social media and use it for research and development two different ways, even as a small business or one without an R&D budget.

The first approach is to use social media monitoring to gather intelligence about your company, your product or service, your competitors, or your industry. By listening to online conversations about certain topics your customers might be talking about, you can gather competitive intelligence that can inform your decision making and produce a better offering.

Let's say you make custom handbags and sell them from your brick-and-mortar location along Fisherman's Wharf in San Francisco. You have a couple dozen styles of bags, most of which sell fairly well, depending upon the time of year. But you need to keep up with what customers want and need in a handbag. You need some R&D or at least some market research to know if what you're planning to produce makes sense for the new spring line you intend to roll out in the coming weeks.

So you go to a free monitoring solution like SocialMention.com or even invest a little money in something a bit more sophisticated, like uberVu, which can be had for around $40 per month. You enter some keywords and tinker with a search until you start to see some relevant results for conversations occurring from users in or around Northern California (see Figure 10.1). "My handbag needs more dividers. I can't keep my stuff organized," is a phrase you see that pops up a couple of times. "My purse should come with a pocket on the strap for my mace," is an interesting suggestion.

Figure 10.1   Social media monitoring platforms like uberVu (shown) can pull conversations from online sources based on keywords or keyword phrases and can help keep your R&D staff informed. Source: www.ubervu.com.

But then you see a theme emerging as you dive into more results. You notice that when people are talking about what their handbag or purse needs, they say that the purse needs to be big enough to hold an iPad inconspicuously. And there's your new product idea harvested from raw data on the Web.

A second approach to using social media for R&D is to openly participate in social media with that intent. Build purposeful relationships and connection with your actual customers so you can turn to them as your focus group. The social media monitoring approach tapped into random conversations. Even though you can filter by geography, keyword, and the like, depending upon your monitoring or online market research solution, you can't easily identify any of that feedback as coming from actual customers or prospects.

As an active social media participant, however—building followers on Twitter, fans and likes on Facebook, readers of your blog, or even subscribers to your email newsletter—you're growing your potential focus group every day.

Let's say you keep it very simple: just Facebook. You log in each morning and post an update to your store's page that lets folks know things such as you're expecting a shipment of accessories, you have some material samples in the store for customers to check out and see if they like, or you're running a 10% off special. Then you go find a couple of handbag photos from new fashion shoots on a couple of blogs you subscribe to and share the links on Facebook.

You check in at lunch and then in the afternoon to respond to any comments, maybe post another update about the store, or tell everyone that they should swing by the store because the bakery across the street just put out fresh French bread. You tell your customers and friends they should "like" your store on Facebook because you'll be sharing some news and discounts there from time to time. Over the course of a few months, you accumulate 150 or so fans.

When it's time to find out what folks like or dislike about last year's line of handbags, or what they'd find useful in new versions for the spring season, you simply post the question on your Facebook page:

"What about your handbag could be better? Any need for more/bigger/smaller pockets? Are you carrying more accessories that we should account for?"

Chances are, you won't get a lot of responses the first time you ask, but you can keep asking, ask folks to subscribe to an email list specifically for "New Product Ideas & Feedback," or even incentivize participation by offering discounts to anyone who answers.

No, these two scenarios don't require big budgets, lots of scientific testing, or even geeks in lab coats. But they are legitimate research and development practices any business can use by implementing social media for R&D purposes. And neither one is very expensive at all.

The key to being successful in using social media marketing for research and development is planning to do so. Set those goals. Write those objectives. Implement whatever plan fits your resource allotment and measure according to what you want to get out of your social media R&D efforts.

How to Plan For Research and Development

You didn't think we'd say, "Go plan for this," without giving you a little help, did you?

Planning for research and development is as complicated as you want to make it. We prefer to keep it simple. There are four general steps to conducting research:

1. Set the goals for the research.

2. Establish the important questions to ask.

3. Research and collect answers to the important questions.

4. Analyze the answers to make decisions.

How does that translate to practical application?

Make a list of the product or service feedback items you might want to ask customers about. Make a list of the information you'd like to know about your customers or prospective customers (think market research). Look at that list and pick the one or two major areas you wish you could solve with a little customer input or feedback.

Those one or two major areas need to be addressed in your goal or goals for your social media R&D efforts.

Let's say your top priority is to get new product feature suggestions. Now start identifying the important questions that you need to ask your customers. Is the handle sturdy enough? Would you change anything about the colors used?

You don't need to be a market researcher to ask questions, but you should probably try to ask questions that allow your audience to give the most unaided feedback. For example, asking "Is the handle sturdy enough?" might be better asked by saying, "On a scale of 1–10 with 10 being most sturdy and 1 being least sturdy, how sturdy would you rate the handle?" The previous question almost implies you don't think it is and could bias the answers. You may also want to add the question, "On the same scale, how sturdy do you think a handle should be?" This will give you an indication of your customers' preferences and feedback on how sturdy they perceive your handle to be, which gives you a point of comparison.

After you've listed the questions you want to ask, you just need to deliver them to an audience to answer. You might do this with a quick online survey you ask customers to fill out, anecdotally through questions you ask customers on social networking platforms or blogs, or even by just asking the questions of individuals directly and making note of the results.

Analyzing the results can be done easily if you have people fill out an online survey. It generally consists of tabulating the answers to show averages and consistencies in issues, then looking at the results with the mind-set of discovering insights and trends the answers seem to hold.

If the majority of your customers say the ideal sturdiness of a handle is 8 on a scale of 1–10 but they rated your handle a 4, then you've discovered an insight that can help improve the product to the audience's liking.

Market research questions are a bit different than product research questions. While product questions are focused on just that—the product—market research questions are generally more focused on the customer.

You can certainly try and aggregate and average basic demographic and psychographic profiles of your audience, but be sure to add technographic questions, like what social networks do they use, do they read blogs, how apt are they to visit company websites from their mobile devices, and so on. You can also focus on deeper market research questions like what they think of your competitors, how they feel about your price, and so on.

The important thing is to focus on the questions you want answered—the goal of your research—and not deviate from that too far. The process of asking questions does not require 50 questions if you really only need to ask 5. If that's the case, then ask the 5 and be done with it.

Your customers will thank you.

And you will be able to give yourself a nice pat on the back, too. Saving money on market research or even harvesting ideas for new products and services without spending hundreds of thousands of dollars in traditional R&D doesn't get handed to you very often. Social media marketing does just that.

Using your online connections with customers to drive innovations and product development ideas also begins to walk your company down the road of measurable monetary return on investment, too. When you develop a new product or begin selling one with a crowd-sourced feature improvement, you can track sales of those new offerings and match dollars to effort.

The only other of our seven benefit areas for social media marketing that offers a relatively simple direct line from activity on the social web to bottom-line dollars is our next area of focus: driving sales or leads.

Endnotes

1. Battelle, "2011 Global R&D Funding Forecast," http://www.battelle.org/aboutus/rd/2011.pdf.

2. "How Companies are Benefiting from Web 2.0: McKinsey Global Survey Results," McKinsey Quarterly, September 2009, http://www.mckinseyquarterly.com/Surveys/How_companies_are_benefiting_from_Web_20_McKinsey_Global_Survey_Results_2432.

3. Marketing Sherpa, "2010 Email Marketing Benchmark Report," http://www.marketingsherpa.com/EmailMarketingReport2010ESum.pdf.

It's All About the Benjamins: Social Media Marketing Drives Sales

Ironic, isn't it, that the key to selling through social media is not selling at all? Walk into the social event screaming about your products and services and you'll be asked to leave. But listening to the conversations, assimilating into the community, and building trust and relationships over time makes you the resource those participants turn to when they're ready to buy what you sell.

As we've covered in other areas, social media marketing can have an impact on your bottom line. Still, the traditional marketer in you probably wants to scream, "Just tell me how to sell stuff, already!"

Okay. We will. But we won't do it without first making sure you're hearing us, loud and clear:

Stop thinking like a traditional marketing nimrod!

Yes, you can turn on a Twitter or Facebook profile and start dropping links to your online sales portal and drive sales. If you have a product that already has a recognizable brand name, high demand, or some timely news item or endorsement that puts the product top of mind for consumers, you'll even make some money and see a nice return on something so simple.

But if your product is like 99% or more of the products out there, you're not likely to attract much of an audience for your traditional, one-way, sales-spewing fire hose. Without some level of recognition that joining the conversation, engaging with your customers, and treating social media as a two-way, or even multidirectional, line of communications, any success you have will be short-lived.

The spray-and-pray approach in the social media realm requires a heck of a lot more than the typical prayer for success. Brands that are just yelling through megaphones and never turning it to their ear more often than not find themselves ignored. You can't afford to be ignored if you're going to invest time and money into social media marketing.

So you have to remember the fundamentals:

- Listen first.
- Be responsive.
- Be honest.
- Provide value.
- Sell last.

This doesn't mean you should sit around on your hands and not sell for months, weeks, or even days. It just means there's a lot more work to do in building relationships, establishing trust, and building an audience through social channels for success to work. You don't just open the door and ask if someone wants to buy. Remember that social media marketing is about building relationships, not receipts. The receipts will come, but only if you invest the time and attention it takes to build relationships with your customers. Think lifetime value, not sale value.

Still, there are those of you who either need to see short-term gains or want to illustrate some dollar value through social channels before you invest more than cursory interest in social media marketing. Some of you might even think, "I'm not cut out for this conversation nonsense. I want to figure out how to sell stuff through social media." All is not lost, but we have to frame the possibilities for you.

First, understand that there's a difference in driving business *from* social media sites and driving business *through* social activity. The majority of this book is focused on the latter. For the former, you can buy advertising on Facebook, LinkedIn, and many other social media sites. Often, this type of online media is more effective than traditional advertising or even standard online media purchases (such as banner advertising or pay-per-click ads on search engines) because the social networks allow you to hypertarget. For instance, Facebook advertising allows you to choose targeting qualifications based on almost any type of user data it collects (see Figure 11.1). Think about all those interests you listed on your Facebook profile. When composing an advertisement for Facebook, you can target using those interests. What this means is that if you know your ideal target consumer is a 40- to 50-year-old male in Arizona who enjoys golf and gardening, you can deliver your advertisement only to Facebook users who meet those profile requirements.

Figure 11.1   Facebook advertisements allow you to hypertarget based on interests listed in users' profiles. The site's advertising tool also shows you the potential audience available based on your targeting before you deploy the advertisement.

Hypertargeting is only possible through social networks because they are the only types of websites that ask users for more than basic demographic information. Although dozens of factors go into an advertisement's effectiveness, Facebook advertisements have been known to provide higher clickthrough rates than Google pay-per-click advertisements, lower cost-per-lead than traditional channels, and higher returns on awareness and recall than other mediums. Facebook's own Advertising Case Studies site lists a 70% year-over-year sales increase for online scrapbooking site How Fast Time Flies.[1] Portland, Oregon-based Daddies Board Shop, a local skateboard retail shop, used Facebook ads to expand its geographic target to a global scale and drove $45,000 in new revenues.[2]

How can this happen with a little box in the right sidebar in Facebook (see Figure 11.2)? Because of relevancy. The ads for How Fast Time Flies weren't served up just to women age 35 to 65. They were served up to women in the company's target age group that listed "scrapbooking" and similar interests on the network. So, the advertisements were seen by a more interested audience. This increased the chances that the audience would click and convert. Social networking sites have more information about their users and can thus better target messages to users. In advertising, relevancy always wins.

Figure 11.2   Facebook advertisements are typically relegated to the right sidebar, but are often more effective than larger or more prominently placed website banners because of hypertargeting.

Nothing's Wrong with Advertising

Cantera Real Estate in Austin, Texas, took Facebook advertising and relevancy to new levels in 2010. Owner Jim Olenbush noticed a preponderance of stories in the news about violence in Mexico. The drug-related murders and shootings reached such a dangerous level by the fall of 2010 that affluent Mexican families were considering immigrating to the United States for safety. Putting two and two together, thinking strategically, and following a No Bullshit mindset, Olenbush turned to Facebook advertising. He did some research, but mostly assumed that affluent Mexicans would likely have Facebook accounts. He took out advertisements for houses for sale in the Austin, Texas, area and targeted them to Facebook users in Mexico City and Monterrey. He told us the results have been extremely profitable.

"We invested about $300 to $400 over three or four months," Olenbush explained. "Facebook even suggested bids of like 25 cents per click and I would lowball it and put in bids of 10 cents. No one else was really focusing on those markets for Facebook ads at the time, so we got lots of impressions. One person moved to Austin and bought a house from us for $1.1 million. While our numerical conversion rate for Facebook clickthroughs wasn't very good, I spent $400 to make commission off of a $1.1 million house. That's a really high return."

Another tactic Olenbush uses is to target companies that announce they are moving corporate operations to Austin. He immediately takes out real estate ads for Austin houses and directs them to be delivered to Facebook users whose profiles and interests include the name of the company relocating. Cantera Real Estate typically spends less than $100 on these types of advertisements for relocating companies but has closed seven deals in the year leading up to April of 2011.

As this real estate advertising example shows, achieving conversions, leads, and sales from social media platforms is possible, even with very little lead time. We asked Olenbush what type of activity he was pursuing to embrace social media marketing like the purists preach—long-term engagement, content-driven, relationship building—and he responded that, in essence, he wasn't.

"I don't have the personality for it and the time involved is considerable for [what I perceive as] vague results," he told us. "Facebook ads can run while I'm out meeting with a client. I was looking for a way to use Facebook and advertising that made sense to me."

And that approach is perfectly fine. If you can use a traditional method like online display advertising on a new media channel like Facebook and see positive results, we would be insane to recommend you not do it. If no one in your organization, including you, has the interest or desire to engage in conversations with customers regularly and in the online realm, then advertising on social networks may be a good alternative for you.

But understand that advertising is advertising. It typically does little to foster trust between your audience and you, build relationships with customers, or engage them in any sort of unique or interesting way. The one benefit to advertising mechanisms on social media sites is that they allow for hypertargeting. Having that laser focus on your customers or prospective customers and delivering them relevancy—the right message at the right time and in the right place—often delivers you conversions or sales.

Advertising Is Outbound. Social Media Is Inbound.

That laser focus, though, is not exclusive to advertising on social media sites. The other side of the coin—driving business *through* social activity, not just *from* social media sites—offers your business hypertargeting as well. In fact, social interaction done well attracts more than just impressions or eyeballs. It attracts customers who consciously engage and interact with your brand or organization. Advertising makes you throw up a message, drive impressions (which is an incredibly vague metric), and hope the user or viewer then consciously interacts with the advertisement by reading, watching, or listening to it with some level of comprehension. This is outbound marketing, the kind that takes place when a company sends a message outward to its customers.

Social media interaction and engagement, on the other hand, is inbound marketing, the kind that takes place when customers or audience members approach the brand or company because they want to interact. Inbound marketing is achieved through social media marketing when your business asks and answers questions, provides information or engagement through content, or simply shows up when audience members are having conversations about the industry, the company, or sometimes anything at all. By having a social presence—a seat at the online table, if you will—your company becomes one that consumers are accustomed to seeing and hearing from, interacting with, and even trusting. Think about it: Instead of advertising that interrupts the audience, consumers begin to see your company's name pop up on Twitter, Facebook, or even in their email Inbox because someone they know has shared a great piece of advice they found on your blog. Over time, they see it consistently enough that they click through and consume a piece of your content. They decide you're being very helpful and the advice or value you are providing is interesting to them. Then they subscribe to your blog, follow you on Twitter, or "like" you on Facebook. Your quarterly webinar, coupon special, or event promotion comes up and they see it, offering up their email address to receive access—and you have yourself a new business lead.

The consumer in this case has come to you. He has taken notice because your marketing actions—providing content, engaging with the greater community online—are not interruptive, but participatory. He likely found you through a recommendation from a friend, which is exponentially more reliable than other mechanisms of product or service discovery. Consumers like this take their time in getting to know you, investigating your content and interactions over time to ensure they can trust you're not just in it for a short-term buck. And when they do come to you, they're far more ready to listen, convert, or purchase than almost anyone clicking through a display advertisement.

Case Studies in Social Media Marketing for Sales

Jeff Moore of Moore and More Print in St. Louis reached out to TKO Graphix in Indianapolis after seeing photos of the company's vehicle wrap graphics on the photo-sharing site Flickr.com. Moore's company also did vehicle graphics and admired TKO's work. He connected with Josh Humble, TKO's social media manager, and met with Glenn Burris, one of the company's national account representatives. And a relationship was born. Humble and Burris told us this story in April of 2011.

Just a few weeks after the people from each company connected—simply because of a photo posted on Flickr—Moore referred a large advertising agency to TKO that was in need of a project beyond his company's means. The referral led to a wrap and graphics project that involved 4,000 vehicles in more than 200 locations across the United States. The total sale for TKO Graphix? Almost $2 million.

But social media marketing success doesn't have to be measured in millions of dollars. Sometimes it can be enacted around something as simple as competition and measured in small business numbers. Take Miss Shirley's, a casual dining spot in Baltimore that's especially popular on Sunday mornings. It's one of those Sunday breakfast-and-brunch restaurants that, no matter what time you come—before church or after—there's always a wait for tables. In the spring of 2010, Miss Shirley's marketing agency, MGH, recommended a way to turn the Sunday morning wait time into more business. The restaurant would use Foursquare, which beckons users to check in and let their networks know where they are physically located; the service then rewards the person who checks in most frequently with the imaginary title of "Mayor" of that location. Anyone who earned the mayorship of either of Miss Shirley's two locations would be entitled to skip the wait and be seated immediately.

We learned of Miss Shirley's Foursquare idea from MGH's Ryan Goff, who told us they got the word out to customers using social channels like Facebook, where the restaurants had about 5,000 fans. They also used their email list and reached out to Baltimore area bloggers to help spread the word. A printed card with an explanation of how to download the Foursquare application to a smart phone and the process of checking in to participate in the promotion was distributed to guests in the restaurant.

"The restaurants got a ton of buzz and media coverage from the Foursquare campaign," Goff said. "A lot of people were talking about skipping the wait at Miss Shirley's. We changed the conversation. It was already a great breakfast place—we just implemented some ideas that added a fun competition to the mix for patrons."

Over the course of the first three months of the promotion, Miss Shirley's saw a 427% increase in check-ins at the restaurants. (People were checking in before the company offered incentive to do so.) More important, however, Miss Shirley's saw an 18% increase in sales. After all, to check in at Miss Shirley's on Foursquare enough to earn the title of mayor, you had to come more often than just on Sunday mornings. The program drove people to frequent the restaurant more often, which logically led to increased use and sales. And each Sunday morning, one active Foursquare user and their guests could spend more money at Miss Shirley's without the wait.

The PIs and the KPIs

It would be easy to get caught up in the key performance indicator in the Miss Shirley's story. A 427% increase in check-ins is phenomenal. But that measure only proves one thing: The restaurant convinced customers to use Foursquare. What the heck does that have to do with driving business for Miss Shirley's? Any metric you track, and percent increase in check-ins is one you might want to monitor, is either proof that you are accomplishing your objectives or it is a performance indicator (PI). Key performance indicators (KPIs) will have a direct correlation to the objective you're focused upon.

For instance, if you track brochure requests from your website over time and see that the number of brochure requests per month has a direct correlation to the number of sales in each month, then brochure requests is a KPI. If lots of people download brochures, but there's no direct correlation between brochure downloads and sales, then it's just a performance indicator. Sure, it might be one you want to continue to monitor and report on; but if fluctuations in its numbers do not correlate to sales fluctuations, keep looking, because something will. In this case, maybe the number that correlates with sales is follow-up phone calls to a dedicated number posted on the brochure or information cards returned from the brochure.

In the case of Miss Shirley's, check-ins were a KPI. It's reasonable to assume that the more times a person checked in, the more money the restaurant made. After all, most people don't stop into a restaurant without spending something.

The Carlton Hotel in New York City is a different story. Many of its social media KPIs revolve around the number of people who visit employee profiles or the company pages on LinkedIn. Here, the staff is focused on optimizing their pages for keywords to attract LinkedIn users looking for group, conference, and executive event space. By optimizing company pages and individual profiles as well as using LinkedIn's premium (paid) features to track and reach out to prospects in 2010, the hotel drove $186,550 in new corporate and group business in just three months of trying.[3]

Not every company has products or services that tally $2 million for a single sale, or a Sunday wait time worth competing to circumvent, or Manhattan real estate to rent out for corporate or group events. Nevertheless, these types of financial transactions can absolutely happen in your company. Whether it's showing off your work through photo- or video-sharing sites, applying a game application to your locations, aggressively seeking prospects on LinkedIn, or just being present and accounted for when potential customers are asking questions about the topics you're qualified to speak to, both planned and serendipitous moments of social media marketing sales success happen daily.

But serendipity, which transpired in the case of TKO Graphix, isn't predictable. You can't afford to roll the dice and hope to get lucky, can you? This brings us back to the No Bullshit approach. By planning to succeed using social media marketing—establishing goals, laying out measurable objectives, and developing strategies and concepts built on tactics and tasks that focus on accomplishing the objectives and goals—you build in strategic communications through social media channels that don't need serendipity to work. This happened in the cases of Miss Shirley's and the

Carlton Hotel. Their success wasn't happenstance or the result of one-to-one networking. It was planned for and calculated.

Seeing the social media marketing world through a strategic filter enables you to plan and calculate your success, too. On a tactical level, this can be done by attaching clear calls-to-action to all of your blog, Facebook, or Twitter posts, converting the public into prospects by giving them reason to volunteer their email address, or even using customer care and outreach through social channels to softly push up-sells and add-on offers. No, you don't want to be pushy or turn into a call-to-action spam monster, but, for example, if a customer says she's worried about the longevity of the product, you're well within the bounds of relevant messaging to say, "We do offer a service plan and warranty."

Putting Metrics Around Sales

Your plan for using social media marketing to drive sales should be steeped in measurable objectives that prescribe what metrics you will focus on, just like any of the previous six benefit areas have. But don't limit yourself to measuring just direct sales. Anything that moves the needle on the bottom line—that sells a product or service or leads to the sale of a product or service—should be quantified, reported on, and tracked to help you understand what your return on investment in social media marketing will be. Keep in mind you're not limiting yourself by measuring ROI—by now you should understand it's not about ROI, but what you get out of social media marketing. But sales is the primary area we can apply financial metrics to and report as a monetary return.

Some other areas to consider measuring include the following:

- Leads
- Cost per lead
- Lead value
- Nonsales conversions
- Cost per conversion
- Repeat purchase value
- Retention rate
- Average order value
- Time to close
- Referrals

Although many of these might wind up being KPIs rather than final program metrics, each one can be tracked and monitored over time to help you fine-tune your social media marketing efforts related to sales. Some can also be tracked and compared with similar metrics from other channels to prove efficiencies. You might find that you get twice as many leads using pay-per-click advertising, but pay three times as much for them than those you garner through blogging or social networking activity. Even subtleties in your measurements can uncover insights that save your company thousands of dollars or make your cost-per-acquisition exponentially smaller. Something we think is lost on many marketers is going beyond the top layer of metrics and assigning a value to some of the measures considered "soft." Let's start simple and focus on the lead. A lead could be a person's email address or a phone number or even just the name of a company. These are superficial, or "cold," leads unless there's more information or context added. If the lead is a name and email address accompanied by information that he or she filled out in an online contact form, now you have a "warm" lead. If it's someone who approached you at a trade show booth and says, "I need a product like yours. Let me see it," then you have a "hot" lead. They're interested in buying and have said as much.

Good salesmen believe in strong metrics and can typically tell you the value of each of the three kinds of leads. Some will say a hot lead is worth $15.00. Others will say something like, "I need six leads per day/hour/week." What they're referring to is a conversion rate. These marketers know that on average, and as a simple example, it takes 10 leads to get one successful sale. If each sale is worth $500, then each lead is worth $50. Yes, you need to factor in profits, overhead, and so on, but you get the point.

That same salesman or marketer can also tell you how many conversions or sales he needs to make a profit, a weekly quota, and so forth. So he'll come to a trade show and know that he needs to close $50,000 in business during the three days. If each sale is worth $500, he needs 100 sales. If it takes 10 leads to get one sale, he needs 1,000 warm leads. Let's hope there are a lot of people at this trade show!

You need to treat your social media marketing the same way. Look at your website analytics and conversion rates. If it takes you 10,000 unique visitors to convert 100 customers, you have a website conversion rate of 1%. Let's say your average customer spends $35.00 when purchasing from your company's site. If, over time, your Facebook activity drives 5,000 unique visitors per month, then you can do some quick math:

5,000 visits = 50 customers
50 customers at $35.00 each = $1,750.00 revenue per month from Facebook

Now let's say that you filter your website analytics and learn that customers coming from Facebook actually convert at a 1.5 percent rate and spend $5 more per visit than regular visitors.

5,000 visits = 75 customers (1.5% of 5,000)
75 customers at $40.00 each = $3,000.00 revenue per month from Facebook

Keep in mind that some of these numbers are impossible to track unless you plan for them first. But knowing what you want to measure before you start—which happens when you follow our strategic planning recommendations we started with in Chapter 1, "Ignore the Hype. Believe the Facts."—enables you to set up your website analytics and sales tracking to measure the information you want to collect.

Let's say you don't sell things on your website. The math is no different, but the place you look for the numbers is. Jason had a professional services client who once told him, "If we can get a prospect on the phone, we're pretty confident we can close the deal and get a new customer." Jason helped the client figure out how many deals the client closed after phone contact with prospects (turns out it was about 55%) and the average value of the deals (around $75,000). The ensuing content strategy revolved around building premium white papers and webinars that interested audience members had to register to download or attend. A required field in the form was the person's phone number. After several months of building a base list of email subscribers using a corporate blog offering good, but basic, free content, the client's webinars were bringing in 100 to 200 participants, while the white papers pulled in about 200 to 300 registrations. Removing duplicates, current customers and prospects, and other unqualified leads (like junior-level audience members), each content effort was delivering between 25 and 40 new prospects. Apply the low number and assume you have the same 55% conversion rate to a $75,000 account, and each content effort was worth $1,031,250. The strategy and ensuing content executions cost the client around $65,000—less than the revenue from just one conversion.

All this might sound like complicated math, but it really doesn't have to be. Ask yourself how much you're paying to acquire a customer, then how much that customer is worth. Keep in mind that a customer often isn't worth just the initial purchase price. Happy customers buy from you again and again. The only things you really buy once are coffins and headstones. Every other customer has a larger lifetime value. The day you can place numbers around those two things—acquisition cost and customer value—your ROI becomes more easily measurable.

Understanding those factors not only helps you put metrics around driving sales and leads through, but can also clarify efforts to measure in the other six areas social media marketing helps your business. Building backward from customer value and acquisition cost, you can look at branding and awareness metrics like impressions or conversational market share, compare those metrics with sales volumes, and see where correlations arise. If you see that more impressions have a direct impact on leads or sales, you can begin to associate financial metrics with those goal areas. We still recommend you look for the results of each of the seven benefits of social media marketing while answering the more broad question of, "What do I get out of it," rather than the financially focused, "What is the ROI?" But sometimes the opportunity to connect dots to intrinsic value and extrinsic value arises. Look for it.

We Know What It Can Do; Now How Do We Do It?

This chapter and the previous six chapters have been focused on the seven major benefits social media marketing has for businesses. Social media marketing can

- Aid in branding and awareness
- Protect your reputation
- Extend public relations
- Build community
- Drive customer service
- Funnel research and development
- Drive sales and leads

We've talked a lot about planning, setting goals, accounting for measures of success, and applying metrics to what your company does in each. You now have a better foundation of what strategic planning is and how it applies to social media marketing.

But strategic planning is only half the battle. Executing on your plan, incorporating social media marketing into the day-to-day operations of your organization, and moving toward a more socially aware and enabled business is the other half. You need to understand how to take the goals you lay out for your efforts and activate them within your company. We'll now look at developing internal and external social media policies and then move through important ideas on managing and activating social media marketing efforts.

After all, if you have a plan on paper but fail to put it to action then what you get out of social media marketing is just a plan on paper. That isn't enough.

Endnotes

1. "How Fast Time Flies," http://ads.ak.facebook.com/ads/FacebookAds/ How_Fast_Time_Flies_CaseStudy.pdf.

2. "Daddies Board Shop," http://ads.ak.facebook.com/ads/FacebookAds/ Daddies_Board_Shop_CaseStudy.pdf.

3. Emily Molitor, "How the Carlton Hotel Leverages LinkedIn for Business Development," November 8, 2010. http://smartblogs.com/ socialmedia/2010/11/08/the-carlton-hotel-leverages-linkedin-for-business-development.

12

Remedy Your Fears with Sound Policy

If we've managed to inspire you to start using social media, but you're still unsure, this is your chapter. Hopefully you can see that although social media might be a little unpredictable at times, it is possible to keep some semblance of sanity and normality while following the company's mission and messaging standards.

We'll admit, social media might sound like some big, Wild West free-for-all. But that does not mean your company needs to abandon its identity, history, traditions, practices, or procedures. Incorporating social media doesn't mean you no longer have to follow the law, government regulations, or sound business practices. There are places on the Internet where it is wild, but that's not where your company wants to (or should) be. Some people online might take certain liberties with language, ideas, and degrees of nakedness, but that's not the kind of thing your company wants to participate in.

This chapter is all about establishing a sound, easy-to-follow social media policy that lets your employees use social media to reach your customers, but, at the same time, keeps them from engaging in inappropriate behavior, visiting inappropriate sites, and not representing your company or brand in the best possible light.

Many companies have created a social media policy to deal with how they will respond to customers via social media, what kinds of communicating they will do in social media, and which employees are allowed to use it and what they are allowed to do and not do. These companies include the BBC, Dell, the *Washington Post*, the New Zealand State Services Commission, the U.S. Air Force, the U.S. Navy, and the International Federation of Red Cross and Red Crescent Societies.[1] Several social media practitioners, such as Dave Fleet, document these policies and write frequently about them (see Figure 12.1).

Figure 12.1   Social media professional Dave Fleet writes about the need for and creation of corporate social media policies. They're important tools that can save you a lot of time and headaches in the future.

Obviously, these companies have recognized the need for a social media policy. They are embracing the opportunities the social web offers companies. These organizations recognize the power of allowing employees the freedom to interact with customers but also give the employees a framework to guide those interactions.

Why Do We Need a Social Media Policy?

In short, you need a social media policy to protect yourself, regardless of your company's size or how comfortable you are with employees operating as extensions of your brand. Chances are, you already have other policies that guide employee behavior. There are policies about sick days and personal days, workplace attire, and workplace safety. There also needs to be a policy about how your company communicates with the outside world.

Maybe your policy is that no one outside the social media practitioners may use social networking on behalf of the company (see Chapter 14, "This Is NOT a Sandbox. It's a Business," for more on who should be involved in your social media efforts). Maybe your policy requires that everyone can communicate on behalf of the company using social media, but needs to go through a special certification and training course first. And maybe you want to take the Zappos approach to social media and let everyone in the company talk about whatever is on their mind. If you work for a small company and you can trust everyone to do and say the right thing, that's great. But if you work for a larger company whose employees don't know each other, you can run into all kinds of problems where different messages and answers get sent out to customers, internal discussions are taken out into the general stream, and people may even inadvertently send out information they weren't supposed to.

In November 2010, National Hockey League general managers (GMs) were feeling their way around Twitter and Facebook, figuring out what they wanted their players to be able to send out to their fans and followers. During a GM meeting, they were discussing their concerns about what to do with Twitter and applying policies around the social network because their players were tweeting inappropriate comments or even giving away team information. Washington Capitals' GM George McPhee told *USA Today* that a couple of years before, one of their players tweeted that he wasn't going to dress that night, which gave their opponent the jump on knowing the Capitals' lineup.

Although knowing whether someone is playing in a game that night might not seem like such a big deal, sending out proprietary business information that's worth millions or billions of dollars is. Although a spat between two players that gets aired right before game time might not seem so important, an inappropriate or outrageous tweet from someone's personal account could result in damage to the employer's brand, especially if that person is closely associated with that brand.

The NHL is still struggling with its own social media policy, while other professional sports leagues deal with it, too. With specific focus on Twitter, the National Basketball Association (NBA) doesn't allow players to tweet during a game (see Figure 12.2 for the kinds of tweets NBA players are likely to send out after a game), the National Football League (NFL) requires players to stop tweeting 90 minutes before game time, and Major League Baseball bars tweeting by players and managers 30 minutes before a game starts. This year, Chicago White Sox manager Ozzie Guillen was suspended after he tweeted an angry response to a bad call during a game against the New York Yankees on April 27 (see Figure 12.3).

@swish41
Dirk Nowitzki

Great win last night. Fun game to be a
part of. Jkidd with a huge 3 at the end.
Gotta do it again tonight. Go mavs

5 Feb via ÜberSocialOrig   ☆ Favorite ↻ Retweet ↩ Reply

Retweeted by   and 22 others

Figure 12.2   Dirk Nowitzki of the Dallas Mavericks sends out tweets before and after most games. The NBA doesn't allow players to tweet during games.

@OzzieGuillen
Ozzie Guillen

This one going to cost me a lot money this is patetic

27 Apr via txt ☆ Favorite ↻ Retweet ↩ Reply

Retweeted by   and 100+ others

@OzzieGuillen
Ozzie Guillen

Today a tough guy show up a yankee stadium

27 Apr via txt ☆ Favorite ↻ Retweet ↩ Reply

Retweeted by   and 100+ others

Figure 12.3   Chicago White Sox manager Ozzie Guillen was suspended for two games after he tweeted during a game against the New York Yankees on April 27. Major League Baseball bars tweeting by players and managers 30 minutes before a game starts.

Right after Super Bowl XLIV (the New Orleans Saints beat the Indianapolis Colts 31 to 17), one Indianapolis PR "professional" sent out a rather denigrating tweet about New Orleans and their "flooded shit hole of a city" (see Figure 12.4). The uproar that followed over the next 48 hours nearly cost this person her job and helped contribute to a major exodus of clients from her agency. The day after the tweet in question, her employer fielded phone calls from angry clients and angry tweets from Indianapolis and New Orleans demanding that the woman be fired. She blogged and tweeted an apology to the people of New Orleans and

Indianapolis, but her original tweet and the resulting backlash reinforced for a lot of companies why they needed a social media policy at all. Unfortunately, for some companies, this uproar might have stopped them from joining the world of social media in the first place.

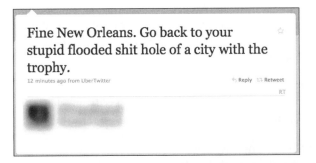

Figure 12.4   One Indianapolis PR professional angered a lot of people when she sent an insulting tweet after the New Orleans Saints won Super Bowl XLIV. The fallout caused her and her employer a lot of grief and reminded people that you're always "on" when you're on social media, even on a personal account.

We're not advocating that you avoid using social media because one rogue employee decides to tweet out something hateful and nasty. Rather, create a social media policy that establishes guidelines for how employees can use and enjoy social media. And spell out the consequences for moving beyond those guidelines.

Several companies have already begun spelling out what they expect of their employees and how they should view their online communications. The United Kingdom government's "Twitter Strategy for Government Departments" says *"while tweets may occasionally be 'fun,' we should ensure we can defend their relation back to Our objectives."*[2] SHIFT Communications, a PR firm, says their employees shall *"(p)ost meaningful, respectful comments—in other words, please, no spam and no remarks that are off-topic or offensive."*[3] And the *Washington Post*'s social media policy reminds its writers that by being journalists, they *"relinquish some of the personal privileges of private citizens. Post journalists must recognize that any content associated with them in an online social network is, for practical purposes, the equivalent of what appears beneath their bylines in the newspaper or on our website."*[4]

Similarly, the *Post* takes one of the best approaches to making sure its social media strategy lines up with its day-to-day mission of being a top-notch newspaper.

> "When using these networks, nothing we do must call into question the impartiality of our news judgment. We never abandon the guidelines that govern the separation of news from opinion, the importance of fact and

objectivity, the appropriate use of language and tone, and other hallmarks of our brand of journalism."[5]

A social media policy like this might have helped the Indianapolis PR professional understand what kind of effect an inflammatory tweet like hers would have had, even if she were tweeting as a private citizen. Because her name had already been linked to her employer's—she even had it in her Twitter bio—the policy would have spelled out what was considered appropriate and inappropriate, as well as what happens when people violate the policy.

Although none of the organizations we've mentioned here discuss what will happen to people who break any of the guidelines, Dell is a little more specific in what will happen if people violate its policies.

> "You will be held accountable for the information You share in online activities. Be careful what You share, publish, post, or otherwise disclose. You are personally responsible for what You share and should remember that anything You post may be public for an indefinite period of time (even if You attempt to modify or delete). Try to ensure Your online communications reflect Dell's brand attributes of openness, responsiveness, integrity and optimism."

Dell didn't specify what will happen, but its policy does remind employees that they themselves, and not Dell, are personally responsible for what they publish. They also remind people that their messages are public for an indefinite period of time.

The Question of Ownership

Who owns your content? That is, if an employee sends a tweet or writes a blog post for your company on company accounts, who owns it? Your company does. This is true of any work that any employee generates, whether it's an engineering technical manual for your latest widget, a brochure about why every household needs the widget, and even the press releases that are sent out announcing the widget. Because social media is just one more written channel in this instance, anything created on the company's social media channels is also the property of the company.

This also means that the company blog posts your employees write, the company tweets they send, and the websites they design are all owned by the company. Their names may be listed as authors, but that doesn't mean the content belongs to the employee. However, they should be allowed to use these posts and examples as part of their professional portfolios, although they wouldn't be able to use that material for another company.

In a similar vein, some companies have taken to deleting old blog posts whenever the author leaves the company. We recommend against doing this for a number of reasons:

- It seems petty, like you're not willing to admit the author worked there or you're trying to erase all traces of her existence.

- The search engines already know the information is there, and you're getting a lot of benefit by having this content on your website or blog. Deleting the content eliminates any search engine benefits you were getting.

- Their posts contain valuable information that is still useful. Presumably you hired this person because he is smart. Just because he is no longer there doesn't mean the information is now invalid or not worthy of your server space.

What Can Employees Do at Home?

Your company's comfort with employees having permission and access to social media gets a little stickier if you allow your employees to associate their place of employment with their personal social media accounts or allow them to communicate through them for work purposes. Of course, even if your company doesn't participate in social media, that doesn't mean your employees aren't using it at home after work hours, and you certainly can't—in most cases—tell them what they can or cannot post on their personal accounts.

But if you communicate openly with your employees that they are allowed to utilize social media accounts and acknowledge their place of employment or communicate through them for work purposes, then you have the right to apply some company policies and expectations for their behavior there. In exchange for the privilege of talking openly as an employee of the company, the employee must surrender his full freedoms to post whatever he wants. That type of approach works well with many existing policies we've written and reviewed.

Depending on the type of industry and its various regulatory or governing bodies, however, a company must be aware that the courts are often ruling on behalf of the employee. In fact, one woman, Dawnmarie Souza, successfully won a suit filed on her behalf by the National Labor Relations Board (NLRB) against ambulance company American Medical Response of Connecticut, Inc. Souza was fired for posting critical comments on Facebook about her boss. The company had an Internet policy that prevented workers from disparaging the company or its supervisors in a blog or other social network. The judgment led the company to agree to change that policy, as well as another policy that prohibited its employees from depicting the company online at all.[6] The NLRB said that both of these policies violated legal protections that allow workers to talk about their salary, working hours, and working conditions with co-workers.

However, this does not mean that employees can discuss private or secret information, such as patients' private information, proprietary company information, or trade secrets. Even if you do not have a corporate social media presence and policy, it's at least a good idea to address these issues in the company handbook. This brings to mind a valid point. If you have a company handbook, ethics policy, or other document that governs employee behavior, often the simple way to add a social media policy is to review those documents and add the words "and online" in strategic places. Communicating on social media channels is no different than communicating over the telephone or talking to someone in person. If you're in a highly regulated industry and have a policy that employees are not allowed to divulge private client information to anyone, then they're not allowed to do that on- or offline. The Internet does not make the rules go away. Just clarify the fact that the policies you already have apply in the online world as well, and you'll probably be just as risk-averse as you were before social media was a factor.

Telecommuting Is Not the Same as Personal Networking

It's worth mentioning that an employee who works from home and uses social media as part of his job responsibilities should be covered under your social media policy. This is completely different from an employee who communicates from home during personal time. Your social media policy can cover what employees say or do during their work hours, even when they're working at home or another off-site location.

It's up to you whether you allow people to update their personal social networks from work, during work hours, even if they're using personal phones on their own time to do so. We generally favor that employees who get breaks and lunches be allowed to update their networks, whether it's from their workstations or their smartphones.

What Should a Social Media Policy Include

The best way to tell you what social media policies should include is to tell you what they should *not* include. This is not the place to start your employee code of conduct or employee manual. Don't start including an entire code of conduct that each employee is supposed to follow. You should already have one of those. If you don't, hire an HR consultant to write one for you. Similarly, if any policies or codes of conduct already exist elsewhere, and you still feel the need to explain a specific social media policy, then simply reference the existing policies in your new one.

Now, the hard part: What should your policy contain? There are two basic ways you can approach this, and we favor one over the other. One option is to write the entire policy up front, dealing with as many contingencies as possible *as generally as possible*. Don't write a rule or process for every single social network, every possible type of interaction you have with customers, and the types of things you are allowed or not allowed to say. Rather, leave it as general as possible, referring to "social media" and understand that it means any and all social networks and blogging.

However, keep in mind that this approach is going to take a very long time because you're going to have people who want the policy to cover every eventuality for every possible usage—both current and future—of social media. The problem is that typically people who undertake this kind of approach (1) don't know very much about social media, so they get bogged down in trying to figure out how it works and create rules that don't even apply, and (2) don't really understand how their co-workers are going to use social media, so they may end up creating rules that will never apply or will completely run counter to the reason you need to be on social media in the first place.

The best practice is to create an overall code of conduct that tells employees what sorts of behavior you expect from them and what kinds of things they are allowed to say and share and what kinds of things they need to keep secret or not say. Next, create different policies (or sections) that deal with different facets of social networking.

Remember Erik's friend who works at a university where they've been debating using social media for six months? This is the part that's taking so long; they haven't even created a single account on a single network, but they've managed to spend six months creating rules on how they're going to use it.

In May 2010, Jason was interviewed by *Inc. Magazine* about some items to include when creating a general social media policy. Even though he recommends that you create individual policies that deal with major social networking tools, like Facebook, Twitter, LinkedIn, and blogging, the policy should evolve based on need and use, rather than remain a static set of arbitrary rules that your committee will debate and argue over for months that never actually come into play. You'll find that the three-week argument about Yandex, the Russian search engine, will prove to be moot, as no one in your company will ever use it.

The best approach is to create your overall code of online conduct, and then add new sections or specific policies as the need arises. Base your policies on need and actual usage; don't write them well in advance to cover that one instance that might or might not ever happen. Remember, if you do it right, your code of online conduct should cover the overall best practices of online communication without getting into the fine details of each and every network. This is helpful because you're trying to govern employee communications, not the technological aspects of a certain platform.

Finally, as the need arises, create separate policies (or sections) on both the personal and company usage of

- Blogs and blog commenting
- Facebook
- Twitter
- LinkedIn
- YouTube

But don't spend a lot of time focusing on the fine details about how each tool should work. They change frequently, and you would have to have someone who is constantly updating each tool. Rather, they should focus on best practices and general guidelines, just like the online code of conduct. An example of a good policy statement might be the following:

- When posting real-time updates about company news, be sure the news has been announced and permission to post has been granted by the communications department.

An example of what we wouldn't want you to waste time writing is

- Do not tag the company in personal Facebook photos.

Instead, write a general policy such as, "When posting images or information of a personal nature, please refrain from incorporating the company into the messaging."

Your policies do need to include information about how, or even whether, employees may represent the company on their personal networks. For example, even if it's with the best of intentions, if an employee of a large fast-food chain responded to allegations of animal cruelty or poor hygiene, his response might be seen as an official statement on behalf of the entire corporation, even though he's the assistant fry cook at the Duluth, Minnesota, restaurant.

Your social media policy also needs to

- **Be positive and proscriptive.** Focus on what employees can do, instead of being negative and restrictive, detailing everything employees can't do. That doesn't mean you can't have anything negative in it, but the overall tone needs to be positive.

- **Discuss consequences for violations.** People have been fired for things they said on social media channels, regardless of how ill-advised the firing might have been. People have been fired for writing about their personal interests and hobbies outside of work, which is none of their employers' concern. Similarly, people have been fired for sharing information they shouldn't have, which *is* their employer's concern. In nearly every case, these firings have been a complete surprise to the people who were fired. Your social media policy needs to avoid any confusion and surprise by stating up front what will happen if policies are violated.

- **Remind people to be authentic.** We've talked about authenticity throughout this book. Employees should not, even if they are trying to help the company, hide their identity, their name, or their relationship. They need to state who they are and where they work. People should also state that their messages are their own viewpoints and not those of their employer.

- **Encourage people to be on their best behavior.** You know how you would react if an employee made racist or sexist comments in the workplace. You should apply those same standards to their online behavior as well. Although your employee doesn't speak for the company, the association with your company can make you look bad if your employees are making racist, sexist, or other disparaging or mean comments online. Remember the Indianapolis PR pro who made the statement about New Orleans after Super Bowl XLIV? Although she was communicating on her own time with her own Twitter account, plenty of clients, as well as members of the general public, saw her employer whenever they saw her. Encourage employees to use their best judgment.

- **Remind people to do their jobs.** Communicating with customers is great, but if it's not in the person's primary job description, then she's not getting her work done. For example, answering customer technical questions and complaints is important, but the PR person should not spend the bulk of her time doing it. She either needs to turn it over to the customer service department, or she needs to stop doing it. (And if there isn't anyone who can handle technical questions and complaints online, then get one. This is a symptom of a bigger problem.)

- **Remind people to maintain privacy.** Even if you don't work in an industry that has strict privacy rules—Health Insurance Portability and Accountability Act (HIPAA), attorney-client privilege, investor information for publicly traded companies—you should honor the privacy of your customers or the regulatory requirements. Never discuss specific customers, never share their problems or questions, and definitely don't link to them unless you have their permission.

- **Spell out who is responsible for making final decisions about issues that have not been covered.** This needs to be someone who is already familiar with social media and understands the marketing and customer communication very well. That means it either needs to be someone in one of the four departments we've already discussed—marketing, PR, sales, or customer service—or someone who is in charge of the social media department.

What Should You Do About Privileged Information and Avoiding Giving Advice?

The fear of violating privileged information is the one reason most businesses, especially regulated ones, stay out of social media. Your social media policy needs to address what is considered privileged information or professional advice (something doctors and lawyers can't just give willy-nilly), and what things you can and cannot discuss on a social network. For example:

- A customer complains on a hospital's Facebook page about his treatment or bill. It is *not* acceptable to address the matter on Facebook, the same way a cable TV company might because a response essentially confirms that the person was a patient. Instead, write a response that says, "I'm sorry, we can't answer any questions on Facebook because of privacy. I realize it's inconvenient, but could you call our main number and explain your situation? They will be able to connect you with the right department."

- Someone writes a comment to a Facebook page with a legal or medical problem. In about 200 words, they ask you a basic question, and you are 99% certain you could solve her problem in about 200 words in return. The problem is, your professional ethics forbids this kind of behavior. You need to honor that and say, "I'm sorry, I'm not able to answer that question directly. I don't have enough information to give you the best answer, and don't want to give you the wrong answer. You could make an appointment to see me, and I can help you."

- A relative of a patient or client sends you a message on Facebook mail, asking about his relative's case. This one is a no-brainer: You can't share any information over the phone (unless you've been given specific permission from the patient/client) and definitely not by email, Facebook, Twitter, blog posts, sky writing, the Pony Express, or interpretive dance. It does not matter what channel, you just can't do it. A simple, "I'm sorry, I'm not able to discuss that," will do.

Now, one thing you *can* do is discuss hypothetical situations as educational blog posts, for example. We once worked together for a legal client who wanted help with his blogging. They wrote blog posts that were common questions people might search for, thus helping this attorney to be viewed as an expert by his potential clients. Many of these posts were answers to frequently asked questions, and even similar to cases he handled on a regular basis. But they were always written as generically as possible. They always included a disclaimer that this was not legal advice, and that if the reader needed further information, he or she should contact an attorney.

With this kind of social media, you can never name names or even discuss specific situations, but the lessons people could learn can be valuable. Just make sure to remove any identifying information, and you can avoid violating any kind of privilege. Of course, finding the best people to handle this kind of responsibility is something you need to take seriously.

Trust Employees, but Not Everyone Should Speak for the Company

We know, we know. We've said several times before that you need to trust your employees and that if you don't have any employees you can trust, you have a hiring and management problem. We said you need to be able to trust your employees to talk with your customers because they will be the best evangelists for your company and can put a human face on your corporation.

But there will be some employees who, let's face it, just shouldn't speak to the public. They might be good at their job, can manage the internal processes extremely well, but when it comes to letting them be the face of your company, they are at the very bottom of the list of people who should be trusted with this responsibility. Some hard questions are likely to come up, like "Can I help out with the Facebook promotion?" or "Why can't I be on the social media team?" That means you'll have to have some difficult conversations with these people. If this is the case, this might also be a good time to consider an internal social media certification program or limiting social media to certain departments or job descriptions.

Who Should Enforce It?

Enforcing a social media policy is going to be left up to two people: the person who is in charge of your social media efforts and your legal department or compliance representative, or both. In fact, this is where your legal and compliance departments are going to become important. After all, they understand what it's going to take to keep your company out of trouble and its executives out of jail. So they're the ones who will know better than anyone whether a tweet violates privilege or a blog post is going to reveal proprietary or sensitive information.

People might think it's rather self-explanatory and easy to figure out. Remember the Washington Capitals' hockey player who tweeted that he wasn't going to dress for a playoff game that night? Although it may seem rather innocuous and a great way to keep fans involved in the team's goings-on, it also accidentally revealed some valuable information to the other team.

Similar things can happen. An innocent tweet from the CEO of your company about a great meeting he had with the CEO of a competing company can possibly signal a merger, a sale of one company to the other, or—in a worst-case scenario— even be a red flag to the FTC that price fixing and collusion is taking place. This is why the social media person needs to work closely with the legal and compliance departments to make sure she understands what is acceptable communication and what is not.

This isn't to say that the lawyers have to review *everything* that is going to be published through social media channels. They don't review every email or listen in on every phone call, so they don't need to review every tweet that goes out. There might be cases when even a two-hour delay is too long, and the effectiveness of a message will be lost. This is why the legal department needs to educate the social media department about what is acceptable communication. This is also where the social media people can educate the lawyers about the importance of customer communication and sounding human. So if any issues come up, especially if they have been spelled out in the policy, then it is up to either the social media head or the legal department to deal with any fallout, along with human resources.

In Ozzie Guillen's case, the Major League Baseball head office and commissioner Bud Selig decided the suspension. In your company's case, you need to appoint someone who will recommend and handle disciplinary measures if your social media policies are violated. However, because social media is still relatively new to you and your company, we don't recommend firing someone for mistakes he makes, especially as your company is still learning to use this properly.

For example, social media agency New Media Strategies was fired by Chrysler after one of its coordinators sent a tweet that was intended for his personal account. After he was fired, and after Chrysler fired New Media Strategies, the social media world was abuzz, not with sympathy for the PR mess Chrysler was in, but for the young man who managed to tank his career in just 140 characters. Many perspectives in the online conversation that followed thought the two organizations overreacted.

Of course, there are scenarios where you would normally have to fire someone anyway, whether it happened on social media or not. Those situations are better decided internally and should be an overall part of your corporate policy, and not just limited to your social media policy.

Let's Be Clear on the Responsibility

Because social media is a relatively new way for people to communicate and the lines between what is public and what is private are often blurred, social media often gets inaccurately blamed for violations of company policy or mistakes made by its users. In the case of New Media Strategies, some media reports and even blog posts about the incident called upon companies to review whether or not they should use Twitter or hire agencies to tweet for them. This line of thinking shows bias against the medium, not the user.

The coordinator mistakenly sent a personal tweet over a client Twitter channel. This is easily done if you're not familiar with the Twitter application you're using. But the blame for the incident is not appropriately aimed if it's aimed at Twitter. The coordinator's lack of care or understanding of the application he was using is to blame. Twitter had nothing to do with the mistake. It is merely the channel.

Similarly, in the summer of 2011, U.S. Representative Anthony Weiner (D-N.Y.) posted a lewd photograph on Twitter that was intended to be a private message to a female follower. The mistake Weiner made was confusing the syntax of a direct (private) message on the platform with that of a public reply. The media coverage that encircled the Congressman after the incident included several sensational exposés and media indications that Twitter was too risky to use, that politicians shouldn't be using the platform, and that this was another case of social media being bad for us.

What those media outlets did in their coverage was blame the tool, not the craftsman. The only person to blame for Anthony Weiner's misstep was Anthony Weiner. He could have texted the message, emailed it, or printed it off and mailed it in an envelope. None of those channels would have been blamed. But because many media members, and the general public, didn't yet have a comfort level with Twitter as a common communications channel, the chic thing to do was to blame the channel, not the culprit.

If your employees make a mistake on a social network, it does not mean your company should go run and hide from the social network. It means the company should do a better job of educating and empowering its employees to use the networks appropriately.

What If People Spend Too Much Time on Social Media?

There is a possibility that, appropriate use or not, your employees will spend more time on social media than is necessary. When this happens, their work suffers. This is where the social media director, the person's supervisor, or both (see Chapter 14 for more information on models of social media management) will need to step in and have a discussion with the employee about getting his work done and not letting social media take over his job.

Of course, sometimes this becomes necessary, like if a customer service person takes on all social media complaints and can't answer phone calls. Or a marketing person spends a lot of her time building an online community centered around a particular brand. In some cases, the person's new duties will need to shift and change, *as long as his efforts are producing a positive return for the company.*

But there are times, as with any new tool or process, when it's easy to let this become a distraction and a problem to be dealt with. In this case, deal with the distraction the same way you would with any other workplace distraction. Don't let the fear of people spending all day on their Facebook accounts keep you from adopting social media. This is what your policy should address, as well as regular performance reviews and a good line of communication and regular updates between employees and managers. It's perfectly acceptable (even encouraged) to include a statement in your policy that reads something like, "Although you have access to social networks from your workplace, you are still accountable for the job duties assigned to you and within the time frames they are assigned. Be mindful of your workload, expectations, and deadlines or the social media access may be removed."

In reality, though, social media time spent is no different than many other workplace time-sucks. Being involved in too many committees or having too many meetings can be just as distracting, as can taking on too many projects. Social media is not to blame for this problem, but rather the employee's work habits and time management. Work with the employee to better manage his or her time, rather than eliminate social media access.

Having a social media policy can ultimately save you and your company a lot of time and headaches if you establish who can and can't use social media, what kinds of messages they can send out, and what consequences will happen if the policies are violated. Although it might seem rather harsh and violates the social media hippie viewpoint of "everyone needs to participate in the conversation," they aren't going to bail you out when your company gets into trouble because someone didn't do what he was supposed to.

Trust everyone, but have a policy that deals with those who cannot or do not comply. Remember that even though social media offers a vast world for you and your employees to explore and even play in, social media for your company is about business.

Endnotes

1. Koka Sexton, "100 Examples of Corporate Social Media Policies," May 14, 2011. http://www.kokasexton.com/word/100-examples-of-corporate-social-media-policies.

2. "Template Twitter Strategy for Government Departments," http://www. scribd.com/doc/17313280/Template-Twitter-Strategy-for-Government-Departments.

3. Shift Communications, "Top 10 Guidelines for Social Media Participation at (Company)," http://www.shiftcomm.com/downloads/socialmediaguidelines.pdf.

4. Staci D. Kramer, "WaPo's Social Media Guidelines Paint Staff into Virtual Corner," September 27, 2009. http://paidcontent.org/article/419-wapos-social-media-guidelines-paint-staff-into-virtual-corner.

5. Staci D. Kramer, "WaPo's Social Media Guidelines Paint Staff into Virtual Corner," September 27, 2009. http://paidcontent.org/article/419-wapos-social-media-guidelines-paint-staff-into-virtual-corner.

6. Sam Hananel, "Woman Fired Over Facebook Comments Settles Suit," February 8, 2011. http://www.huffingtonpost.com/2011/02/08/woman-fired-over-facebook-comments_n_820487.html.

13

Assign Responsibility and Be Accountable

This is where everything we've discussed in the last 12 chapters is finally coming together. But there is one question remaining: Who owns social media? If you adopt social media in your company—and if you've made it this far in the book, we hope this is something you're considering—you're going to need to choose where social media lives, who will be responsible for it, who can participate in it, and who has the final say about how it's implemented.

Ultimately, this needs to be someone you trust, someone you can rely on to speak for the company, to be the face of the company, and to deal with your customers. If you don't have anyone at all in your company who fits that description, then you've made some poor hiring decisions. We talked about this in Chapter 2, "It's Not Them; It's You!" but it bears repeating: If you don't have any employees you trust to talk directly to customers, you don't have an employee problem, you have a management problem. And it all started with the people who hired untrustworthy employees.

But assuming this isn't a problem, and you have identified the right people in the intervening 10 chapters, you now need to start looking at who will manage your social media efforts on behalf of your company.

The Question of Ownership

We've skirted the question so far: Who should be in charge of the social media efforts at your company? We sort of made a case for marketing in Chapter 5, "Make Some Noise: Social Media Marketing Aids in Branding and Awareness," but that's because we're both marketers. But we've been able to make a case in the other chapters that PR should be in charge of it, or customer service, or sales. The crisis communication employees, who are often in the PR department, may be asked to take over during a major crisis. Or maybe it's the community leaders and brand managers who are in charge of the messaging.

How's this for a no-bullshit answer? There is no one answer. The answer is going to be right for your company, for the people you hire, for the personalities who will handle it, and for the level of trust you actually do have for each of them.

Maybe your sales force is a little older and they think Facebook is stupid. But if your target market is women between the ages of 50 and 60, that's Facebook's fastest growing demographic. Your salespeople are missing out on a great opportunity by ignoring Facebook. So they're not the best candidates. Or your marketing department is going through an internal power struggle right now and you know that introducing social media to the mix is only going to create more problems than it solves, so that might not be the best place to put it. Your customer service department is wildly overworked and understaffed and there's no budget to give it to them right now, although that might change in six months. But rather than put it off for six months, you decide to press on and see if you can lighten their workload in the meantime.

Ultimately, you're going to have to choose which department might be best suited for managing a social media campaign.

A Quick Review of the Pros and Cons

Looking at the pros and cons of the different departments and how to overcome some of the downsides will help you find the right answer for your company. Keep in mind that these are generalities and not hard-and-fast truths, so it's important to take a look at your own departments and staff before you base a decision on what we're telling you here. These are just general guidelines to give you a place to get started (see Table 13.1).

Table 13.1   Pros and Cons of Social Media Responsibility by Department

	Pros	Cons
Marketing	Understands how to create a persuasive message, knows how to measure ROI, is most willing to try out new tools. Used to speaking to customers in their own language.	Most likely to blast unwanted commercial messages. Not experienced at solving customer problems. Easily distracted by other new tools. Can easily slip into marketing jargon.
Sales	Consummate networkers who are likely to embrace social media if it helps them avoid the phones. Also more likely to use social media to build relationships with potential customers. This helps them avoid their customers' gatekeepers.	Most likely to avoid social media if they don't see immediate results. Also likely to try blasting commercial sales messages in pursuit of quick results. May be a new way of thinking for old-school salespeople.
PR	Most appropriately trained employees to deal with real-time communications, speaking on behalf of the organization, and building relationships with customers.	Don't usually think in terms of sales and ROI, but in reads, listens, and views. Must be careful not to look down on small-time bloggers and social media practitioners.
Customer Service	Experienced at handling customer complaints and problems.	Not experienced in writing persuasive marketing messages or using sales techniques. Might not be trained to follow up on sales and marketing questions.

Marketing

Upside: This is the most likely place to put it because social media *marketing* is basically what you're trying to accomplish. These are the people who typically understand how to create a persuasive marketing message, are used to measuring the results of a campaign or overall performance, and are often more than willing to try a new tool or toy if it will help them increase market share. They are also adept at speaking to customers in their own language, helping them identify pain points, and showing them how to solve these problems.

Downside: They're often willing to try a new tool or toy even if it *won't* help them. They can get easily distracted, so while they think marketing on Twitter and Facebook sounds cool today, they could be distracted by the newest tool tomorrow, without actually making the others work first. They are also not prone to thinking in terms of customer service because they're more focused on gaining new customers. These are also one of the two most likely groups to start blasting commercials via social media, thus alienating your potential customers. They are also most likely to revert to marketing jargon in their messages, so watch out for this.

Sales

Upside: Ultimately, these employees are most dedicated to seeing sales numbers go up as a result of a new campaign or effort. These people will most likely buy in if they know that they're going to see more qualified leads, more closes, and higher revenue. A lot of salespeople are consummate networkers, and social media is the ultimate networking tool that lets them get in touch with potential customers and lets them bypass the gatekeepers.

Downside: A lot of experienced salespeople (read: older) are so used to jumping on the phones day after day that if they don't think they'll see immediate results, they won't try it. Because social networking is all about building trust and relationships, they might not have the patience and time to build those, relying instead on face-to-face meetings and phone conversations. There's nothing wrong with those, but this is a paradigm shift for a lot of old-school salespeople.

Public Relations

Upside: Public relations professionals are typically the individuals within your organization who have the most experience and training in communicating not just with the public, but in crisis situations. That background gives them the right pedigree to manage and balance real-time and potentially viral conversations that involve happy or unhappy customers. The disciplines of public relations—crisis communications, media relations, event management, community relations—have very logical parallels in the social media space as well: responding to detractors, blogger outreach, event management, building community.

Downside: PR people typically don't think in terms of marketing, ROI, and sales. They think of eyeballs, readers, viewers, and total reach. PR people have their own ways of measuring results, but they often don't cross over to sales and profits. You also want to make sure the PR people don't make Target's mistake of turning up their noses at "nontraditional media" (see Chapter 2) and possibly alienating a few thousand bloggers all at once.

Customer Service

Upside: Because a lot of people like to use Twitter and Facebook to complain, who better to be on the front lines communicating with them than your customer service people? These staff members respond immediately to complaints, questions, feedback, and compliments on a daily basis. Not only will they help solve the problems customers are complaining about on social media channels, it also lets your customer service efforts be more visible. That shows your potential customers that you're responsive to problems, and the happy customers will tell their networks, which means you can spread your message to thousands of other people, via the people they most trust: their friends.

Downside: Customer service employees have the opposite problem marketing does: They focus on fixing current customer problems, not gaining new customers. So they're not experienced in writing persuasive messages, measuring ROI, or trying to win market share. Customer service people might not be trained to follow up with sales or marketing questions from noncustomers.

Who Should *Not* Be in Charge

Who are the people who should not be in charge of social media efforts? The legal, IT, or compliance departments. It's not that we have anything against those people. We're sure they're nice people. It's just that in our experience, the legal department will often take days or even weeks to answer a single tweet, by which time a customer's problem will either resolve itself or turn into a bigger problem, which PR has to deal with. (In fact, if your legal department feels they need to approve every single tweet before it goes out, that's a sure sign you're not ready for social media. Or you need to convince your legal department to loosen their ties a bit.)

The IT department isn't equipped to deal with customer service issues, sales questions, marketing issues, or talking to media types. And compliance makes sure that your products or services follow the law. They don't deal with customers or media types either. In fact, IT is often a hurdle that needs to be overcome when trying to implement a social media campaign. We talked about this extensively in Chapter 2.

Even though these people might insist that they need to be involved, we're going to recommend against it for the most part, *unless* you work in a highly regulated industry. And then—and only then—the legal or compliance departments should have a seat at the social media table, but they still should not be in charge. If their indecisiveness or thoroughness gets in the way of you successfully interacting with customers, take away their seat. They can give advice and guide, but they should not be a hindrance to your responsiveness to your customers. We've already seen what happens when the lawyers get involved in talking to customers. Unless you want to have a big social media crisis caused by people who don't like the way the legal department handled a customer service problem, you won't let them get the keys to the social media car.

But if you think they need to be in charge because you're worried about the risk to your company, put this book down. You're not ready for social media, and you might never be.

The Ideal Setup

The best setup might be to take a "tiger team" approach and select one or two people from each department to serve on a committee. Put the committee in charge of your social media efforts. Pick a representative from each department who should have influence in your social media campaign and let that team manage it. Although the people on the committee would continue to serve in their regular day-to-day functions, the social media responsibilities would be added to their day-to-day responsibilities and become a normal part of their job. They would devote the appropriate amount of time to any social media matters that came up.

This is a nice democratic solution that will keep everyone involved. It will also crash and burn in about four months, if you're not careful. If you take the social media committee approach, consider a few caveats before launching it:

- Don't make this a democratic committee where everyone has an equal vote. The only thing slower than the seven-year itch is a committee. Remember Erik's friend who worked at a university with a social media committee in a single department? After six months of regular meetings, they still haven't started a single profile on a single network. If you want to kill an idea, give it to a committee. To kill it extra brutally, make the committee write a mission statement first.

- Put one person in charge of the entire social media effort. This person should be in charge of the committee and the social media campaign, and should ultimately be responsible for making sure everything gets done. Everyone else can make recommendations and give input, but this needs to fall squarely on the shoulders of one person. He or she will make the decisions and create the messaging and the editorial calendar. You don't have a democratic method in any other department in your company; there is always one person in charge who makes sure everything gets done. This committee needs to follow the same model of management.

- A social media committee can also serve as a clearinghouse for the different departmental functions. Any customer service issues can be forwarded to the customer service department, any leads can be forwarded to the marketing or sales departments, and any serious crises can be sent on to the PR department or elevated to customer service management. This might mean that only one person is handling social media, and he'll farm out the different issues as he sees fit; this is the hub-and-spoke model of social media management. It also means that someone in every department has access to a social media account. Tools like CoTweet let several people participate in a hub-and-spoke model.

- Don't create a committee if that is the normal procedure for any of your interdepartmental efforts. That is, if your standard operating procedure is to create a committee, then don't do it here. What often ends up happening is the same people end up serving on several committees, which means they'll view this as just one more assignment and not give it the attention this needs if you want it to see a positive ROI. You're better off only putting a few people, or even one person, on this assignment and reducing her regular workload to let her fit in her extra responsibilities.

Of course, the best course of action is to make social media a department all its own. Rather than just creating a committee, move one or two people to the new social media department and let them lead the charge. The department should be independent of any of the others because they each have different missions themselves: Marketing is about getting sales leads, sales is about closing the deal, and customer service is about fixing the problems created by sales.

The problem with letting one department run social media is that the others might feel slighted and either fight for control or try to go rogue and do their own social media program. Also, keep in mind that it could take at least 6 to 12 months before you begin to see noticeable results. You will meet some initial goals along the way: adding X people to your network or getting X visitors to your site per month.

Once you decide which approach you want to take, it's a matter of finding *who* you want to have serving on your committee or new social media department.

Social Media Management Is for Senior Staff, *Not* Interns

Social media is *not* only for young people. It's not an entry-level position, it's not only used by entry-level people, and young people are not the only ones who are good at it. The minute you think that, you'll start running into problems because there are plenty of Generation Xers and baby boomers who are on social media.

There are a number of companies who turn their entire social media efforts over to interns and entry-level employees because they mistakenly believe social media is a young person's game. They think the geezers in management can't grasp the complicated tasks of sending 140-character tweets or reading complaints on Facebook.

Even though the younger employees might be whizzes at Twitter and Facebook, they don't necessarily know how to create an extended strategy, have experience responding to customer complaints, understand how to market and sell enough to be able to do it effectively online, or even know how to calculate the ROI and do basic market research. The net result is that the companies have a Twitter and Facebook presence, but not much else to show for it. They don't know the ROI of their efforts, there are no goals to measure, and their strategy is a one-sentence statement to "do more social media."

It's real simple: Managing social media is not for rookies or the twentysomethings who just started with your company three months ago. Now, we're not saying that these young employees shouldn't *do* social media. If you can get them to be a part of your social media team, that's great. They should be using it because they really *do* get social media and the idea of collaboration and rapid-fire communication. But they should not be in charge of something that would, by any other name, be a major department with a serious undertaking.

Think of it this way: The new PR associate doesn't do media interviews during a major company crisis, the marketing intern doesn't oversee the entire spring launch for your new product line, and the new corporate attorney doesn't defend your company in a civil suit three months after graduating from law school. You would never dream of letting new employees do anything like that, so why would you let a rookie handle one of the most public-facing communication channels your company will ever have? Other than PR and marketing, no other channel reaches so many people so permanently and widely as social media.

By using a more experienced employee, you're able to draw on his real-world, full-time work experience. He can recall similar situations, can understand the gravity of what he's doing, and has experience building and executing campaigns, measuring the results, and speaking with customers with a sense of purpose and company mission. Although we've known a lot of great twentysomethings who are really smart and could make a social media campaign sing, they're few and far between.

Who Are the Ideal Social Media Practitioners?

There is no one good social media person, but there *is* a limited field of possibilities. Typical social media people are generally going to come from marketing, PR, or sales. They're used to dealing with the public and are generally outgoing and easy to get along with. They're used to multitasking and can manage the sometimes fast pace of social networking and conversations. They also spend a lot of time, or are willing to spend a lot of time, attending conferences, visiting local and regional networking events (Chamber of Commerce, business networking, and so on), and are comfortable being in large groups of people.

Social media people tend to be more social in nature and view these online networks as extensions of their real-world connections, rather than a replacement or substitute for it. They're happy to meet people outside the office and will evangelize for the company.

This is important because your social media people are going to be performing a number of different functions for your company: public relations, sales, marketing, and customer service. The big four functions that can use social media to their benefit are the same four functions that this one person will employ as your social media mouthpiece. So they need to be customer-focused, sales-minded, public-facing, brand experts. They're going to be a self-starting, self-motivating, revenue-generating, problem-solving, media-earning *force majeure.* So they need to be the kind of people who can handle this all on their own without a lot of input from someone else. This is also why the social media person is not going to be found among the ranks of the most junior employees.

Typically when asked the question, "Who should be in charge of social media in my company?" we answer, "The person most passionate about doing it." If that person happens to be a seasoned communicator who falls into the previous description, you've got your answer. If she doesn't, then you have a candidate who might need some additional oversight. But passion compensates for a lot. Let the person who wants it lead the charges.

What If Your Employee Becomes a Social Media Rock Star?

Those passionate leads often fast-track themselves to becoming influential within their own market. If the social media industry breeds anything, it's microcelebrities. Few influencers in any industry are as lauded or stroked as those in the social media world, deserving or not. If your company is widely known or your industry is a large one, you can almost count on an active and visible social media evangelist for your company becoming quite the hot ticket for conference speaking and beyond. It happened to Frank Eliason when he started the @ComcastCares account on Twitter and began handling people's customer service complaints. It happened to Scott Monty when he became Ford Motor Company's social media director and to Chris Barger when he took the same position at General Motors. Amber Naslund is another notable industry influencer in the social media world, and she is the vice president of social strategy for social media monitoring software company Radian6.

Some employers worry about what will happen to their employees when they become a big name in their industry or within social media circles. This is a viable concern. After all, with this kind of microfame comes more opportunities for speaking at conferences, being interviewed by bloggers and media members, and being asked to contribute to industry blogs and trade journals. These situations make those individuals more attractive in the job marketplace and potentially put your company in the position of allowing them to build a personal platform, only to leave.

The best way to consider this employee is as one more marketing channel, as one more way to get the word out about your company. If she is speaking at a conference, then she'll be "Janet Haverstand from ABC Company." If he writes a guest blog post or a trade journal article, his byline will read, "Bob Masterson, director of social media for ABC Company." And, of course, any traditional media mentions will always carry that person's name and job title. Remember, these are things your PR department wants, and your employee's presence in online and traditional media is making their lives easier. These mentions and appearances can then lead to increased awareness for your company, which can lead to more sales.

For example, both of us speak at a variety of conferences and trade groups, regardless of industry. We're often approached after a talk to send more information about our companies. And from time to time, one of those contacts will turn into a project or ongoing client. It's a marketing and lead generation channel for us, and it can be for your company as well.

Think about the benefit Comcast got when Frank Eliason went to a conference to talk about @ComcastCares (or even now, in his role as VP of social media at Citibank). Former Comcast subscribers who left because of poor customer service got to hear about how the cable giant was improving its customer service. And what if that led to even a small handful of subscribers returning to Comcast? Now, Frank was speaking at that conference anyway, but Comcast got a little something extra in return in the form of returning revenue that could vary between $50 and $100 a month.

Understandably, the concern most companies have is that the employee is not going to be able to get her work done, will get an unmanageable ego, or will be recruited by another company and hired away.

This isn't an employee management handbook, so we can't tell you a lot about time management or hiring practices or even how to deal with someone with a huge ego. Our hope is that yours is the kind of company where the managers have a good relationship with their employees and they can talk to the employee before any of these things become a problem. The managers should talk with the employee about her workload and meeting her deadlines, about her expectations, and about working well with others. And hopefully your company can match or even exceed a competing offer from another company.

On the other hand, you should also be proud that you were able to train and develop an employee to become such a highly sought-after person that other companies want to hire. You already know that no one stays at a company for their entire career anymore, so the idea that someone leaves for greener pastures shouldn't be a surprise. But your hope should be that your former employee is going to still be in a position to help your company through referrals or even more orders, like if she gets hired by a client of yours.

So it's important that you let your employees shine, rather than trying to hide their brilliance. Let them be the voice and face of your company and let them become rock stars. If they feel like you're giving them a chance to be awesome and to spread their wings, they're more likely to work harder to earn that trust and belief in what they're doing. That can only lead to bigger and better ideas from them, more exposure for them, and, ultimately, more exposure for your company.

The Models of Social Media Management

Regardless of who is going to be in charge of social media, or maybe because of it, it's important to decide what kind of social media management model you want. A lot of approaches are going to be based on your own company's dynamics, internal relationships, strength of personalities, and whether you think the people involved can work well in a particular model.

According to Jeremiah Owyang of the Altimeter Group, there are five different models of social media management. (Figure 13.1 gives a basic illustration of what each of them means.)

- *Decentralized* means that no one department manages or coordinates the social media efforts. Each department does its own thing without any guidance or coordinating clearinghouse. The departments may collaborate with each other.

- *Centralized* management puts one department, like corporate communications, in charge of managing all social media efforts. The benefit is that the messaging is centralized and consistent. The downside is that other departments might have a tough time responding to customers.

- *Hub and spoke* means that several cross-functioning teams report to one centralized position. These teams can be different individuals or business units. This could be a tiger team approach, where representatives from different departments all work on this as a committee. The central point monitors all the channels and assigns tasks to the appropriate department or person, who would then respond appropriately. There are online tools that a manager of the hub-and-spoke model can use to assign tasks as needed.

- *Multiple hub and spoke* is like regular hub and spoke, but used with larger companies and multinationals with different locations. This could be a company with offices in different countries and different identities or even a franchise operation where each location gets to maintain its own identity but coordinate its messaging through a centralized hub.

- *Holistic* management is the ultimate in trust in your employees. It means that everyone has the ability to communicate on social media. No one person is in charge, and everyone has the keys to the car. In Chapter 2, we talked about how Zappos shoe company used this model to great effect and was sold for $928 million while selling $1 billion worth of shoes per year. The one change we would make is someone should be able to remove certain people from social media duties and monitor the social media metrics to make sure goals are being met.

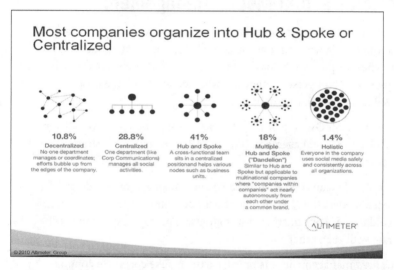

Figure 13.1   The Altimeter Group identified several widely used models of social media management, as they are found in different companies around North America.

All of these models require some form of collaboration and cooperation on the part of the people involved and even from those who aren't involved but still need to contribute information or answer questions, like a customer service representative forwarding information to the social media member. This is why it's important to find people who are willing to work together as a team when choosing a model. Although it might be possible to choose a model and say "this is the way we are going to work," it's also likely that you might just want to choose a team and let them determine their own model.

But don't let the democratic process and social media feel-goodery get in the way of actually getting something done. Remember that this is a business decision, and like all business decisions, it needs to happen quickly enough to actually see a decent ROI. That's not going to happen if everyone gets an equal vote and voice. Pick one person to lead the charge and let the others advise them.

Hold Your Team Accountable

This is where goal setting and measuring results with analytics and social media monitoring services will become important. Knowing what you want your committee to produce and asking for the goals and objectives up front will set the stage at the beginning of your endeavor:

- **Clearly defined goals**—Goals have to be crystal clear and singular. A good rule of thumb is to never include the word *and* in a goal statement. If you have one, split it into two goals. This clarity helps your team develop a litmus test. Is it helping us reach the goal? If yes, move. If no, move on.

- **Measurable objectives**—Where goals are general, broad, but directional, objectives are specific and measurable. "We want to increase sales," is a goal statement. An objective would be more like, "We want to increase sales by 25% through visitors from social media websites by December 31."

- **Strategy**—This is where you build the blueprint or road map for your success. Identify your audiences, where they are online, and the needs you can fill for them. Then delineate which channels you'll use, how they'll integrate, and what calls to action or drivers you'll push in each one. Map out a content strategy for the channels you choose and build milestones in to continually measure and optimize your efforts.

- **Tactics**—Tactics are the steps taken to implement the social media strategy. This is where specific topics and messages formulate into blog posts, Facebook activations, and more. It's where monitoring and responding happens. Think of these as your to-do lists.

Meet with your social media team or the director on a regular basis. Make sure the goals are being met and discuss any changes in the strategy that need to be made to reach them. Give your social media team the flexibility and leeway needed to meet those goals—social media tools are changing on a regular basis, after all—but hold them accountable and make sure those goals are met, both in terms of ROI and profits as well as the size and growth of the network.

Whether you choose one or two people or you create an entire committee or department, finding the right kinds of people to run your social media efforts is necessary if you want to see a positive ROI and increase in sales and your customer base.

Assigning responsibility and holding both yourself and your employees accountable for social media marketing is sort of the glue that holds your efforts together. The management and reporting will keep your organization on course and navigating through the waters, sometimes treacherous, sometimes not, of social media. And that just leaves the last piece of the puzzle for your company to be ready for the social web.

This Is NOT a Sandbox. It's a Business.

Eric Brown owns an apartment complex in southeast Michigan. In 2004, he stopped using traditional means of advertising and pushed most of his marketing budget into pay-per-click (PPC) advertising. He didn't start out with $100 and play with Google AdSense, Google's advertising system. He studied PPC advertising, learned how to do it by reading blogs, watching videos, and following the helpful Google how-tos on the AdSense website.

In 2008, Brown started his first blog to promote Urbane Apartments. He didn't throw up a basic Blogger.com site (a free blogging platform owned by Google) and experiment. He went at it after following his same pattern of success with pay-per-click advertising. He studied, learned what blogging could do, and set out to make it drive business.

Eric Brown is a no-bullshit kinda guy.

"The bottom line for me is, was, and will always be, did we rent more apartments," he told us. "Because if we didn't, the practice of social media marketing is just a hobby."

Like Eric Brown, you probably can't afford to waste time, effort, and even money on something that isn't going to move the needle for your business in some form or fashion. So listening to some social media consultants—those who have the hippie tree-hugger gene—can be frustrating.

Even social media's poster boy, Chris Brogan, espouses the value of experimentation. His main consulting firm is even called New Marketing *Labs*. He uses any of several side projects to experiment with blogging, business models, monetization strategies, and more. He's good at experimenting and passing learning on to others. But you're not a highly paid marketing consultant who gets paid to break stuff and report back on what fell out. You're trying to grow more checking accounts or subscriptions or get more people to buy policies, houses, or cars. You can spend all day, every day just selling your product or service and still not meet your quotas or goals.

Where in that world do you have time to exercise trial and error? Nowhere. That is why you need to be like Eric Brown.

You Know What It Can Do, Now Decide What You Want It to Do

In Part II of this book, "How Social Media Marketing Really Works," we focused on the seven major outcomes social media marketing can produce for your business. If you don't have them memorized by now, you should. This is the point in your own strategic planning process where you ask yourself, "Okay, what do I want social media to do for my company?"

Deciding your goals now will guide your decision-making for the near future and probably for the distant future as well. Even though it would be superhelpful of us to fill the rest of this chapter with answers to the question of what you want to do with social media, it wouldn't be very useful because we can't possibly know your business. Only you understand the challenges you face and the opportunities that might lie ahead.

But we can help your thinking to better answer the question, "What do I want social media to do for my business?"

Do this:

- Write down the top five problems you're facing in your business.

- Take each, one by one, and look at our seven outcomes. Will enhancing branding and awareness solve the problem? How about protecting reputation? Facilitating public relations? Building community? Improving customer service? Driving R&D? Increasing sales?

- Now look more specifically at the top five communications problems you're having. Be sure to consider internal communications and vendor and partner communications alongside those with your customers.

- Do social channels like blogs, social networks, video sharing, collaboration platforms, or social media monitoring services help solve those?

You'll start to see potential solutions emerge that will help you decide what social media marketing can do for *your* business. Write these down and focus on them as potential areas to focus on and solve business or communications problems using social media marketing.

Certainly, you'll need to prioritize and, depending upon your comfort level using the tools and technologies available, you might be ready to dive headfirst into a full social media marketing program. But you might also still be rather unsure what you're going to get out of your activity here, whether or not you can achieve your goal or goals, and what the unknowns you'll encounter along the way are.

It's easy for social media marketing consultants to recommend experimentation. It means they don't have to think about the what-ifs. Remove contingency planning and the strategy process is simple: Just roll the dice. Our guess is that not many of the social media advice-givers out there were ever Boy Scouts, whose motto is "Be Prepared." The sometimes prevalent attitude that social media is a sandbox and it's okay for businesses to just play there until they figure it out is a polite way of telling you to potentially throw your business away. Although we're all for starting a personal Facebook account, turning the security settings up as far as they'll go, and learning the platform a little at a time, we don't recommend launching a Facebook page for your business without knowing what you want to get out of the channel first.

"We have a Facebook page!" is often announced as a sort of social media success story by business owners and marketing managers. But ask them what they get out of it or what it's for and they look at you as if you have three heads. After taking the knowledge in this book to heart, you should start your Facebook page with an understanding of the seven outcomes a business can see using social media marketing, decide which one fits your audience, your needs, and the environment of Facebook, and then launch the page with a purpose. If you do, you won't say, "We have a Facebook page," but rather, "We drive sales through our Facebook page." Or perhaps, "We handle customer service issues on Facebook, which amplifies our support and responsiveness, thus growing our online audience and positive brand sentiment."

The same will hold true for following the strategic planning process for other individual channels within social media or for your social media marketing efforts as a whole. The more social your brand becomes, the more time you'll need to answer the question, "What does your business use social media marketing for?" because you'll use it for many business objectives.

Done Is Better Than Perfect

Marketing guru and author Seth Godin talks about the need to "ship."

"Real artists *ship*," he says, echoing Apple CEO Steve Jobs. But artists aren't the people who paint, write, sing, or perform. Artists are entrepreneurs and businesspeople who create new products and new ideas.

When you ship, you bring your new products or services to market. You put them out, not when they're perfect, but when they're done—sometimes even before they're done. When it's "good enough," it's good enough to ship.

But having your social media marketing efforts being good enough to ship shouldn't be confused with them being scatterbrained and without direction. A Twitter stream with a purpose, even one that doesn't quite have the right content to really attract the audience volume the company wants to have, is infinitely better than a Twitter stream with no defined reason for being.

Planning will take care of the distinction between immature and idiotic. You will grow into your social media marketing program. And growing indicates you will experiment with ideas and even make some mistakes along the way. But it doesn't mean you're playing. Remember what adding the word *marketing* to *social media* does: It makes it about business.

This is where social media's genetic link to the technology world helps those of us in marketing and business. Technology startup companies and entrepreneurs are taught to iterate, to innovate—launch the product and see where the audience takes it, making improvements and adding features over time. This approach, rather than reaching a "final" point and then sending the product out for sale, gives your offering the capability to launch earlier, but also your product team the power to get actual customer feedback to make early improvements. The process typically strengthens the product in the long term and helps companies generate interest and revenue earlier in the life of the product or service than traditional launch sequences provide.

In social media marketing, this iterative process allows you to take your plan to the public—to launch—but remain poised to listen, respond, and adjust your execution accordingly. Although it is true that listening to your audience is the first step in being a strong social business, listening doesn't end after step one. You must continue that listening, not just along each step of a campaign or execution, but always.

> *Listening to the conversations surrounding your product or service should become like breathing for your company. You should do it naturally.*

This listening will help you take a product, service, or even campaign from good enough to ship to good enough for the customer to buy. But it won't take a product, service, or campaign to that point if it doesn't have a direction in the first place. Let the competitors play. You're here to do a job. But that job takes more than a plan. You have to translate that plan into action. The best-laid plans only go awry because someone didn't take the ball and run with it.

Turn Your Plan into Action

This section of the chapter might be the most important few paragraphs we can share with you. By our estimation, 90% or more of all social media marketing plans fail because people who write them don't move the plans from being written on paper to actually being performed by human beings. Executing a social media marketing plan sometimes seems troubling because of the diversity of tools and the often-present fear of technology among those in the organization. Imagining what your organization can do is the easy part. The hard part comes when you actually have to roll up your sleeves and make that imagined view come to be.

Social media marketing is not a strange, magical place that has different rules and processes from other areas of business. If you know how to manage a project, you know how to manage a social media marketing project. The steps you'll take to execute a strong social media marketing plan may include some activities your company has not performed before, like daily social media monitoring. But those activities are just tasks to be assigned to team members. Remember, this ain't rocket surgery.

Actualizing a plan takes two primary steps: getting everyone on the same page and then assigning tasks with deadlines. Adding steps and layers to that process, as many managers do, only complicates things. Why add layers of to-dos when sometimes all it takes to execute an important part of a strategy is to just put tasks one through three on someone's list? Both steps are necessary, but let's not make this harder than it seems.

First, let's get everyone on the same page. If you've read a lot of business books or understand how to write a business plan, you'll recognize this as the crafting of the mission and values statements step. Although you're not going to pound out a 56-page diatribe, complete with financial projections and spreadsheets, you do need a rallying of the troops and a constant reminder of what you're trying to accomplish for each social media marketing effort your company puts forth.

When activating a customer service pilot project for a health-care company, Jason had a number of team meetings where the goal of the pilot project was shared and discussed, along with several if-then scenarios should the effort start out slow or even ramp up faster than expected. With every member of the pilot's team present at these meetings, Jason was, in essence, sharing the mission and value statement for the project with the team, earning buy-in from them, and covering all the elements a strong business activation plan includes. When the project launched, there was little need to regroup and retool based on an initial slow start because the team anticipated it and plowed through ideas to compensate. Three months later, the pilot was elevated to a full customer service support feature for the company.

But it's not just about meeting and talking. Activating social media is about clearly defining goals and expectations for each member of the team. The key to activating a plan is ensuring everyone from the CEO to the janitor understands the goal of the project, its audience and message, and their respective role in achieving the goal. When one person fails to keep their eyes on the prize, the effort suffers and the prize is harder to achieve.

In his 1999 book *Implementing Your Strategic Plan*, C. Davis Fogg discussed 18 key elements to moving a plan to action.[1] Key 1 was developing an accountability system. Certainly, in complex organizations with silos, multiple departments, and sorted reporting, accountability can be confusing. But what accountability really boils down to is dividing up the tasks and responsibilities behind a certain effort and assigning them to someone to complete by a given deadline. Developing a strong accountability system for a social media marketing effort simply requires enumerating the tasks at hand, accounting for a few you might not see (contingency planning), charting them out on a timeline that ensures tasks are accomplished in an appropriate order, and then assigning the tasks to the right team members. The more complex the program, the more complex your accountability and scheduling will be. But shrugging off that action plan, calendaring, and assignments because they're hard? You might as well go do something else for a living.

Keep in mind your accountability system should include some important facets:

- A clear delineation of the task
- A clear understanding of who will perform the task, in coordination with whom, and using what resources

- A specific deadline and explanation of subsequent tasks dependent upon the assignment given

- A reminder of the overall goal, and success metrics, of the project

Team members who buy into your system and purpose, who believe in why you are doing what you're doing, will take those assignments, run with them and the project will move along as needed. As a manager, you should always install checks and balances, reporting, frequent interludes of motivation, and reminders of the goals of your projects. But with the above information and intentional team members, you won't have to fret much about activating.

Fogg's book goes into great detail on organizational management and outlines how to create plans within plans and build out complex activation structures for your strategies to see reality. We don't think activation needs to be quite that complicated. Whether you enumerate the tasks required to accomplish your strategic plan, then route them to a project manager and insert them into a Gantt chart or dump them into a project management software like Basecamp, you assign the tasks to the right people in the right order and accomplish your plans.

Planning for the Unexpected

All this talk about planning, though, makes us a little nervous. It's as if we're saying you can script social media marketing. You can't. Remember that success in the social media world does include participating in two-way (or multiple-way) conversations with consumers. It requires you to engage and be responsive to prospects, customers, the media, or even competitors. And sometimes it even requires you move with those audiences, changing your products, services, and communications along with their needs, moods, and direction. And those changes aren't typically accounted for in a written plan.

This is the core reason you hear a chorus of social media evangelists constantly singing about changing your company's culture. The scripted, predictable way of doing business—often directed or at least affected by a company's legal department—is a thing of the past. By not being flexible, responsive, and even interesting in how you communicate with customers, you're saying to them, "We stick to the script." Unfortunately, empowered online consumers do not, and they resent it when you do. Worse, your company will look stupid when you're sticking to the script and the customer has taken the conversation and their problems in a whole new direction.

Although we'll discuss the culture of being social more in Chapter 15, "Being Social," when it comes to your action plan, you need to ensure that those responsible for first-line customer interactions are empowered to act. They need to be able to respond quickly and decisively to customer needs and concerns, and they even need to be able to vary from the script sometimes to deliver the experience today's consumer expects. This requires that those frontline employees have decision-making and diplomacy skills. They need to be able to differentiate between doing what's right for the customer and knowing where the company has to draw the line to avoid being taken advantage of. Certainly, a system of management feedback can be incorporated into most situations that the social web will present, but real-time decision making is now a critical need when companies are hiring frontline employees.

You might find yourself in a situation like Scott Monty did on December 9, 2008, when the recently hired social media lead at Ford Motor Company awoke to find online message boards and blogs denouncing his company. In the midst of a highly scrutinized but impressive rise to the top of the marketing world as the first true director of social media at a Fortune 10 company, Monty had to stare down an angry public that morning.

A website called *The Ranger Station*[2] reported Ford's legal team had threatened it in a cease-and-desist letter and demanded its URL and $5,000 be turned over to the company. The reasons, as Monty would find out throughout the day, were not made clear to the audience and the issue raged out of control.

What Monty didn't do that day was follow the script. He quickly investigated internally to find out what letter had been sent to *The Ranger Station*. He reassured the public through messages posted on Twitter that he was on it. He even called Jim Oakes, the owner of *The Ranger Station*, to hear his side of the issue and get a well-rounded perspective.

At the end of the day, Monty discovered that the site was allegedly selling counterfeit Ford products (stickers) and the legal team simply wanted them to stop. Oakes panicked, not wanting to give up his URL or $5,000 (which the legal team added as a "we're serious" kind of threat), and turned to his readers to help defend against the big company coming down on a little website. Monty convinced the legal team to separate the counterfeit product issue and the URL/money threat, worked with Oakes to ensure he understood the reasons for the letter, and then posted a Ford response to the matter online, including a recording of the phone call with Oakes that assured everyone that the controversy was understood and addressed.[3]

None of the expert handling of a communications crisis situation would have happened if Monty was simply ticking off to-dos on the Ford social media strategy. To his credit, he spent a good deal of time that day continuing to nurture Ford's vibrant online community with news, notes, and tidbits about lots of items other than *The Ranger Station* controversy, but Monty also went off script to tend to the real-time, real and live nature of Internet conversations and community reactions (see Figure 14.1).

Figure 14.1   Ford's Scott Monty didn't follow a strategic plan's script in assessing, responding to, and mitigating public outcry around a cease-and-desist letter sent to *The Ranger Station*. He even responded to individual forum posts, like this one on SubaruForester.com, to clarify the situation.

Sometimes You Can't Do It Alone

Ford Motor Company is an exception to the rule. A company that size has the resources and manpower to offer up case study after case study of doing social media marketing right. Not to discount Monty's leadership or ingenuity, but most of us would trade budgets with him with confidence that we could rock social media marketing's socks off, too.

Your company probably won't have the same resources or opportunity. In fact, the vast majority of the people reading this likely work at businesses or for organizations that have zero dollars budgeted for social media this year and just as many people on board to run it all. Those factors, coupled with the fact that (this book notwithstanding) you may not have the requisite understanding and experience to lead a social media marketing effort, and you'll find yourself coming to one conclusion: You need help.

We're the first to admit that we often tell business owners that social media is relatively easy to use, the tools are often free, and volumes of both free and premium information are out there to help anyone figure out how to use the social web for business. The barrier to entry here is not high, in either cost or know-how. Although the tools and technologies might be easy to use, how you use them—and how often—can be downright difficult. Keeping up with the do's and don'ts, the ins and outs, and the changes in technologies keeps us busy, almost 24/7, and it's our jobs to stay informed. Even then we miss a lot of information and opportunity, so we can imagine how difficult it is for someone to manage all of this *and* do their regular job. So there are times that, despite all the books you and your staff are reading and the goals and measurements you're setting and watching, that you need outside help. There are times that hiring a social media consultant or agency is going to be a good step for you.

We don't see this any differently than the typical kinds of outsourced help you seek. Small businesses often outsource human resource functions, bookkeeping and accounting, and even a lot of their marketing efforts. Big businesses hire agencies and contractors to manage seasonal projects or fill temporary jobs. It makes sense to turn to people who have the expertise to help you navigate the social media landscape, define your goals, develop your strategies, and even execute the tasks to accomplish them.

But the explosion of social media marketing avenues, coupled with the economic recession the world has faced in recent years and the roster of social media agencies, consultants, and experts has exploded. For every one experienced marketer out there offering social media marketing as a service, there are 10 who haven't a lick of marketing experience. They may well know social media, have built well-read blogs, or have accumulated tens of thousands of followers on Twitter, but look beyond to their marketing and communications experience and the cupboard is as empty as their stares when you ask them about channel integration.

The Social Media Group, a Canadian agency headed by Maggie Fox, developed a useful tool to discern social media vendors called the Social Media Request for Proposal (SMRFP)[4] in January 2010 (see Figure 14.2). Version 2.0 of the document was released a year later and includes the following questions or topics we think are pertinent to ask when looking for outside help with social media marketing:

- What social media services do you provide?

- Please outline your social media strategy process.

- Provide a case study of your strategy work that resulted in a social media initiative and the business results achieved.

- Please detail your methodology/workflow for handling online crises.

- Please provide two to three top-level campaign concepts for Company/Product/Service ABC that allow us to see your concept development and creative-thinking abilities.

- Please detail your creative process as it relates to social media campaigns.

- What methodology do you use for measuring the success of your social media programs for clients? Can you give us an example?

Although this list provided only a small sampling of the 100+ questions listed in the SMRFP template, as you can see, these are not questions easily answered by a random blogger who suddenly decided he is a marketing consultant. Why? Because

Training
RFP QUESTIONS

1. What format does your recommended training take (i.e. workshops, presentations, walkthroughs, webinars/online learning)?
2. How do you measure progress and evaluate training effectiveness?
3. Do you have experience working with any Learning Management Systems (LMS) for online training? If so, which ones?
4. Please provide testimonials or feedback from past training participants.
5. Please provide sample curriculum/outline.
6. Please provide a training case study.

IN-PERSON PRESENTATION QUESTIONS

1. What internal processes do you have in place to ensure your staff are kept current on social media innovations and best practices?
2. Who are your preferred technology partners for online training?
3. Do you have instructional designers on staff?
4. Who would deliver training and what are their qualifications?
5. What types of materials, guides or manuals do you provide to compliment the training?
6. Do you provide a method for ongoing training of new hires or new staff?

Social Media Marketing
RFP QUESTIONS

1. Please provide two to three top-level campaign concepts for Company/Product/Service ABC that allow us to see your concept development and creative thinking abilities.
2. What are your in-house web design/build capabilities?
3. Please provide a sample of a measurement document or final report (with specifics removed).
4. Provide case studies from at least two social media marketing campaigns.

IN-PERSON PRESENTATION QUESTIONS

1. Please detail your creative process as it relates to social media campaigns.
2. What is your process for validating social media campaign concepts?
3. How do you incorporate existing applications, websites, microsites and newsletter programs into your overall social media campaigns?
4. What platforms and software do you use and recommend for social media marketing management?
5. What methodology do you use for measuring the success of your social media programs for clients? Can you give us an example?
6. Tell us about a social media marketing campaign you were responsible for that didn't achieve objectives. Why?

socialmediagroup.com   • Social Media RFP Template V2.0 - 2011 . . .   7

Figure 14.2   The Social Media Group's Social Media RFP template includes suggested questions for a request-for-proposal document as well as in-person questions you can ask prospective consultants and agencies about their practices and methodology.

social media marketing is about driving business. It is not a sandbox and not meant for folly or to be performed by people who don't understand that when you spend resources, both human and otherwise, there'd better be something at the end of the equation that the business wants in return.

Gone are the days of writing off an agency or consultant's inexperience because this thing called "social media" was something no one had heard of. Although it is true the industry and practice are still young, even in their respective infancies, that status provides no excuse for spending your organization's time or dollars experimenting. If this book gives you anything, we hope that it is a clear understanding that social media marketing is a strategic exercise that your company can execute to accomplish one or more of the seven business outcomes we've explained. We hope you know now that social media for your company is less about Twittering, conversing, and engaging and more about setting goals, developing measurable objectives, and executing strategies and tactics to accomplish each.

Understanding this will help guide your decisions and ability to select and hire the appropriate consultants, agencies, or partners to help you. Whether you operate your social media marketing efforts with consultants or agencies or conduct your efforts with internal staffing, still greater questions remain unanswered about who does what and who owns responsibility. Those answers become clearer as you turn the page.

Endnotes

1. C. Davis Fogg, *Implementing Your Strategic Plan*, Amacom, 1999.

2. *The Ranger Station*, http://therangerstation.com/

3. Ron Amok, "Ford, Fansites and Firefighting," RonAmok.com, Dec. 18, 2008. http://ronamok.com/2008/12/17/ford-fansites-and-firefighting/.

4. Social Media Group, Social Media RFP Template, 2010. http://socialmediagroup.com/social-media-rfp-template/.

15

Being Social

As much as we've tried to do so in the previous 14 chapters, diagramming one single playbook or one scientific approach to social media marketing is next to impossible. Sure, we've given you plenty of instructions, ideas, and even some how-tos on what it can do for your business; what your goals and objectives are; and actions to follow through with. But none of that instruction makes your business social.

Mind you, there is a distinction between marketing through social media and being a social business. One is prescriptive, strategically driven, but tactical. The other is a state of being, a culture, a personality. You can cross your T's and dot your I's on your social media marketing strategy and successfully move some needles for your business. But that doesn't make you social as a business. What does being a social business have to do with anything, then? It separates companies pulling off a neat marketing trick from those that people truly want to be associated with.

In *Brand Hijack*, Alex Wipperfürth alluded to the notion that fans of Pabst Blue Ribbon or Doc Martens were not just loyal to the brand, but proudly wore their badges. Companies that "get" their customers are companies that not only succeed, but serve as case studies for the rest of us. They're talked about with a different intensity and vigor. They get more and mostly positive buzz than their competitors.

Being a Social Business Makes Customers Proud to Wear Your Badge

Although we can (and will) list some ideas on how you can now take your social media marketing know-how to go a step beyond to become a social business, the no-bullshit explanation is easy. If your company doesn't like interacting with people—particularly your customers—don't fool with social media marketing. If you as an individual would rather have an administrative assistant respond with a prewritten answer to questions from the public than write the note yourself, then someone else ought to be responsible for social media in your organization. There are people who are good at communicating with others and those who aren't. If you aren't, social media won't be up your alley. Although we would never discourage anyone from trying, if that describes you, factor in some time and patience to deal with the fact you're not going to be good at this right away.

In their book *The Now Revolution*, Jay Baer and Amber Naslund argue that companies must have a "new bedrock" that creates a "real-time culture." The five characteristics of this type of corporate environment include solidarity of purpose, demonstrated trust in employees from management, laboratories and feedback loops for innovation and ideas, a diverse workforce in makeup and in creativity, and reward systems to fuel active participation from employees. Does this sound like your company's culture?

Baer and Naslund present common roadblocks to becoming an adept social business, which include fear of employee and public feedback, blaming internally for external conversations, and the fundamental changes that your business needs to make. If those challenges lie ahead for you, don't worry. You're not alone. It is our belief that most companies today are not inherently social. They still want to control employees, messages, and conversations, even though the company has never had control over them in the first place. They still see random customers complaining about something online and point fingers rather than simply fixing the problem. And they refuse to tear down silos internally or even put traditionally disparate departments at the same table to help understand today's empowered consumer because "that's just not the way we do it here."

The bad news is that those companies are doomed to fail at social media marketing. The good news is that things can change within companies, even gradually, that allow for a more socially adept approach to marketing and, more important, business itself.

Social Media Marketing Is More Than Just Business

The critical point is knowing that business alone is not the answer. Yes, we want you to understand the seven business drivers of social media marketing, choose which you want to focus on for your company, set goals and objectives, build strategies, and so on. But we want you to embrace more than just the systematic checklist in this book. We want you to understand that, to borrow a phrase from Baer, "It's one thing to have social media, it's another thing to *be* social."

Being social means thinking about customers as long-term partners, friends even, who you don't just sell to, but who you know, trust, and value for more than their dollars. It's about reaching for the lifetime value of a customer, not the end-of-month quota. It's about bringing a value system to your company that holds the customer in the highest regard.

Think about small towns like the one where Jason grew up. Pikeville, Kentucky, population 6,903, sits nestled in the Appalachian Mountains in Eastern Kentucky (see Figure 15.1). If you aren't familiar with small towns, think Mayberry in *The Andy Griffith Show*. In many ways, towns like Pikeville (or Mayberry) are perfect examples of the ecosystems that make up social businesses. The lack of population volume means it's easier to know most everyone, but it's also easier to keep up with them, too. That familiarity breeds a bond of commonality that translates to people helping each other and even protecting one another from outsiders or interlopers. Those who want to join the community first have to illustrate they have shared beliefs, needs, and interests and become members by helping others in some way.

These community aspects are found in social businesses. There's a sense that everyone in the company knows each customer and vice versa. The transparency involved in social media marketing plugs the various external audiences into what's happening within the company. It also holds everyone accountable for their words and actions. Take as an example Facebook's terms of service and stance on user accounts, which stem from the ethos of its founder, Mark Zuckerberg. He told author David Kirkpatrick, "Having two identities for yourself is an example of a lack of integrity."[1]

Figure 15.1   Pikeville, Kentucky, population 6,903, has a typical small-town market ecosystem, which mirrors a connected one like social businesses. Photo by Sara Falls George.

In a small town and in a social business, there's no hiding behind a mask. You are who you are and you are responsible for your words and actions. And that goes for the company as well as the customers. Although many perceive this ultratransparency to result in a gross lack of privacy, the environment created when everyone knows everyone and their business means the collective trust is stronger. People in a small town know when someone is trying to pull one over on them. When they know someone is not doing so, they trust them more. By insisting that companies like yours be transparent and honest in your social media marketing efforts, the public forces you to become stakeholders in a greater online community. When you resist, the public knows where to put you on their own personal trust meter.

This familiarity and community then results in an unspoken bond. Everyone in Pikeville, Kentucky, would come to the defense of a fellow townsperson being insulted or attacked by an outsider. Many of them would bend over backward to help a fellow Pikevillian in need as well. Brand advocates are the same way. You only have to look at the sports world to see that when someone in the crowd is wearing the same colors as you, you have a natural tendency to support one another, especially when outnumbered. For a social business, it needn't look far for help when someone insults or attacks the credibility of the company. Remember our example of Sea World San Antonio from Chapter 6, "It's Your House: Social Media Marketing Protects Your Reputation"? When someone attacks your social business, your customers and fellow community members have your back.

Becoming a social business—plugging into that greater consumer community as a participant and stakeholder—only requires that you provide value to the community. Whether through your actions or content, giving to get works here, so long as the intent is perceived as genuine. But once that intent is revealed as not-so-genuine—when customers think you're participating in the community for purely selfish reasons—the cost becomes incredible. Wal-Mart learned this the hard way in 2006 when a folksy blog featuring a couple traveling the country to visit Wal-Marts and interview their inordinately happy employees was learned to be a stunt devised by Edelman, the company's public relations firm. It took the company nearly a year to recuperate and launch more honest social media efforts that the online community didn't write off as violations of its collective trust.

What the marketplace of social businesses looks like is what those of small towns often look like. Jason summed it up in a 2011 blog post:

> "My family didn't buy cars from Dodge, Ford, or Chevy. We didn't buy insurance from State Farm or Nationwide. We didn't bank with PNC or Wells Fargo. And we didn't buy our clothes from JC Penney or Target. We bought our cars from Terry and our insurance from Sharon. We banked with Danny and bought clothes from Jerry. All four people in question sat within four pews of us at the Pikeville United Methodist Church each Sunday.
>
> People buy from who they know, like, and trust. Becoming one of those that others know, like, and trust...that's the point of social business."[2]

For your business to become social, you must add these human layers to your social media marketing. Checking off to-do lists on strategic plans isn't enough to be ultimately successful. Your customers make up the online community we've come to know as social media. Beginning with *The Cluetrain Manifesto* in 1999, that community has insisted companies like yours behave differently to gain their attention, trust, and, ultimately, dollars. You need to have a plan, set goals, and devise strategies and tactics that provide those items of value to your customers. But you also simply have to be better at joining your customers where they live, work, and play, rather than just dropping by and yelling through the bullhorn at them from time to time.

Five Kickstarters to Change a Traditional Mind-Set

So how do you get from bullhorn to best friend? What does it take in terms of actions, time, and investment for your company to become a social business? Unfortunately, the answer is, "It depends." Like any aspect of marketing, a lot depends on your product or service. Then there's your communications, the audience, the competition, the market conditions, and more. But there are steps you can take to drive the elements of that mix you control. We call them kickstarters. When set in motion, they begin to chip away at the traditional mind-set and approach and build a bridge to a new way of doing business.

The kickstarters are operational, even tactical, so they come across as to-dos. And that they are. But each of the five only work if all the stakeholders within and around the company center their focus on the most important core concept your business will ever have: "At the end of the day, the most important person in our company is our customer."

Notice that we didn't say the most important person "to" your company. Rather, we said the most important person "in" your company. If anything, transitioning your company to become a social business is about making your business care about your customers so that your customers care about your business. The people you provide products or services for are not external stakeholders. They are the ultimate internal stakeholder. When you follow the traditional mind-set of company knows best, you disregard the most effective source of easy-to-follow, how-to-be-successful instructions your business has: the customer's.

From a business perspective, especially a social business perspective, the customer is king. So, let's kickstart your company's actions to ensure that belief runs through the organization.

Kickstarter No. 1—Hear, Then Listen

Hearing is a physiological act. Provided your ear drum and subsequent bones and nerves behind it work correctly, you hear. Listening, however, requires thought and decision making. Similarly, social media monitoring is a technological act. Provided you have signed up for some type of social media monitoring service, the data comes into your account and is available for you to review. But it takes action to look at the data, analyze it, and turn it into meaningful intelligence that your company can put to use.

The biggest problem with social media monitoring platforms, from basic and free ones like Google Alerts to complex and paid solutions like Radian6, is that most businesspeople using them think that the tool will magically perform social media actions for them. Even though the technology and algorithms behind such tools are impressive, none of them perform analysis, interpret what actions need to be taken, route those issues to the appropriate internal parties, or follow up to ensure the intelligence is used in an efficient and effective manner. These activities require human action, and those humans are typically housed within your companies. Relying on software to hear is fine, but relying on it to listen is like expecting the hose to wash the car.

Set a time each day or week to really look at the online conversations and feedback your customers are giving you—subtle though some of that feedback might be—through online conversations. Turn the hearing into listening and find trouble areas you need to address quickly and either respond or route them to the appropriate internal party for response. Then follow up to make sure a response happens. Then make lists of ideas and suggestions for the various internal and external stakeholders. You'll need them in Kickstarter No. 2.

Kickstarter No. 2—Share, Then Solve

Now route your list of ideas and suggestions to the appropriate managers or department heads. Share this feedback with your team. If they've never heard information straight from the social web before, take the opportunity to explain to them where you got the feedback, that you're using new online monitoring tools to see what people are saying about the company, and that these issues are coming up in conversations online that everyone can see. If need be, open a web browser and show them where the conversations are happening so they can see the potential impact on the public participating in that conversation.

Now work with those internal teams to address the issues and suggestions, even if only to confirm why the feedback cannot or will not be incorporated moving forward. Collaborate to solve the problems or bring resolution to the questions posed or the ideas offered. Bring various departments, even customers themselves, to the table to discuss and decide what improvements can be made, if new products or features can be added, or how procedures or policies need to change.

Think of this collaboration as the new team building. But add your customers to that team and empower them as well. And no, you don't have to invite all 156,000 people who bought from you in the last five years, but you can select 1, 2, or even 10 loyal customers who know your product well to be an internal voice for the greater prospective audience.

Kickstarter No. 3—Launch, Then Learn

Your collaboration will result in new ideas, new action items, and new approaches for your product or service. Launch that newness, encouraging all the stakeholders involved in building it to watch, share, and participate. Connect the audiences that gave the suggestions and provided the intelligence or opinions you listened to with the new initiatives. Show them you were not just hearing, but listening, and that you now want feedback on how you did.

Then listen again to the customer's opinion on your new products or approaches. Learn where you hit your mark or missed it and iterate through the first two kickstarters again. Like a technology startup, iterate, iterate, then iterate some more. Keep the feedback coming, the team collaborating, and the launches and relaunches happening. Whether this is information and workflow relevant to your product or even just to your communications programs, bringing all the relevant stakeholders into the system and listening, processing, and incorporating their ideas into what you do empowers them with a vested interest in your business.

Kickstarter No. 4—Trust, Then Adjust

The process of getting previously loosely connected parties, internal and external, together should now have created an environment of familiarity—even a sense of community—among the core team closest to your listen-solve-learn process. Trust your team—even those empowered customers—to take those messages, changes, and even products to the rest of the world. Empower the product team to answer questions in industry forums. Let retail clerks remind their Facebook friends of Saturday's sale. Trust that the newfound bond that bridges the gaps of the old guard, siloed divisions makes for more well-informed and even motivated employees.

After the various stakeholders begin engaging online, you can then see who is taking the initiative and who needs further learning, motivation, or resources. Adjust your requests of both internal and external stakeholders to fill gaps in departments or messages. Look to ensure the broader customer base is connecting to all the various touch points their questions and concerns refer to. Have more-experienced communicators or other well-grounded or groomed stakeholders coach less-comfortable ones. Read and react to those who, for all their love of the company, just aren't comfortable being plugged in and turned on.

As with Kickstarter 3, you will need to iterate, iterate, then iterate some more. The more connected, empowered, and valued your employees and customers feel, the more motivated and inclined they will be to behave as social beings on your company's behalf, not just corporate drones turning in their eight hours each day.

Kickstarter No. 5—Give, Then Get

Incorporating the previous four kickstarters in your company gives you an inclusive, iterative process that values the customer first. Now you must give...time, attention, service, content, ideas, encouragement, and support. Give everything you can possibly give to your customers as a company, a department, and an individual, and you'll see something magical happen.

Customers will tell their friends about you. Their friends will reach out to find out more about what you do and what you sell. They'll read your blogs and comment on your posts. They'll retweet your updates and forward your emails to their friends. They will get to know you, learn to trust you, and then buy from you. Before too long, they'll do something else. They'll wear your badge.

These kickstarters can be implemented quickly or over time. They can come from the top down as directives, but more often than not they creep into organizations from the social media evangelists or clusters of socially enabled employees. They spread slowly as more department heads or managers see the intrinsic, and sometimes extrinsic, value these activities provide. The latter approach is often met with roadblocks along the way because a bottom-up approach is "not the way we do it around here." You'll have vice presidents and department heads who passively resist and others who actively work against your attempts to kickstart social aptitude around your company. You can overcome them.

The best path to thwarting your would-be thwarters is to come armed with business in mind. Illustrating customer problems solved or consumer ideas the company can use to improve its offerings will raise some eyebrows as you work to get executive buy-in. Offering examples of other companies moving to social business models often helps.

At health-care giant Humana in 2008, several department heads came together and formulated an approach to social media exploration and application for the company called The Town Square. The informal but diverse group of department representatives formed a "chamber of commerce" for the town that was Humana's social media efforts. They decided they would have only one rule: We share.

From innovation to marketing and human resources to information technology, all department representatives sat on the Humana Chamber of Commerce and shared ideas, vendor recommendations, internal projects, suggestions, and more. Although the core idea was to explore the world of social media together, as a social entity within the organization, the body wound up reinventing the way the company communicated internally.

Having the ammunition you need from examples and proof points will help you pursue your kickstarters. And as you do so, you'll almost assuredly add more proof to the pudding and fuel new arguments for top-down blessing or even endorsement. The more each of those proof points can point to business drivers, the better off you'll be, because...

In the End, It's a Business

We told you in Chapter 1, "Ignore the Hype. Believe the Facts," that we weren't going to fill your head with warm and fuzzies and try to teach you how to use something you're not yet entirely convinced will work. We also told you that the "join the conversation" hype of the hippies and tree huggers left out the business part. But we clarified that they weren't wrong, just not complete in their recommendations. Honestly, as we wrote and edited the five kickstarters, we argued back and forth over how substantive they were. But the full circle of social media marketing and social business recommendations has a nice yin-yang (see Figure 15.2) feeling to it:

- You must be human, join the conversation, engage your audiences, and give to get to be successful in social media marketing.

- You must also set goals and objectives and plan, strategize, execute, and measure to be successful in social media marketing.

- You must further balance the business-driving approach with human qualities to evolve into a social business.

Figure 15.2   The yin-yang symbol from Chinese philosophy can represent the seemingly opposite but realistically interdependent nature of being social and being a business. Image from WikiCommons.

Yin-yang symbolizes the connectedness and interdependence opposite forces have on one another. To be human and to be a business are, in some ways, opposite qualities. To be social as a business, you have to have one to have the other. Humanness begets business because business begets humanness in our new marketing landscape. The more sales oriented you are, the less human you become. In today's world, that often equates to fewer sales or at least a poor long-term sales strategy. The more human you are, the less businesslike you become. If you forget about business in that existence, you suffer as well. It takes one to fuel the other.

You are now equipped with a strategic blueprint for social media marketing. You know the seven things social media marketing can do for your business. You understand step one is to decide which of those you want to focus on. You're ready to establish a goal or several goals for your company or organization. You understand that objectives will follow that must be specific and measurable. You have a blueprint of how each of those seven business drivers is broken down, what activities fall within them, and how they benefit your company. You also have a prescription for developing measures of success for your social media marketing program based on the goals you set forth for it. And you also have some solid ideas on moving beyond the social media marketing strategy to fully embrace the culture and makeup of a social business.

All that's left to do now is to get it done.

Good luck!

Endnotes

1. David Kirkpatrick, *The Facebook Effect*, Simon & Schuster, 2010.

2. Jason Falls, "What Small Towns Can Teach Us About Social Business," SocialMediaExplorer.com, May 16, 2011. http://www.socialmediaexplorer.com/social-media-marketing/what-small-towns-can-teach-us-about-social-business/.

Index

SOCIAL LOCATION MARKETING

Outshining Your Competitors on Foursquare, Gowalla, Yelp & Other Location Sharing Sites

SOCIAL MEDIA ROI

Managing and Measuring Social Media Efforts in Your Organization

OLIVIER BLANCHARD

BLOGGING TO DRIVE BUSINESS

Create and Maintain Valuable Customer Connections

ERIC BUTOW & REBECCA BOLLWITT

#1 BESTSELLER

FACEBOOK MARKETING

THIRD EDITION

Designing Your Next Marketing Campaign

JUSTIN R. LEVY

que®

Biz-Tech Series

Straightforward Strategies and Tactics for Business Today

The **Que Biz-Tech series** is designed for the legions of executives and marketers out there trying to come to grips with emerging technologies that can make or break their business. These books help the reader know what's important, what isn't, and provide deep inside know-how for entering the brave new world of business technology, covering topics such as mobile marketing, microblogging, and iPhone and iPad app marketing.

- Straightforward strategies and tactics for companies who are either using or will be using a new technology/product or way of thinking/ doing business

- Written by well-known industry experts in their respective fields— and designed to be an open platform for the author to teach a topic in the way he or she believes the audience will learn best

- Covers new technologies that companies must embrace to remain competitive in the marketplace and shows them how to maximize those technologies for profit

- Written with the marketing and business user in mind—these books meld solid technical know-how with corporate-savvy advice for improving the bottom line

Visit **quepublishing.com/biztech** to learn more about the **Que Biz-Tech series**